The Craft of
Decision Modelling

The Craft of Decision Modelling

Patrick Rivett

Emeritus Professor of Operational Research,
University of Sussex, UK

JOHN WILEY & SONS
Chichester · New York · Brisbane · Toronto · Singapore

Copyright © 1994 by John Wiley & Sons Ltd,
Baffins Lane, Chichester,
West Sussex PO19 1UD, England

Telephone (+44) 243 779777

Other Wiley Editorial Offices

John Wiley & Sons, Inc., 605 Third Avenue,
New York, NY 10158-0012, USA

Jacaranda Wiley Ltd, 33 Park Road, Milton,
Queensland 4064, Australia

John Wiley & Sons (Canada) Ltd, 22 Worcester Road,
Rexdale, Ontario M9W 1L1, Canada

John Wiley & Sons (SEA) Pte Ltd, 37 Jalan Pemimpin #05-04,
Block B, Union Industrial Building, Singapore 2057

Library of Congress Cataloging-in-Publication Data

Rivett, Patrick
    The craft of decision modelling / Patrick
Rivett.
        p.   cm.
    Includes bibliographical references and index.
    ISBN 0-471-93962-5
    1.   Decision-making—Mathematical models.   I. Title.
HD30.23.R578   1993
658.4'033—dc20
                                    93–10008
                                    CIP

British Library Cataloguing in Publication Data

A catalogue record for this book is available from the British Library

ISBN 0-471-93962-5

Typeset in 10/12pt Palatino from author's disks by Photo·graphics,
Honiton, Devon
Printed and bound in Great Britain by Biddles Ltd, Guildford, Surrey

Contents

Preface   vii

PART ONE

1   Introduction   3

The First Life   Syringe Trouble   11

2   Decisions and the Scientific Method   19

The Second Life   The Pastry Man's Tale   39

3   Logic and Common Sense   51

The Third Life   Berwyn Bank   65

4   Describing a Problem   87

The Fourth Life   The Happy Hamburger Company   99

5   Uncertainty   113

The Fifth Life   Getting a Lift Up   121

6   Deterministic Problems   129

The Sixth Life   Tattie Fabrix   141

7   Forecasting   165

The Seventh Life   Nirvana Residential Homes   173

8   The Analyst   183

The Eighth Life   Competitive Tendering for Conner Mining   193

9   The Anatomy of Organisations   213

The Ninth Life   Buttermere Oil   221

10   Bridge Building   245

PART TWO

11   Focal Points   251

12   The Analytical Process   257

13   Practical Matters   267

14   The Future   279

15   Closing Thoughts   297

Bibliography   A Journey into Serendipity   299

Index   303

Preface

This book is concerned with the analysis of the consequences of decisions and is aimed at teachers and graduate students in management science, operational research, computing, economics and kindred areas such as accounting and finance. The book is not technical in content but presents an attitude of mind regarding management problems and hence we hope that it will also be of interest to managers and executives.

The text stems largely from courses in model building for decision making given in a number of academic institutions and has been greatly influenced by the comments and reactions of many students in different countries. The main recipients have of course been my own post-graduate students at Sussex University but others have also been involved, including students in Texas, Mississippi, Pennsylvania, Cape Town, Pretoria and Hong Kong.

What was evident in all those places was the pleasure and insight afforded by case studies, interactive analysis and problem solving, where there was no obvious standard method or technique. So often a case study can take on the air of a post-mortem. The management corpse is laid pale and lifeless on the slab and the students are taken on a guided tour of the body. What is missing can be any sense of involvement and emotion. However where the teacher is speaking from personal experience and is illustrating the process by side lights and parenthetical remarks, then the corpse can spring to life. The approach of "I was there and this is what happened. This is where I went wrong and this is how we saved our bacon" brings spice to what can sometimes be a dry academic monologue.

The case studies and the anecdotes in this book are nearly all true. They are based on the personal experience of myself and my friends. Where they are not true a confession is made. The relevant words are "based on". Sometimes the organisation can be identified without breaking a confidence but in most cases both it and even the industry are disguised. Fictitious names are used and we trust that there is no firm of chartered accountants named Gessit, Prayhard and Sine, nor any analyst named Tom Tryer. Any resemblances to real persons and institutions are purely coincidental.

The essential characteristic of model building in a living environment is that it is fun. I hope that this fun breaks through and that the occasional lapse from solemnity will be forgiven. Model building really is a wonderful way of earning a living and these pages do try to present a serious message within this context of enjoyment.

The process is not without difficulty. The point is that unlike mathematics there is no single correct answer. The problem itself is always ill defined and will nearly always change during the analysis. Any, we repeat, any, example which is in terms of a problem defined a priori and a single correct answer is misleading. Real life is never like that. This is a human activity and hence the other essential point is that the process of modelling is intensely personal. The method adopted in this text is to try to outline the stages in the research without slavishly defining the successive steps which must follow each other. Model building is not a form of mindless folk dancing in which we all do the same steps together in time to the music.

Model building means so many different things to different people. Philosophically it embraces a spectrum from the classical "hard science", through computer modelling, economic, mathematical and statistical modelling, information technology, soft systems approaches, and systems analysis. In application areas it impinges on accounting, marketing, finance, production, human resources and, importantly, social and health systems and politics. It is unfortunately the case that some researchers with different philosophies do not mix together happily, neither do they have empathy for approaches to problems that are different from their own. There can emerge a tedious scoring of points, a tendency to fight each other and to ignore those massive real problems, economic, social, political and moral, that affect us all.

I have tried to steer a course through this minefield without being dogmatic, patronising or exclusive and always, I hope, acknowledging that approaches other than my rather hard one have their own merits and have equally valid methodologies. This has been my objective and it is for others to judge the extent to which I have steered between the rocks of dogmatism and the quicksands of ineffectiveness.

The first chapter sets out the plan of the book. In the evolution of that plan many friends and colleagues have taken part and their comments and criticisms of early drafts of the text have been of great value. I acknowledge with gratitude the contributions of Dr Peter Bennett, Professor W.W. Cooper, Professor G. Gregory, Professor Brian Haley, Dr Tony Hindle, David Kaye, Dr R. Machol, Professor Heiner Muller Merbach, Dr Bob O'Keefe, Paul Thornton and Professor Stephen Watson.

I am grateful to Penguin Books Ltd for permission to quote from Edward de Bono's book, *I am Right. You are Wrong* (Viking, 1990; Copyright © 1990 Mica Management Resources, Inc.).

Patrick Rivett
Brighton, September 1993

Part One

Chapter 1

Introduction

This book is concerned with the construction of models for decision taking. That being so, the first duty incumbent upon its author is to establish why yet one more book is being written on a topic for which many similar texts already exist, (including one by the author himself). Most texts in this field, however, are largely mathematical or statistical in content. As such they reach a very high standard and there is clearly little need, at present, to add to their number. But another characteristic these texts share, besides technical excellence, is that model building tends to be equated with the creation of mathematical arguments and the texts are high on the mountain tops of research in both altitude and attitude. However, in the paddy fields down on the plains, the labourers are concerned with more earthy matters. "What do our masters really need?", "What is the hidden agenda?", "What data are available?", "Are they tainted or are they fit for human consumption?", "Given all the uncertainties, how can we get an answer in time that is good enough and robust enough?"

We shall therefore operate in the no man's land between the managers and executives who are faced with decision-making problems and the specialist in mathematics, statistics, computing science, operational research and management science. There are many descriptions of those who work in this linking position – operational (or operations) researchers, management scientists, systems analysts, systems modellers and others as well. For all these we shall use the umbrella word, "analyst", and shall term the activity, "operational research (OR)". The person(s) on whose behalf the work is carried out will be termed the "client". These are purely pragmatic and hidden meanings should not be read into them. It is for ease of presentation and they are certainly not proposed as definitive terms.

OR shares this gulf between practice and theory, with other disciplines.

Kant, amended by Marx wrote "Practice without theory is blind. Theory without practice is sterile" and in his preface to *Time Series Analysis* Kendall remarked "There has, nevertheless, tended to appear a rift between sophisticated theory and practical application, and although there exists an extensive literature in scientific and professional journals, there are few books which attempt to treat the subject in its entirety for the benefit of the practising statistician."

Since we are in the paddy fields of practice, the main portion of this book will contain a series of case studies, all founded on and inspired by the experience of the author or of friends and colleagues. In none of these is there any "correct" answer – often the problem itself is fuzzy – there may be different approaches which could be discussed. At the end of most of these studies will be found different forms of report. A note for the files; and a report for the client. These are *not* the "correct" answers, there will be various "answers" to each of these problems.

THE STUDENT

The student who works through this text may have been in employment in some part of the management or research structure. If so he, or she, will be aware that life does not proceed with the stately timetable logic of a university course. Issues are not clear cut, data are ambiguous and it is never the case that the information with which one is presented is necessary and sufficient for the task. It is, nowadays, more likely that one is grappling with too much information than with too little.

Academics are aware that universities do not cover the chaos of real life, nor the culture of commerce, government, social institutions. Their task is the creation of fresh knowledge and understanding, of education and training (these not being mutually exclusive), to criticise and clarify the assumptions of received doctrine and to serve the community.

The student can receive an unpleasant shock on moving from academic life to outside employment, although often it is one of pleasure to be paid for doing something so enjoyable. This text attempts to provide some flavour of this other life.

THE STRUCTURE OF THIS BOOK

The main part of this book will be rather like a club sandwich with a series of narrative sections interspersed with case studies. There are ten chapters, including this one, which will will deal with such topics as the description of problems, the distinction between fixed deterministic and variable probabalistic problems, the problem of forecasting and so on, and between these will be nine case studies. As these have been part of the life experience of the author and his friends, they are termed the Nine Lives. They each illustrate a principle of good practice. There is, however, an important point to make. It is usual for textbooks to have at the end of each chapter a set of exercises based on the material of the chapter and in this way the student knows that in order to work through these exercises all that is needed is the material of the preceding pages. In this book, however, the Lives will not necessarily relate to the preceding narrative. The reader therefore will move alternately along two separate lines which will converge in the final section. It is hoped that this approach will illustrate that rich weaving of theory, concepts, ideas, and problem formulation which form the fabric of professional life and that in so doing we shall show not only what is the attitude of mind of those who do this sort of thing but also why it is what it is.

The final chapters will place the craft in a broader context not only of problem description, but also of education and training, the factors affecting success and failure, ethics, other approaches to modelling and information technology.

WHO SHOULD BE CONCERNED?

In the early sections we shall establish *why* we need to be concerned with decisions and their consequences, *how* this is done and *what* is the approach of those brought up and trained in management analysis. Where mathematics is brought into use, it will be to illustrate, simply, certain points in logic and quantification, since mathematics is the language of quantification and logical relationship. However, the mathematics is not necessary to the argument and can be skipped if it induces nervousness. The purpose is to deal with the concepts behind the quantification. To those trained in quantitative disciplines it can be a shock to be thrust into an industry, (even a science based one) or into a service or a government department and find that most people are not quantitatively oriented, decisions often emerge by stealth and emotion, reason is not the driving force, and much energy is consumed by fighting one's colleagues for resources. The picture of the pure analyst holding the world at bay while he does his sums does not apply. He is not on the bank of the river watching and modelling life as it goes by, but is out of his depth in a frail canoe, shooting the rapids.

Equally therefore, action and reaction being equal and opposite, the qualitative man of experience, successful, and with nothing to be ashamed about, might also appreciate understanding the concepts on which quantification is based and understanding the attitude of mind of the analyst.

Central to all this is not a battery of techniques, it is not a mastery of software and information systems, it is not even a calculus. It is this attitude of mind which sharply differentiates the analysts and makes them different from, but not necessarily better or worse than, the successful experienced manager.

THE HISTORICAL PROCESS

Why analyse decisions? Why be quantitative? The dynamic for this was the first industrial revolution. Until then most enterprises were owned and managed by the same person and occupied the space of a school classroom. The capital involved was the owner manager's, so there was no need to give an account of stewardship. The workers were known to, were hired, fired, trained and promoted by, the same owner manager who also acquired raw materials and sold the goods. It was the industrial revolution which led to change. The capital cost of the machinery involved made it both necessary for money to be borrowed and for stewardship to be confirmed. The needs of power generation moved industry closer to sources of power, water and coal. The increasing fixed cost and decreasing marginal cost increased the break-even level and so the size of units increased. All of this led to fragmentation of ownership between creditors and shareholders and a similar fragmentation of management into specialist functions, purchasing, production, marketing, training, personnel, distribution, while replicated production facilities or vertical integration created problems of complexity. Very soon the thrust of a single owner manager became a complex system, economic, technical, human, political, in which internal power struggles muddied problem definition.

But in all of this, the scientist kept out of management process and those who looked on the problems of managing a complex organisation as worthy of scientific study were rare indeed. It is interesting to note that in parallel with this, and almost contemporary with it, a similar fragmentation was taking place in the sciences. Before the industrial revolution it was just about possible for one man to know the whole of science, (it is claimed that this was Leibniz). Philosophy embraces all human thought. Science was synonymous with natural philosophy and was almost completely physics and chemistry dominated. For various reasons beyond our scope, there was a development, from physics and chemistry, to engineering, mechanical, civil, electrical, chemical and industrial. The interaction of man and machine led to work and method study. But the scientists were rarely interested in the process of communication and control in the industrial or governmental context. It was always assumed that one could learn by trial and error. And so one could, as long as there was time enough and the errors were not fatal. But with large complex systems there is never time enough and such learning becomes trial and catastrophe. Even so, it was not such considerations which persuaded scientists to be involved and interested but rather the approach of World War II (refs 1 and 2).

GENESIS

The physicists who had invented and developed radar had the task of introducing the sets to the army units who would use them as part of the ground defence of Britain. They found that in doing so they were drawn into planning the *operational* use of radar: how should it be integrated with the control system necessary to get fighters into the sky in time to confront enemy bombers? Hence these scientists were called radar (operational) research and then operational research. It was estimated at that time that radar doubled the effectiveness of the RAF and operational research doubled it again.

These quantitative analytical studies spread throughout the British services, Navy, Army, Air Force, and in those of the USA. At the war's end such methods were taken into industry, from industry into government, social services, finance, commerce and banking. But although they are widely practised in many contexts under different names, they are all essentially the attitude of mind of defining relevant variables and objectives, quantifying, and generalising by means of a model. But what are our reasons for doing this? They are to *understand* the nature of decisions, why they are taken and what their consequences are likely to be.

This is where the difficulty lies in the quantitative approach and we must not duck the problem. In practice most decisions are not made in any formal process, they are not even taken: they emerge in a time based (and not an analysis based) process. Many men cannot even remember when, or if, they proposed to their wives (or vice versa in these enlightened days) in what is the most important decision of their lives. The fact that A and B were going to marry gradually emerged. There was no exact moment of decision. Many industrial, commercial, social decisions emerge in the same way. Many are still taken on gusts of emotion.

There was, for example, no relevant quantification before the gadarene rush of building tower blocks, acclaimed alike by architects, town planners, local councillors, central government. There was just an emergence of this as a good thing. Other decisions are taken on political grounds without any quantification at all, such as the secret (not even in cabinet) decision to produce a British atomic bomb and the decision to move to a new system of local taxation (the poll tax). The point is *not* whether or not these decisions were correct, but rather that they ineluctably emerged and it is not possible to trace a moment when formal analysis, logic and quantification were brought together and a formal decision made. Those who work on such problems know that at the time for a big decision to be taken, the choice has often been severely constrained, or even completely removed, by many small decisions which have previously been taken. So the task for the quantitative analyst is how to operate in such a culture. Moreover he has to face the question posed most crudely in the American wall text: "If you're so smart, how come you ain't rich?" And if he ain't rich, how credible is his advice?

Although analysts are not averse to being rich, it is not their prime objective, for otherwise they would not be analysts. Their task is to hold up a lantern in the dark and lantern holders do not always become rich. Running and managing an enterprise is different from that of analysing it. Some even maintain that the qualities needed for each are mutually exclusive. But equally it is not the job of the analyst to be so much at arm's length from the managers he is serving that he is dissociated from them. It is no comfort to the captain and the crew of a ship lost on a foggy night, near the rocks, to observe the navigator rowing for the shore and crying out "It's quite all right, just keep on a steady course and you should be safe – with a probability of 58.4%."

The analyst has to laugh when the managers laugh and to weep when they weep. And still be calm and professional. He has to ride two horses at once. Those who complain that this is not possible are reminded of the words of J.H. Thomas, the former British Chancellor of the Exchequer: "If you can't ride two horses at once you should not be in the (expletive deleted) circus."

There is a final and most important caveat. If we are concerned with decisions and their consequences, then the questions which have to be asked are: what decisions and how do we evaluate the consequences?

All decisions can be related to a problem. Who describes the problem? This book takes the situation arising when the problem has been stated, but in so doing there is an heroic begging of the question. What is the process of problem description? This will be implied in much of what follows but it is important to be explicit. The process of problem recognition and description is completely subjective and there are now established approaches, through what is termed "soft systems", complementary to the hard system approach of the central sections of this book. The proper place to discuss this is not its apparent logical position prior to problem solution, but rather posterior to establishing something of the craft of decision modelling. It is wise to proceed in this way as there is then a natural widening of perspective after the concentration on modelling per se. Unfortunately hard and soft systems approaches (and even moderately squashy ones) can be taken like primitive religious beliefs in a state of hostility to all others. We shall hope to avoid all this with a calm and contemplative approach.

References

1 Rivett, B.H.P. and Ackoff, R.L. (1967). *A Manager's Guide to Operational Research*, Wiley, Chichester.
2 Waddington, C.H. (1973). *OR in World War 2*, Elek Science, London.

Syringe Trouble

The First Principle: It is not enough to think that you understand what you read or hear. You should ask what you were expected to understand and what interpretations others will form.

INTRODUCTION

The point made in this short study is the need to read papers carefully and not to jump to preconceived conclusions. This is why we shall always list the assumptions we have made in reaching an answer.

Take for example a simple mathematical problem: "A man 2 metres tall is standing 4 metres from a lamppost. He observes that his shadow is 2 metres long. What is the height of the lamppost?"

Immediately we have a conditioned response (see Figure 1).

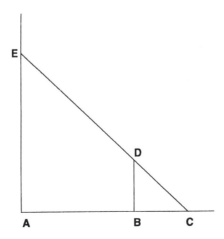

Figure 1

Mathematically:

$$\frac{AE}{AC} = \frac{BD}{BC}. \text{ If } AC = 6, BD = 2, BC = 2, \text{ then } AE = 6 - easy. \tag{1}$$

But now list the assumptions made.

1   The lamppost is vertical.
2   The man is vertical.
3   The ground is straight and horizontal.
4   The man is standing full height, not sagging.
5   He is not wearing a hat nor is he wearing shoes.
6   The light is at the top of the lamppost.
7   There is no other lamp near by also casting a shadow.

Can you think of still more?

The reason these assumptions are made is not because they are all reasonable (assumption 6 is never true). They are made because without them we cannot "solve" the problem. This was all on reflection, obvious. But this next example is not so obvious.

"Name a former president of the United States who is not buried within the USA."

The answer is on page 18. But do *not* look. Try it. Look up reference books if you wish. Ask your friends. Ask the US Embassy. But do *not* look it up until you have completed the whole study, otherwise you will miss the point. If you react to this question as most people do it will be because you have not read it properly.

Anecdote (True)

There was an investigation of the incidence of accidents in coalmines and the factors which might cause them. Part of this work was an investigation of minor "non reportable" injuries which could be dealt with in the first-aid centre at a mine. The study was carried out at a selection of mines, each with different accident rates of minor injuries. In all the mines except one the accident rate had been fairly constant over a period of time. But at one mine the researcher was interested to note that the level of injuries had increased markedly from one year to the next.

He visited the mine and spent some time with the (very attractive) nurse who outlined the different injuries and their possible causes. They had certainly increased significantly in January last. Discussions with mine staff revealed no change at all in mining conditions before, or during, January and the increase was inexplicable.

After work that day the researcher talked to the mine manager in the club bar. He outlined his total frustration and told the manager that the only bright spot in the whole day had been the gorgeous nurse.

"Yes she really is lovely", said the manager. "But you should have seen the one we had before her, a real dragon", he continued.

The researchers nostrils began to twitch and a shiver went down his spine. "How long has the new nurse been here?"

"Started just before Christmas. The best Christmas present the lads ever had", replied the manager.

The researcher had a big smile. "Have a pint of the best", he said.

Moral of the Story

No desk bound analysis, taking in data through the letter box would have solved this problem. No analyst visiting the mine would have solved it from the data in the books and records – no matter how good a mathematician or statistician he was.

It had to be a friendly extrovert researcher who liked meeting people and *listening* to them.

SYRINGE TROUBLE

Introduction

The Regional Health Authority (RHA) for Loamshire serves a large area with many hospitals, 200 medical practices and a full range of domiciliary care services and residential homes. It is, amongst many other things, responsible for purchasing thousands of different supplies, which are then made available through local storage depots to the medical services of the region.

The items with which this study is based are syringes. These are disposable and the RHA purchases thousands of these each month. There are six makers of syringes and the RHA pays the same for them no matter who the maker is and in order to be even handed in its treatment it orders about the same number from each maker.

The process of production at each of the makers is approximately the same and the syringes are delivered in batches of 3000 to the storehouses. It has always been difficult for the makers to control the quality of production not least because there are a number of ways in which a syringe can be faulty. It can leak, causing blood to overflow from the syringe while it is being used, which naturally depresses the patients somewhat. Also they can jam, the needles can break, as can the finger control. Of these, jamming is the most common fault but the RHA has laid down an inspection scheme covering all four faults to weed out poor quality batches. Experience has shown that, in general, batches only rarely have any defective syringes but occasionally a freak batch with as many as 5% defectives will occur.

The storehouses are spread throughout the RHA and they are each supplied by two or three makers. Table 1 shows the pattern of suppliers.

Table 1 Suppliers and storehouses

From maker	Gallop	Horestead	To storehouse Inman	Jones	Killick	Long
Abel	X		X	X		
Baker		X				X
Charles	X				X	X
Donaldson	X			X		
Ellerman			X			X
Fineway		X	X		X	

Note: A cross denotes a supplier.

Stage 1

This is the state of affairs when the RHA director of Medical Relations sends the following memorandum to the Director of Purchasing.

To Mr Patrickson. Director of Purchasing
From Dr Hughes. Director of Medical Relations

It looks as though there may be a serious problem with the syringes which we supply to hospitals, general practices and district nurses. From all of these we are receiving complaints of faults. These complaints do not appear to be confined to any one part of the RHA area and it seems to be a problem which is endemic. Can you look into this and see what can be done to improve the quality of the production at the makers?

This provokes the following response:

To Dr Hughes. Director of Medical Relations
From Mr Patrickson. Director of Purchasing

Thank you for your note. I cannot understand why this matter has arisen as we have a very strict inspection scheme at each maker. Each batch of syringes produced has a random sample of 25 syringes taken from it and the batch is only allowed to be despatched to a storehouse if this sample is totally free of defective syringes.

I am no statistician, just a plain honest man, but this test proves to me that no defective syringes at all should be delivered. My own view is that the medical staff, both doctors and nurses are being clumsy and are mistreating these delicate items.

Dr Hughes does not give up:

To Mr Patrickson. Director of Purchasing
From Dr Hughes. Director of Medical Relations

I have received your note. I feel that before we accuse the medics of being clumsy it would be wise to examine the substance of their complaints. These complaints are not from the doctors and nurses alone. I heard recently that the local MP and her husband who were receiving shots at their home prior to a jaunt abroad had an embarrassing time. She had her blood pour out of the syringe on to a highly expensive carpet while he had the needle break off in a sensitive part of his anatomy. I met them at dinner the other night and they were quite articulate. If we reach the stage when work interferes with my pleasure then something must be done.

The director of purchasing, who is a kindly soul, does now decide to do something and takes the highly sensible step of asking the OR analyst to look into this.

What should you, as Tom Tryer, the analyst, do now?

Stage 2

Identify the maker.

The trouble is that we cannot do this in one go. Tom does, however, discover that the complaints come from three localities which are supplied by the Gallop, Killick and Long storehouses.

You, Tom, the analyst, now have a choice to make. These six storehouses between them are supplied by every maker. Do you assume therefore that all makers are despatching bad batches? What is the alternative? Are there just one or two makers involved? Have a look at Table 1 and check. Go on – *do it*!

If you have done this you will have discovered that there is one maker, and one maker only, who has supplied the three questionable storehouses and that is Charles.

The advice at this early stage in our travels through this book is to keep everything as simple as possible. In fact this is good advice at any time. The statisticians discovered this many years ago with the concept of the null hypothesis as being the simplest statement one can get away with. So we shall go for the single maker assumption and if that does not work, and only then, we shall look for something more complicated.

Stage 3

Identify the source of the faults.

We must not be too simplistic. What is meant by a fault? There are, as we have seen, basically four faults: leaking, jamming and breaking (needle or control breaking). Tom, however, finds that the complaints list does not often differentiate between the type of complaint and when it does the type is fairly evenly distributed between the four with a slight preponderance of breaking.

The next stage therefore is for Tom to contact all the makers, preferably by personal visitation, to discover in what way the production processes at Charles may be different from the others. The source of the problem may be the raw material, the process of making the separate parts, or their assembly.

So Tom goes to all manufacturers and lists their suppliers of raw materials. There are three main suppliers of the metals, plastics and glassware and they all supply equally all the makers. There is therefore nothing specific to Charles.

What about the manufacturing process? The manufacturing equipment is, in its turn, supplied by one company only, so the problem is not the machinery.

Stage 4

Think.

What now? Have we left anything out? If it were not for the complaints which are still coming in, we would be tempted to say that there is nothing wrong. But there is something wrong. There must be something. It does seem that the initial request by Dr Hughes that the key is to improve the quality of production is misguided since there is no significant difference between the raw materials and the production processes at the manufacturers.

Stage 5

Call in Sherlock Holmes.

The great man once remarked that if, of a number of possible solutions to a problem, all but one are impossible, then the remaining one, no matter how unlikely it is, is the correct answer. The only thing which we have not considered is what?

It is the inspection scheme which is applied to each batch of syringes before it is despatched. This, however, does not look at all promising as Tom discovers when he asks Mr Hughes for advice:

To Tom Tryer. OR Analyst
From Mr Hughes. Director of Purchasing

You have asked me about the inspection scheme for syringes. It is very strict indeed. The scheme which is agreed with all makers and which is exhibited at every inspection point reads: "A random sample of 25 syringes will be taken from every batch and each syringe will be tested for its sealing, the flow and for needle fracture in the prescribed manner. A batch will only be passed for despatch to a supplier when a sample shows no defectives at all."
   This seems to me to be quite watertight. If you get 25 out of 25 good syringes, there cannot be any bad ones at all in the batch. My advice to you is to lay off the inspection scheme. I devised it myself and it is obviously strict.

As an analyst you can, if you know some statistics, confirm that out of every 100 batches with as few as 1% defective in each, then about 78 of them will pass the test. And if there are 5% defective syringes in the batch then only 28 batches out if every 100 will pass the test. It would be rare for any batches with more defective syringes than that to pass. It looks as though Mr Hughes may be right. However if he is right then there is no way out because the raw materials and processes are all similar. Therefore he cannot be right and the obvious thing to do is to go again to the Charles factory and look specifically at the inspection scheme.

Stage 5

Visit Charles.
   When Tom goes to Charles he is aware that the problem is most likely to be caused by the occasional highly defective batch passing the test. There are not many such batches, as we have been told, so some time elapses before the solution becomes clear. Each day, Tom observes that the man doing the inspection correctly takes a random sample. Each sample yields no defectives and each batch is passed properly. All this Tom sees day by day.
   Until one day: *Eureka!* On that occasion the operative takes the random sample and starts testing each one. After the first five, the next syringe is leaky. The operative then throws away the whole sample and takes another random sample from the batch. This yields no defectives and the operative then passes the batch.
   At this moment Tom leaps up and asks the operative what he is doing. He replies: "I am very strict about doing this test, Mr Tryer, as I know how important it is. I know that I am not allowed to pass any batch when the sample has any dud syringes in it. No matter how long it takes, I keep on taking samples until I get one with no defects. Do you know that sometimes I have to take three or four samples before I can pass the batch?"

Answer to Question in the Text

US Presidents Bush, Reagan, Carter, Ford, Nixon. Why did you assume the question referred to dead presidents? No *dead* former presidents are buried outside the USA. Any *living* former President will do.

Reflections

When any of us read or listen, we always start with certain preconceptions. If we read an example at the end of a chapter in a textbook, we expect the example to be solved by the material in the chapter. When some of our friends give us information we expect it to be true; but when others do so we expect it to be exaggerated. This is why sometimes it is difficult to understand a joke in a foreign country, because their view of the world is different.

The man and the lamppost problem demands assumptions which are produced because of the demands of the method of solution. The US Presidents question teaches us to read carefully and not make unconscious assumptions.

Incidentally, the syringe problem is based on the first study carried out by the author after he graduated. The words of the man mentioned on page 17 are, as far as memory allows, the actual words used. Alas, this sort of misunderstanding is as common now as it ever was.

Chapter 2

Decisions and the Scientific Method

THE ELEMENTS OF A DECISION

In this chapter we shall outline the nature of a decision, relate it to the scientific method and show how these two interact to produce a quantitative method for analysing decision making.

In any decision there are three elements, all different in nature but which apply in problems large or small, public or personal. These are:

1 The range of choice.
2 The consequences of each of these choices.
3 The objective(s) involved.

There are many decisions on which no one would wish to deploy the whole battery of the scientific method. The problem may be too small or too trivial in its content, for such a sledge-hammer to be used on such a walnut. There are also many cases where the range of choice is so limited, the consequence of each of them so well determined and well measured and where the objective is a single statement, that even though the problem is non trivial, all that is necessary is to take each of the limited number of alternatives and by arithmetic work out their consequences, compare them with the single objective and take the "best" one.

We shall therefore be concerned with problems where one at least of these is true:

1 There is no easily available, acceptable and valid unit of measure.
2 The range of choice of courses of action is uncertain, or, if known, too large to be able to consider each of them.

3 The consequences of these choices are uncertain.

4 There is more than one objective or even, perhaps, no agreed objective(s).

We shall, however, at this time, make the courageous assumption that the problem itself is definable and defined.

MEASUREMENT

Measurement is basic to this book and before proceeding it should be borne in mind that there is no such thing as a neutral value free measure. All measurement involves a view of the world, for the units express what is thought to be important. Measures always say something about the measurer. For example, if a man tells his friends that he has met a superb girl – 36–22–36 – it tells something about the girl (even though the units of measurement are never stated) but it tells much more about the man.

If the output of a factory is expressed in items per day, or items per unit of labour cost, or items per man hour, and if the items are measured in number, cost of the items, selling price of the items, profitability of the items – all these measures will be different. They will all deal with different objectives and they will all be of interest to different people. But each one is redolent with some value system and each one tells something of the people who use it. Similarly the units in which one describes a hospital or a social security scheme tell us much about the administrators. That great cry "Give us the facts and we can decide" is an open invitation to those who want the decision to go a particular way, to present the truth in such units of measurement as to make the choice inevitable. It is still the case that innocent creatures, such as managers or financial journalists, (especially financial journalists) will take, as true, the costs of doing something as that which is given by the accountants, without asking the basis on which the accounts are drawn. The scientist is especially prone to this since he has been brought up to regard "mass", "velocity", "density", as being uniquely definable and measurable. But cost, in accounting terms, is related to purpose. The cost of a car journey, for example, can, like all other costs, be one of three:

1 *The average cost per mile of driving the car.* This takes account of the miles per year that are driven, expresses the fixed costs (that is tax, insurance etc.) on a mileage basis and adds to this the variable cost per mile, fuel, oil, tyre wear etc. to produce an average cost per mile.

2 *The marginal cost per mile.* This uses the argument that the car is there already, its fixed costs have been paid for and the only cost to be considered is its incremental (marginal) cost per mile.

3   *The opportunity cost.* This is concerned with comparisons with anything else we could do with the car. For example, using the car for this journey, when it could have been hired out at a high fee, means we should take into account the loss of income of *not* having this fee.

When we consider all the other ways of treating the implied costs – depreciation, interest charges, allocation of overheads, the cost of garaging and so on – we can see that there can be some thousands of cost combinations. So what *is* the cost of the journey? It can only be evaluated when we know how the cost is going to be used. A far cry from physics where we know uniquely the mass of the car, its velocity and the density of each material used in its construction.

MULTIPLE CHOICE

It is essential, first to make a distinction between an objective and a constraint. In the terms of this book an objective is something attractive which we require to be as good as feasible. A constraint is something which must be satisfied. To some people food is an objective and they require as much of it as they can manage to digest. To others, less greedy, food can be an input sufficient to banish hunger and enough to allow efficient working. It is then a constraint.

Where we have a single measured objective to be optimised and a number of constraints on what we might do, then the problem is that of finding a particular policy, or decision, which is "feasible", (it satisfies the constraints) and also is "best". Having only one objective means that all possible decisions can be analysed and the best one selected. Although this may seem to be a rare case indeed, there are in fact many decision problems of this type and there is a vast literature devoted to them.

For example, consider the problem of selecting a dietary intake for a person. There will be a number of alternative foods, each yielding so much per gramme of intake, of carbohydrates, cholesterol, calories, vitamins A, B, C etc., calcium and so on. Diets consisting of various amounts of each alternative food will yield different total amounts of carbohydrate, cholesterol etc.

The minimum (or maximum) amount of each of these which a diet must achieve is a *constraint* and the single objective could be to find the particular diet which has the minimum cost. This would be an optimising problem which at first sight involves looking at each alternative diet that satisfies the constraints and costing it. However, help is at hand in the internal logic. This logic shows that in such a case there is a specific set of alternative solutions, limited in number, which contains the best one. This problem therefore, which at first sight involves a search for an optimal needle in an infinitely large haystack of choice, is one in which just a set of particular choices need be considered. Moreover there are very efficient ways of going through this set and discovering the "best" one. Because of the mathematical seductiveness of such problems, they have achieved more attention from researchers than their incidence in the real world demands. On many courses such mathematical and computing techniques can take up to half the total time of the course, where as in real life perhaps only about 5% of research time is devoted to such problems. The real point about them is that embedded in the problem formulation is the structure of a set of typical relationships which exist in their own right (see Appendix 1).

It is not always the case that such relationships exist. The logic does allow us (simply because there is only one objective) to eliminate most of the feasible alternatives. Another way of eliminating alternatives is through what is known as dominance. If one alternative is better in every respect than another, then it has dominance and the second alternative can be discarded. This is particularly useful when taking decisions in the face of uncertainty.

UNCERTAINTY

There is a tendency to regard uncertainty or variability as reprehensible and as something of which to be ashamed. But it is uncertainty, and not certainty, which is the nature of the universe. Even in so simple a situation as the conversion of water to steam there is a total uncertainty. For example, if a kettle is boiling water, we know from the rate of application of heat, and the volume of water involved, how many water molecules per second will be turned into steam molecules. But we do not know which will be the next molecule to turn into steam and *there is no way of knowing*.

An insurance company can estimate accurately enough how many of its policy holders will die next week. But it will not know who will be the next one – *nor can any mortal know*. In these two special cases we know more about the group involved (the molecules of water or the policy holders) than we do about the individuals, even though in most cases, dealing with many things is more complicated than dealing with a few things.

The point is that variability and uncertainty are *natural*. Uncertainty is measured by probability, and variability by statistical measures such as variance. At this stage we will content ourselves by discussing probability. Probabilities always lie between 0 and 1 (or 100%). At the extremes a probability of something that is zero means the something cannot occur, and a probability of one means that it will certainly occur. The probability can be taken as a degree of belief and it is easiest to estimate probability when we have historical data. There are three different classes of problem:

1   If we know from history that on average 1% of the product of a machine is defective, then the probability that one randomly selected unit is defective is also 0.01 (or 1%). This class comprises those cases where we have a background of history and we assume that the future will be an extension of the past. This is when we feel most at ease about stating a probability and the prosperity of insurance companies is testimony to how successfully it is done.

2   At a different level we have cases where we can estimate probability theoretically. These show how difficult it is to estimate a probability of something of which we have no experience. The reader is asked to make an informed guess as to these:

(a) Twenty-six people selected at random are in a room. What is the probability that two of them share the same birthday (*not* including the year of birth)?

(b) A straight rod, 1 metre long, is broken at random in two places – all points in the rod are equally likely to be chosen. We will then have three pieces of rod. Sometimes we can make a triangle out of them (Figure 2.1).

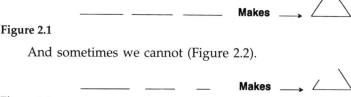

Figure 2.1

And sometimes we cannot (Figure 2.2).

Figure 2.2

What is the probability we can make a triangle from the three pieces? The answers to these are at the end of the chapter. Do not look yet. Think. Estimate or just guess. Then, and only then, check.

Appendix 2 at the end of the chapter gives the proof of the answers. In these two cases we can prove mathematically how often something should happen, without experimenting. An experimental way of answering the birthday problem would be to get a few hundred random groups of 26 people and see how often the event happens. For the other problem one could break randomly a few hundred 1-metre rods. Sometimes this is the only way to estimate a probability, but it is very interesting that exact mathematics can estimate something as shaky as a probability. An entertaining and perceptive account of the use of probabilities in day-to-day life is given in ref 1.

3   A final problem category is where there is no history and mathematics cannot help. For example, what is the probability that a research team

will produce a certain drug before a rival company? If they do, what is the probability that they can market it successfully at £10 a litre and, if they do, what is the probability that sales will exceed 1 million litres a year?

Here we are making guesses. (Always beware of the person who talks about something being a "calculated" risk. It usually means that no calculations at all have been made.) In sharp contrast to the facility with which insurance companies can estimate historical probabilities are the problems of Lloyds Insurance, where the unique event has to be covered. There are processes (ref 2) by which we can work towards a guess but there is little confirmatory evidence of how successful the processes are. In Chapter 5 we shall discuss some situations where in order to solve a problem we shall need to make such guesses. But this should always be done with great caution. One of the temptations to which all modellers are subject is that where seductively elegant methods are available they may be used carelessly and without regard for the assumptions that have to be made.

OBJECTIVES

There are some points now to be made about *objectives*. The first disposes of a natural enquiry as to why, in this introduction, objectives are taken at the last. The conclusion drawn from management texts is that the first stage on the road to salvation is to state our objectives and that not a step can be taken without knowing these. However real life is an anti-climax. A household shopper who insisted on knowing the objectives involved in going shopping before he or she sets out (not just a shopping list but *why* the goods are being bought), would soon have a starving household. Objectives evolve and emerge during a study.

Once upon a time every office displayed an organisation chart in pyramid form. Although such a chart is now less common, we can consider an organisation as a pyramid. At the lower levels the decisions taken will have consequences quickly manifest (low gestation period), the consequences will have a short life span, and they will not be sensitive in determining the performance of the organisation, they will only encompass a part of it and for those involved there will only be one simple objective and one simple criterion of performance.

The disappearance of the management chart reflects a movement in organisations away from the command structure implied in Figure 2.3 towards a more cooperative approach. These new, amorphic, structures will nevertheless within themselves have the same nuances of gestation, strategic and tactical, but will work them out within a different context.

Within the traditional structure as one ascends the management pyramid and approaches the top, decisions are in general not quickly manifest, the consequences last longer, they are sensitive, they encompass the whole and there are many objectives and criteria which are not capable of being placed in a common scale of measurement (Figure 2.3).

The top level is concerned with setting long-term strategic goals, the middle works out tactics within this strategy and the bottom (one fervently hopes) does what it is told. Hence, strategic planning, corporate planning and long-term planning are all synonymous.

All objectives should include, at least three perspectives:

To ensure survival, to encourage growth and to define a collective of good things which we can call eudemony (or well-being).

But they must always include methods of quantification. It is of no use to tell a subordinate that staff morale is important, or that objectives include innovation or customer satisfaction, without stating how each of these is to be measured. Otherwise the subordinate will only know how well he or she is doing by gusts of emotion from superiors.

It is easy to be confused about objectives and to confuse symptoms with reality. In addition there is a transition between means and ends. Each level of management has ends to achieve and its subordinate group provides the means of achievement. But at that subordinate level, their means become the ends and the next level down are the means. This translation goes through any system like a domino effect.

One of the difficulties with objectives is the hidden objective. It would be miraculous if the objectives of each employee coincided with the group objective and we are, each of us, subconsciously or consciously liable to push things our own way. Often we cannot determine objectives by rational

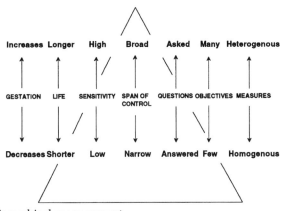

Figure 2.3   Hierarchical management

discussion. How many could imagine that choosing a life partner could be analysed against a stated set of objectives in such a way that the choice could be left to one's mother? Similarly with choosing a house or a job. Possibly a good way of gaining an insight into one's personal objectives is to analyse how one spends one's time or one's money. For these involve decisions and choices. Equally, a good way of understanding the mores of a foreign country is to look at the decisions handed down by their courts. The best way to understand the real, as distinct from the pretended, objectives of a group is to analyse the choices they make. There will always therefore be more than one objective for a group since the individual (unstated) objectives will never be identical.

MODELS AND SCIENCE

There is a problem in using such a term as scientific method. It can be taken to imply a ritualistic process of step by step analysis and hypothesis testing. It is also implicit in such a process that results can be confirmed or refuted. As will be seen, for us confirmation is impossible in the sense that one can say to sceptics, "If you do not believe me, try it for yourselves." They cannot try it for themselves since we operate in a changing environment and during a study the world will change. Even carrying out a study changes the world. As Herodotus wrote, "No man can ever step twice into the same river."

There are many ways of understanding the world around us and the scientific method is a subset of such ways. Discussion of what the scientific method is, can give rise to heated debate. For our purposes here we shall describe science as an organised logical approach to understanding the world around us and central to this is the model. Models are often mathematical or statistical in nature – sometimes it is even difficult to decide whether papers on physics, chemistry, biology or engineering are on these subjects or on mathematics, and most creative work in economics is mathematical. But mathematics is the language, the content lies behind the language and the content gives understanding. Since *understanding* is our objective, we must always remember that the mathematics is the vehicle that takes us to our destination and is not our destination itself. In this book there will be mathematical models, but they will always be our servant. In an age where in much of management research the mathematics becomes an end in itself, this is an important point to remember.

But *what* is a model and *why* have a model? The answer to the *why* question is that there is too much information and too much complexity in the problems we tackle. We have to simplify. A model's first quality is to cut out irrelevance and to simplify. This is what every person of experience does in every day's work. A model implies a filter function on information. For example if one is driving a car through dense traffic, much information coming through the eyes and ears is filtered so that our minds do not even receive it. The fact that a woman on the pavement is wearing a white hat, (or even that she is wearing only a white hat), the fact that a man has an Old Etonian tie, or that the car on the left is a rare Alvis, are all filtered out as irrelevant. But when driving in the country, the sights, sounds and smells are all received and treasured. The information filter depends on environment and purpose, and the model will be different according to environment and purpose.

Models therefore simplify. Newton produced a law of gravitation, in which the attraction of two particles for each other was proportional to the product of their masses divided by the square of their distance apart. But such a law applied to every particle of a body affecting every particle of another body would have involved intractable amounts of arithmetic, even with today's largest computers. Newton's law simplifies this quite savagely by locating attraction by and for a body at a single point – the centre of gravity. It is only by this great simplifying statement that science can deal with gravity, the force that holds the universe together.

Economic models, however successful, are all abstractions. The economy works by the actions and interactions of millions of people and billions of transactions. The Keynes model and other economic models replaces the millions and the billions by a set of relationships and statements.

Such modelling has always been the approach of mankind to complexity, there is nothing new about the idea. The Greeks created a model of the movement of stars and planets with the earth as the centre. This was a physical model of 52 concentric invisible spheres rotating around each other and driven by friction by the outer sphere (those who have played with a spirograph will know the rich and amazing paths that can be traced in this way). The planets were assumed to be attached to these wheels and very good approximations were obtained by the astronomers. Using this model, for example, Ptolemy estimated the distance of the moon from the earth as 29.5 times the earth's diameter whereas, the accepted figure today is 30.2. In parallel with this, but independently, the Babylonians had a totally different approach. They have left behind tablets containing records of hundreds of years of planetary movement, floods, earthquakes, crops, pestilence. By statistical analysis they were able to predict eclipses and planetary movements with great accuracy. (Incidentally this was all done on a number base of 60. The heavens were divided into six equal sectors with 60 parts in each – hence our 360° for a circle.) Very cumbersome arithmetic was performed, but because they had so much historical data, great accuracy was possible (ref 3).

These two astronomical models show interesting similarities and differences. A similarity is that they both put the earth, and the observers themselves, at the centre of things. We are put at the origin. Sometimes, when modelling, we only get a valid result when we move ourselves away from the centre and realise that we are part of the problem. As we are reminded in the *Rubaiyat of Omar Kayam* "Who is the potter, pray, and who the pot?" Another similarity is that both the Greeks and the Babylonians thought that this was a good problem and worthy of attack; in fact they recognised the same problem.

Today we ourselves have a great capacity to ignore – even to be unconscious of problems which are at present unsolvable. There is not a single management problem on which research is now in progress which has not existed for thousands of years. For example, the word "unemployment" did not even exist a hundred years ago, because it was not something worth noticing. But unemployment itself existed. Conflict studies are of recent origin, but conflict has always existed. It was almost totally ignored because we did not yet feel ready to study it. Ignorance of the problems that surround us is either because our value system ignores them or because we do not feel able to cope with them.

A final similarity of the Greek and Babylonian approaches is that although both models are based on real life observations, both models were closed. In neither of them would it have been possible to break out of the bounds of experimental observation and to deduce the existence of stars which had not been observed. An important quality of a model should be its capacity to reach out into the unknown or the unknowable.

There is an important difference between these two approaches to modelling the same problem. The Greek model tried to *explain* what was happening while the Babylonian model only *described* it. This distinction between the explanatory and the descriptive is fundamental and is seen in a study carried out in an American oil company (ref 4). The company had a large number of urban filling stations and the sales at the different stations varied widely. What was causing this and how could they estimate what sales might be at new sites? A university OR team went to hear the work the company had already done on this problem and to get more closely acquainted with it. There had, it seems, been two previous attempts. In the first, a group of motivational researchers had interviewed motorists to determine their psychological relation with the filling stations on rival companies. From this emerged the importance of the filling station attendant as a substitute father figure. This conclusion was thought to be fascinating but not of much use in solving the problem.

A second study had created a mathematical model. A team of economists interviewed 12 of the top marketing managers in the company and asked them to list what in their personal experience were the three most important factors affecting the sale of petrol. (A very sensible start.) Between them the 12 men listed 24 different factors, (at which point the economists should have stopped to draw breath). Nothing daunted, they formed the model:

$$S = a_1x_1 + a_2x_2 + a_3x_3 + \ldots + a_{24}x_{24} \qquad (2.1)$$

The S are the sales at a particular station and, the x's are the 24 different factors listed, e.g. traffic flow, number of pumps, number of attendants, use of screen wash, trading stamps, price and so on. As there were more than 24 stations in the cities concerned it was technically possible to estimate the a factors so as to give the best possible fit to the sales data. When this was done it was found that the sales model – a *descriptive* model – could estimate sales to within ± 50%. Not a very useful result.

At this point in the presentation, an analyst in the team, who was a physicist, made the remark that if Einstein could explain so much of physics in one equation, $E = mc^2$, what was so difficult about selling petrol that it demands 12 times as many factors as Einstein needed? He further remarked in a phrase which should be exhibited on the office wall of every decision analyst and decision maker: "The more variables you need to describe something the less you know about it."

The research team visited all the stations (notice the importance of personal observation). They discovered that the stations were at road junctions, as management folklore held that stations in the middle of a block did not sell as much as those at a junction. The roads formed a rectangular network (Figure 2.4).

The team observed the usage, at each station, from cars passing through the junction. For each road of entry into the junction there were four routes

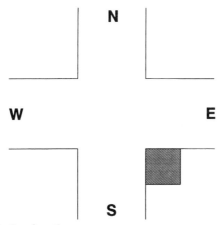

Figure 2.4 Petrol station location

out, (including going back the same way on a U turn) and so there were 16 routes in and out. The number of cars on each route using the station were logged and it was found that nearly 90% of the sales were always from cars on the same three of these 16 routes. In Figure 2.4 these were S to E, E to S, and S to N (driving on the right). They now had a descriptive model with only three parts to it. But what was the explanation?

The team had also noted the added time for cars on these 16 routes, if the station was used. They found that when the 16 routes were put in the rank order of added time and then in rank order of proportion of cars using the station, the two rank orders were the same. The deduction was that drivers used the station not primarily for price, trading stamps or even as a result of advertising campaigns, but for their own personal time convenience.

There was now an explanatory model which was then used to go beyond the limits of experience and observation in a way which the Greeks and Babylonians could not do in their own research. The extrapolation from the model was important. Part of the folklore of marketing was that it was useless to locate a new station at a road junction, where there is already a station, because the sales are taken up. But reference to Figure 2.4 shows that the three major routes for the other locations do not include any of the routes for the present station. All three major routes for each of the four corners are mutually exclusive. So not only are these other three sites good, they will be purchasable more cheaply because folklore has misled rival companies into thinking that they have little sales potential.

This is the power of an explanatory model, and is why one should always start modelling by listening to people, by reading about the problem area and by thinking. Modellers should start by trying to think of explanations that make sense and clarify their minds about the real objectives of people involved. It is particularly important not to impute objectives to others because they make sense to the model builder. The cultural values of the model builder are not necessarily those of the people he is working with. We should always think first, and the greatest scientists have always been those who have thought first and carried out the least experimentation.

Explanatory models are therefore cost effective and even when we have a descriptive model we still have to explain why it makes sense. There are many illustrations of the perils of descriptive models. One of the most famous (and probably apochryphal) is based on observational data of the numbers of storks in Scandinavia each summer, before they migrate, and the local birth rate. It was observed that there is a good relation between these two (Figure 2.5).

But is this a cause effect relation? Do we reduce the birth rate by shooting storks? What is the explanation? It is that in a dominantly agricultural community, prosperity is related to crops and harvest, which in turn are related

Birth Rate

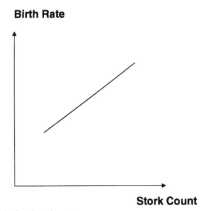

Stork Count

Figure 2.5   Storks and the birth rate

to how good the summer is. If the summer is good the storks stay longer. If the summer is good prosperity is high. If prosperity is high the birth rate increases. The two variables, stork numbers and birth rate, are not linked by cause and effect. They are each linked to a third variable, prosperity.

These various examples suggest the simplifying nature of a model, and the way in which variables can be reduced in number and attention concentrated on key issues. This concentration of attention is certainly central to any process of control which might follow the research.

Other factors have also been implied, for the model not only encompasses causes and effects, bearing in mind that we rarely have the luxury of a physics type experiment where there is only one cause which is allowed to vary. Within the model itself the factors and relationships are in different categories.

Some of the variables involved can be manipulated and controlled by management. For example a doctor's surgery can choose how many ancillary staff, such as practice nurses, secretaries, computer analysts, receptionists, cleaners, it might employ. Such variables are called (rather uninspiringly) controllable variables. It should be noted that controllability is relative, not absolute. For the manager of a petrol station the price at which he sells petrol is not controllable (by him), but, for the marketing director of the oil company, it is a controllable variable.

This relativity of the controllable and uncontrollable is basic and important. "Uncontrollable variable" is also a relative term, and it splits into three categories. There are some uncontrollable variables (like selling price for the filling station manager) which are controllable but by someone else who is beyond our own control. This someone else may be capable of being influenced in our favour (for example, someone on our "own side", or a civil servant in government) or it may be a malevolent opponent. This is the case in competitive situations.

There are those uncontrollable variables which might be termed "natural", that is, variables such as rainfall or harvest size which are related to nature and for which historical data are available. Within the modelling process, the task of the analyst in this case is to forecast, in probabilistic terms, what these variables may be.

Finally, there are uncontrollable variables for which adequate historical variables are not available, of the type termed by insurance companies Acts of God. Major natural disasters are such. In most cases one puts these on one side and then carries on regardless. Even in these cases there should be a contingency plan available for dealing with them. Although it might be thought that such action is only common sense, it is rare. There is, for example, almost no robust contingency plan by which the affluent countries can spring rapidly to the aid of a developing country when a large disaster occurs. Money is flung at it and vast numbers of blankets and top coats are left to rot because there is no adequate transport system. There is no forward contingency planning.

There will be, to begin with, an awful lot of variables and it can be depressing, at the early stage of analysis, to be presented on a daily basis with yet more variables. It is impossible, in one's mind, to deal with more than six or seven variables and so some process of variable reduction has to take place. This can be of different fashions:

1 Variables can be examined and tested for their relevance and for their sensitivity (see for example the Third Life on page 65). The analyst can only do this cooperation with those who know the problem area.
2 Variables can be examined for their internal relationships. For example, all our bodies are of different sizes, shape and weight and a list of variables describing our own personal appearance could run into dozens. However, a multiple store offering men's suits off the peg, may only consider three quantitative variables – chest measurement (for the jacket) and waist and inner leg for the trousers. This is because all the other variables, hips, knee to foot, crotch to knee, neck size etc. are closely enough related to the basic three. The "closely enough" is critical. These three variables get a fit which is good enough for most of us and if we want a better fit (or if our own shape has unusual correlations within it) we have to go to the bespoke tailor who will take more measurements. We can see therefore that the accuracy of the model is related to the purpose of it. If one is fell walking one needs a simple weather forecast – cold, warm, or hot, some rain or no rain. But gas or electricity producers, where one degree of temperature can seriously affect offtake, need a much more accurate model.

The variables chosen therefore are related to *how* the model will be used. Part of this "how" involves the imposition by external forces of constraints. Scheduling patients into a hospital is within a set of constraints – physical (numbers of beds for different specialties), human (numbers of consultants by specialty, doctors, radiographers), balance (for social or political reasons there could be a minimum number of geriatrics). Constraints can be too easily accepted as "given" and must never be accepted with docility.

The other part of the "how" is the reason for doing all this. What are the objectives? These were discussed earlier and are absolutely crucial. Sometimes objectives can be symptoms, often they are emotional, but mostly they emerge during a study. The problem as first given to a research team nearly always has to be changed and the most common reason for the rejection by management of a research team's proposals (apart from those given in Chapter 13) is that the team has "solved" the wrong problem.

THE ANALYST

Before we proceed we must bring from the wings and on to central stage a missing person. For basic to all of this, as applied to decision making and modelling, is the overwhelming need for the analyst to visit and observe what is going on and to be personally involved wherever possible.

The place of the analyst is central. This does not mean that he or she is central to the model created. The analyst is not the sun in the management astronomical system. But the analyst does listen, see, feel, sense in a personal way and is part of the problem – no one is just an observer or an arithmetic engine. We all influence and are being influenced. It is not common for the analyst to be discussed as a participant in what might be termed "hard", or "classical" management science. In one of Agatha Christie's detective stories, written in the first person, it is the writer who is the murderer. This pivotal role of the analyst is important enough for us to consider it more widely in Chapter 8. At this stage we only make one point about the role of the analyst – namely that when data can be made available in profusion at the touch of a button, it is tempting to sit back and carry out pre-packaged analyses. Never, never, never do this. Always go to the source of the data. The true anecdote on page 12 illustrates this.

We always have three dimensions involved in a decision. There is at least one measurement – often money, but it can be life, health, comfort, morale, innovation, market share, sales and so on. But always at least one measure. There will also be the effect of time. Is this a one-off decision? Is there a sequence of interlocking decisions? Does time affect value – either increasing it, as with wine stocks, or decreasing it, as with value depreciation. Besides the unit and time, there is also probability. Are we dealing with fixed quantities and deterministic relationships? Do we know for sure the consequences of our actions? There is always the trinity of factors – measure, time and probability, and the following chapters will develop these.

Before moving on, a word of caution: it must never be forgotten that we are dealing with people. Behind the data sheets and computer printouts, behind the graphs and the tables, behind the mathematics, are people in all their emotions, in all their contrariness and bloody mindedness and in all their humanity. The man or woman can always beat the system.

In Mario Puzo's book, *The Godfather*, there is a scene in which a senior gangster, the Capo Regime, has been discovered leaking information to a rival gang. As he is being taken away to be executed he turns to the Godfather and says: "Godfather, it was only business. There was nothing personal." The reply of the Godfather was: "Everything is personal."

Everything is indeed personal.

But why go to the extent of modelling – why do advanced statistics, mathematics and sophisticated Information Technology have to be summoned to help? Surely it can all be done by a logical mind, common sense and experience? Chapter 3 will answer that question.

APPENDIX 1

There is an important point to make about problems where all the relations are linear. This will be illustrated by a small, almost trivial, problem which does, however, make some important points.

Suppose we have two food stocks, Xylate and Yuck, which are each sources of vitamins A and B. One unit of Xylate contains 6 units of vitamin A and 3 units of vitamin B, while one unit of Yuck contains 4 units of vitamin A and 8 units of vitamin B.

Each unit of Xylate costs £50, each unit of Yuck costs £30 and we need to have a mixture of Xylate and Yuck with at least 24 units of vitamin A and 24 units of vitamin B at minimum cost. We can put all this in a table:

	Produces	
	A	B
One unit of X	6	3
One unit of Y	4	8

The algebra tells us that x units of X and y units of Y will produce a mixture with $(6x + 4y)$ units of vitamin A and $(3x + 8y)$ units of vitamin B. The cost of such a mixture is $50x + 30y$. Since we need at least 24 units each of A and B we can graph all this (Figure 2.6).

All mixes of X and Y are points in the diagram and if we want the minima of vitamins A and B to be 24 then, to satisfy the vitamin A minimum, all

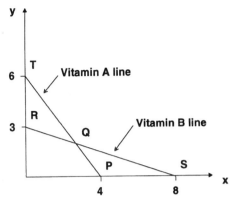

Figure 2.6 Diet mixtures

mixes must be above the line RQS and for vitamin B above the line TQP. There is an awful lot of possible mixes. So far as cost is concerned, we have to minimise $50x + 30y$. For any given cost, say 150, all points on the line $50x + 30y = 150$, will have that cost. This line joins $x = 3$, $y = 0$ to $x = 0$, $y = 5$ and for any other cost, say 200, all points on the line $50x + 30y = 200$, i.e. the line joining $x = 4$, $y = 0$ to $x = 0$, $y = 6\frac{2}{3}$ will have that cost.

All these equal cost lines are parallel and as they move up their (equal) cost is increasing. We need to minimise the cost of the mixture which means to find a point (i.e. mixture) on a parallel line as low as possible (to minimise the cost) but still on or above both vitamin A and vitamin B lines (Figure 2.7).

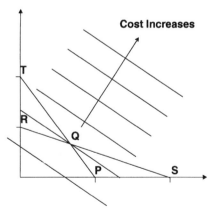

Figure 2.7 P logic

It can be seen that the best (least cost) point is Q, where $x = \frac{8}{3}$ and $y = 2$. That is, with a cost $193\frac{1}{3}$. It cannot be done any cheaper *but*, observe the logic. There are two straight lines involved, the vitamin A line and the vitamin B line. There is a set of parallel (equal cost) lines. Depending on which set of lines we have, the problem will always be solved *not* by some point out of an infinitely large set of possibilities, but by one of three only – each time the relevant P, Q or R. If X is much cheaper than Y, then the cheapest mixture could be only X at S. If Y is much cheaper than X, then the cheapest mixture would be all Y, at point T. Otherwise the best mixture is at Q.

In this way, the logic, if necessary with no quantitative data at all, tells us that there is not an infinity of choice but only one of three alternatives (at S, Q or T). Where these alternatives are, depends on the quantities. But there are always three possibilities from the internal logic *even before any data are collected*.

In addition, the "best" solution is never inside the diagram and always on the border. More than this, even, it is always at a corner. There may be more equally good ones but they will be on the border or at another corner. The method of search for the best recognises this and hunts from corner to corner, always getting a better answer until a corner is reached from which it is impossible to improve by moving to any other corner. The optimum has then been reached. It is this same principle that is followed in vastly more complicated problems.

APPENDIX 2

Birthdays

It is easiest to consider the probability of there being NO pairs. Take the first person and their birthday. When the next person joins there are 364 dates out of 365 which will mean no pair, that is the chance of no pair is 364/365. If there is no pair out of the two then the third person has 363 dates out of the 365 for there to be no pair, and so the chance of no pair in three is:

Chance of no match in the first two, times the chance of no match between the third and either of the first two. That is, $364/365 \times 363/365 = 0.9918$.

In the same way the chance of no match among 4 people is: $364/365 \times 363/365 \times 362/365 = 0.9898$.

As might be expected this probability decreases each time a new person joins in and by the time there are 25 people present the probability has declined to 0.50 or 50%.

The Stick Problem

For a triangle to be possible none of the three portions can be greater in length than the other two combined. Let the stick be of length 1 metre and suppose that the first and second break points are, respectively, lengths x and y from the left-hand end (Figure 2.8).

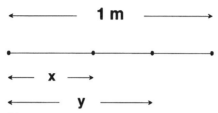

Figure 2.8 Stick breaking

If the first break point is in the left-hand part of the stick then the second break point must not be in the same half otherwise one portion will be of length more than 0.50 m. In addition if it is in the other half it cannot be more than 0.50 m away as if it is the central portion will be more than 0.50 m in length. Similarly, if the first break point is in the right-hand portion of the stick then an identical limitation occurs (Figure 2.9).

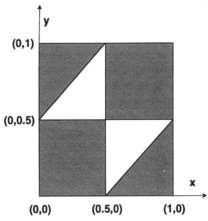

Figure 2.9 Probability diagram

The probability as revealed from Figure 2.9 shows the combination where a triangle is impossible as the shaded area and as can be seen the probability required is 0.25.

References

1   McGervey, J.D. (1986). *Probabilities in Everyday Life*, Ivy Books, New York.
2   Lindley, D.V. (1965). *Introduction to Probability and Statistics. Part 1, Probability*, Cambridge University Press, Cambridge.
3   Toulmin, S. and Goodchild, J. (1963). *The Fabric of the Heavens*, Pelican, London.
4   Ackoff, R.L. (1978). *The Art of Problem Solving*, Wiley, New York.

The Pastry Man's Tale

The Second Principle: Always question the assumptions which lie behind the question given and also question the origin and scale of each measurement in the data.

INTRODUCTION

The questioning of data is a two-edged sword. There may often be quantitative data latent in a qualitative statement and it is wise to investigate the validity of all prior statements and descriptions which have led to the posing of the question.

The other edge of the sword is that the data we use relate to a particular origin and scale of measurement. In the First Life we saw how important it is to collect and handle at least a sample of the data we use. But data are never pure, unsullied, virginal numbers that can be taken as unbiased and "true". Not only do we have to go to their source but we have to comprehend the implications of scales of measurement. Sometimes a problem is immensely clarified by looking at data in a fresh way. We therefore have two anecdotes this time. They are both venerable but no apology is offered for their age. One relates to the reign of King Charles II and the other is one of the great classics in the early years of OR.

First Anecdote (True)

This anecdote illustrates the capacity for self-delusion which is, alas, a trait of scientists in general and even OR analysts. It is recorded (ref 1) that Charles II once "invited Fellows of the Royal Society to explain why a dead fish weighs more than when it was alive. The fellows responded with ingenious explanations, until the King pointed out that what he had told them was not true".

Second Anecdote (True)

After the surrender of France in 1940, the Germans occupied the ports in the Bay of Biscay. From these they mounted a submarine offensive on the British (and, later, the Allied) convoys bringing supplies of material and men from Canada and the USA to Britain. At that time submarines normally travelled on the surface, for speed, in order to charge their batteries and to receive radio messages. They only submerged when they were in action.

Coastal Command of the British Royal Air Force, based in Devon and Cornwall, operated a patrol of aircraft carrying depth charges. These depth charges were pre-set to explode at the depth at which they had the greatest radius of kill. If set too shallow, the result was spectacular fountains of sea water. If set too deep, the water pressure reduced physical impact. In practice the depth setting was about 100 feet.

The operations were very similar. The aircraft by visual sighting (and later by radar) would spot a submarine. It would adjust its course for an attack and then drop a stick of depth charges. Meanwhile the submarine, on spotting the aircraft, would crash dive.

However, few submarines were being destroyed. The operational research section of the RAF (led by Professor Patrick Blackett, FRS – later to be a Nobel Laureate in physics) flew with the aircraft and, with the help of cine cameras, analysed the circumstances which might lead to an increase in their success rate.

Their logs had the details of the attack:

- Time and place of sighting.
- Height and course of aircraft.
- Course of submarine.
- Time when the submarine submerged.
- Time when the run in to attack began.
- Time when the depth charges were dropped, together with height and course of aircraft.
- The result.

The first analyses were related to the time elapsing since the aircraft spotted the submarine, but this analysis yielded nothing of significance. Eventually time was measured from the critical moment of truth, that is when the depth charge(s) exploded. This was when the depth charge was at 100 feet. Visual observation enabled the horizontal error to be evaluated and the vertical error could be estimated by how long the submarine had submerged when the depth charge exploded.

Therefore, when time was measured backwards from the moment when the first depth charge exploded, a clear result was obtained. At that moment of explosion, 40% of submarines were either still on the surface or had been submerged only long enough to take them down to 20 feet. It was now clear that the setting of the depth charge should be reduced, not only because on a vertical measure the explosion would be closer to the U boat, but that in any event the accuracy of drop was ten times better when the U boat was still visible than when it had been submerged for more than 15 seconds. As the lethal radius of a depth charge was only 19 feet, increased accuracy was vital.

Considerable discussion and argument was necessary before it was agreed to reduce settings: first 50 ft, then to 33 ft and finally to 25 ft (in 1942). The effect of reducing the setting (ref 2) is vivid:

Period	Total no. of attacks	Sunk (%)	Seriously damaged (%)
Sep. 1939–June 1941	215	1	4
July 1941–Dec. 1941	127	2	13
Jan. 1942–June 1942	79	4	19
July 1942–Dec. 1942	346	7	9

This is a fascinating story of the interaction of the RAF, OR and politics. For our purposes the single facet, from this multi-variegated example is that the real illumination was first gained when the data were re-arranged from a new base point.

Moral of the Stories

Before you start to answer the questions given ask some of your own.

Ask (tactfully) what are the underlying premises behind the question and, when you collect data, do not unthinkingly accept the origin, the scale and the units of the measures.

THE PASTRY MAN'S TALE

Introduction

Mr Hugh Patrick runs a meat pie factory in the north of England. An important source of his sales is bakery shops which sell bread, cakes, tarts, pies etc. Patrick has four salesmen, Williams, Exman, Young and Zeller, who have developed their own techniques and approaches. As a firm believer in competition Patrick allows all his salesmen to call on any of the bakery shops and to sell as many as they can. When they make a sale the pies are immediately delivered from the salesman's truck.

Having taken a course in business studies, Patrick decides to set up a special experiment to see which (if any) of his salesmen is the best. Over a 40-day test period (these bakery shops are open 7 days a week) four bakeries are selected by Patrick, namely Ackerman, Breadmaster, Collins and Doughboy. The salesmen must each call on these four bakery shops, which are chosen because they encompass high, medium and low sales figures. Each salesman must call exactly three times on each of these four during the test period while, of course, continuing his other work on all the other bakery shops (Patrick has obviously taken classes in the analysis of variance). Finally, in order to avoid collusion or other factors affecting order size, salesmen must decide when to call without reference to each other. Indeed it is not in their own interests to collude.

Table 1 shows the sales achieved by each salesman in each of the shops during the test. You, as a student in the local university are given this table by your head of department, Professor Berwyn, who plays golf every week with Patrick. He is due to have a round with him tomorrow and needs an answer today.

Stage 1: Look at the Data

Can you write a brief note which would be given to Patrick?

Stage 2: Discussion of Data

The obvious next, and only, stage in the work is to select the salesman who sells most. After all, although we are told that the shops encompass different levels of sales volume each salesman is treated exactly the same, he (or she) has to call exactly three times on each of the four shops. Twelve visits in all.

The total orders by each of the four competitors is:

Williams	489
Exman	581
Young	550
Zeller	325

Exman is a clear winner – indeed looking at Zeller's performance one wonders how he spent his time and what he has been up to. If we require further detail, These total orders can be broken down as shown in Table 2.

This table shows the variation in sales per shop and it is apparent that it was wise to give each salesman a fixed quota of visits to each shop.

Table 1 Salesmen's performance

	Williams			Exman	
Day	Bakery	Order size	Day	Bakery	Order size
2	Ackerman	11	2	Breadmaster	18
11	Collins	48	8	Doughboy	40
15	Breadmaster	68	9	Ackerman	29
18	Doughboy	36	15	Collins	57
21	Ackerman	24	16	Ackerman	24
25	Collins	57	25	Breadmaster	58
27	Collins	33	26	Doughboy	136
30	Doughboy	77	28	Ackerman	34
34	Doughboy	64	29	Collins	27
35	Breadmaster	42	37	Doughboy	60
37	Ackerman	11	38	Breadmaster	28
40	Breadmaster	18	39	Collins	70
	Total orders	489		Total orders	581

	Young			Zeller	
Day	Bakery	Order size	Day	Bakery	Order size
6	Doughboy	74	2	Collins	35
7	Collins	42	2	Doughboy	47
10	Ackerman	6	3	Ackerman	8
13	Doughboy	104	4	Collins	35
16	Doughboy	56	8	Breadmaster	64
18	Breadmaster	28	8	Collins	20
21	Collins	93	11	Ackerman	9
27	Breadmaster	22	19	Breadmaster	15
31	Ackerman	14	19	Doughboy	27
31	Breadmaster	18	29	Breadmaster	27
34	Collins	72	31	Doughboy	28
35	Ackerman	21	38	Ackerman	10
	Total orders	550		Total orders	325

Table 2 Breakdown of orders

		Shop			
Salesman	Ackerman	Breadmaster	Collins	Doughboy	Total
Williams	46	128	138	177	489
Exman	87	104	154	236	581
Young	41	68	207	234	550
Zeller	27	106	90	102	325
Total	201	406	589	749	1945

Table 3 Orders by salesmen and by day number at all bakeries

Day	A	B	C	D
1				
2	W-11	X-18	Z-35	Z-47
3	Z-8			
4			Z-35	
5				
6				Y-74
7			Y-42	
8		Z-64	Z-20	X-40
9	X-29			
10	Y-6			
11	Z-9		W-48	
12				
13				Y-104
14				
15		W-68	X-57	
16	X-24			Y-56
17				
18		Y-28		W-36
19		Z-15		Z-27
20				
21	W-24		Y-93	
22				
23				
24				
25		X-58	W-57	
26				X-136
27		Y-22	W-33	
28	X-34			
29		Z-27	X-27	
30				W-77
31	Y-14	Y-18		Z-28
32				
33				
34			Y-72	W-64
35	Y-21	W-42		
36				
37	W-11			X-60
38	Z-10	X-28		
39			X-70	
40		W-18		
Total sales	201	406	589	749

So the prize goes to Exman and our note to the professor is simple.

To Professor Berwyn,
Subject: Mr Hugh Patrick.

The orders achieved by the four salesmen over the four weeks were:

Williams	489
Exman	581
Young	550
Zeller	325

They each called three times on each of the 4 shops selected for the test.

The arithmetic is impeccable. The differences are significant. Award the prize to Exman and fire Zeller.

Stage 3: A Note of Caution

But Wait! Ask: what lies behind the data?
These orders are obtained from bakeries which are selling the pies day by day. Therefore the stock of pies in each bakery will diminish as days go by and the bakeries will therefore order replenishment in the light of their existing stock when the salesman next calls. A salesman who calls when stocks are low, that is, when some days have elapsed since the last salesman called, will be at an advantage compared with a salesman who by chance calls the day after another salesman visited the shop. There is therefore a hidden handicap and we must take account of the time elapsed since the previous call and re-cast Table 1 as Table 3.
In Table 3, A, B, C and D are the four bakeries and W, X (for Exman), Y and Z are the four salesmen. Thus on day 3, Zeller obtained an order for 8 pies at Ackerman. Take the elapsed time between visits and let t = the days since the last visit by any salesman; we take the day as zero when all the shops were brought up to full stock at the begining of the test, i.e. Day 0 (see Table 4).
Zeller is a clear winner (Table 5). There is no need to ask how he spends his time and it would be disastrous to fire him. However, his figures do look curious as so many of them are whole numbers. Look at the data. Why is this? It appears that Zeller often calls on the day following a previous visit by someone else (when the divisor $t = 1$). Is there any advantage in this?

Table 4   Orders by shop

Day	Salesman	Sales at Ackerman Quantity Q	t	Q/t	Day	Salesman	Sales at Breadmaster Quantity Q	t	Q/t
2	W	11	2	5.5	2	X	18	2	9.0
3	Z	8	1	8.0	8	Z	64	6	10.7
9	X	29	6	4.8	15	W	68	7	9.7
10	Y	6	1	6.0	18	Y	28	3	9.3
11	Z	9	1	9.0	19	Z	15	1	15.0
16	X	24	5	4.8	25	X	58	6	9.7
21	W	24	5	4.8	27	Y	22	2	11.0
28	X	34	7	4.9	29	Z	27	2	13.5
31	Y	14	3	4.7	31	Y	18	2	9.0
35	Y	21	4	5.2	35	W	42	4	10.5
37	W	11	2	5.5	38	X	28	3	9.3
38	Z	10	1	10.0	40	W	18	2	9.0

Day	Salesman	Sales at Collins Quantity Q	t	Q/t	Day	Salesman	Sales at Doughboy Quantity Q	t	Q/t
2	Z	35	2	17.5	2	Z	47	2	23.5
4	Z	35	2	17.5	6	Y	74	4	18.5
7	Y	42	3	14.0	8	X	40	2	20.0
8	Z	20	1	20.0	13	Y	104	5	20.8
11	W	48	3	16.0	16	Y	56	3	18.7
15	X	57	4	14.2	18	W	36	2	18.0
21	Y	93	6	15.5	19	Z	27	1	27.0
25	W	57	4	14.2	26	X	136	7	19.4
27	W	33	2	16.5	30	W	77	4	19.2
29	X	27	2	13.5	31	Z	28	1	28.0
34	Y	72	5	14.4	34	W	64	3	21.3
39	X	70	5	14.0	37	X	60	3	20.0

Table 5   Summing up: orders received per day since last call

	Ackerman		Breadmaster		Values of Q/t Collins		Doughboy		Overall average
Williams	5.5 4.8	5.5	9.7 10.5	9.0	16.0 14.2	16.5	18.0 19.2	21.3	12.5
Exman	4.8 4.8	4.9	9.0 9.7	9.3	14.2 13.5	14.0	20.0 19.4	20.0	12.0
Young	6.0 4.7	5.2	9.3 11.0	9.0	14.0 15.5	14.4	18.5 20.8	18.7	12.3
Zeller	8.0 9.0	10.0	10.7 15.0	13.5	17.5 17.5	20.0	23.5 27.0	28.0	16.6

Assumptions

1 That the data given are correct.
2 That salesmen have no knowledge of who else called, where they called and the sales they achieved. (Discuss why this is important.)
3 That the objective is sensible. If some lines of pies are more profitable than others, then equal size of orders does not mean equal contribution to profits. (Discuss the implication for the research if there is a difference in profitability of different lines and the object is to select the salesman who contributes most to profit.)
4 The price list from which the salesmen offer pies to the different shops is the same and there are no discounts for the quality.
5 There are no days when shop sales of pies to customers are likely to be higher than on other days. There is no trend and no cyclic effect. In statistical terms this means that shops sales to their customers are *stationary* and purely random about a mean which is constant for any given shop but not, of course, constant for all shops. (Discuss how you would deal with the problem if there were trends and cycles in the data.)
6 The age of a pie does not affect its attractiveness.

The note to Professor Berwyn is now longer than we first thought but we must still keep it short as the professor will not want to have a quick look at a ten-page report while he is ankle deep in a sand bunker.

To Professor Berwyn.
Subject: Mr Hugh Patrick.

The test was properly carried out, so far as I can judge. The superficial (and wrong) result is that Exman won:

Orders achieved per salesman:

Wiliams	489
Exman	581
Young	550
Zeller	325

But, since our assumption is that salesmen effectively called at random times on each of the four shops, the time interval between successive calls on any given shop is highly variable (from 1 day to 7 days) and this will affect orders received – it is almost certainly easier to get a large order when shop stocks are low. If we assess the orders achieved per salesman in terms of the lapsed time since the last visit, then Zeller, (who in the first analysis looked by far the worst), is the winner.

Average order per day of lapsed time:

Williams	12
Exman	12
Young	12
Zeller	17

There are assumptions I have had to make which we can discuss (these are listed above). The most important is that shop sales are stationary over time. If Mr Patrick wants a confident answer then we ought to examine shop sales on a daily basis throughout the test, so as to examine orders received in the light of stock in hand.

References

1 Wolpert, L. (1992). *The Unnatural Nature of Science*, Faber, London.
2 Waddington, C.H. (1973). *OR in World War 2*, Elek Science, London.

Reflections

This little example shows the importance of units of measurement and also of the selection of a base point for the data analysis. We should always list the variables considered together with their units of measurement. In this case we have the following.

Uncontrollable Variables

1 Which salesman calls on which bakery and when.
2 Customer demand at each shop (pies per day sold).
3 Salesmen's techniques and approach.

Controllable Variables

1 In the form of this test – none. But we can control the schedule of activities of the salesman as much as we wish.
2 Prices per pie charged to bakeries and any volume discount. (Price per pie in volume ranges.)

Objective Measure

Pies sold to the bakery per day elapsed since the last salesman called.

In a subtle way the base point will influence our thinking and selection of a base point means we must understand what is going on and make a hypothesis *before* we start to analyse the data. The hypothesis will then affect the measures we use. The alternative is to take data as measured by someone else and this *always* implies accepting a hidden hypothesis.

Further Work

1 Suppose there is a cyclic effect. If days 5, 12, etc. are Saturdays when sales are higher, how would you amend the analysis?

2 Suppose you suspected that one salesman might have got information on when the others were calling and adopted a non-random strategy. Would this help him? If so, how would you test for randomness of calls?

3 Suppose the pies vary in their profit margin. What changes would you make in the analysis?

4 Suppose that sales decline day by day after a delivery of pies because the customers notice that their quality is deteriorating. How would your analysis be changed?

5 Criticise this experiment and propose a better one. In what way is it better?

Chapter 3

Logic and Common Sense

Common sense, which can be quite uncommon, is built by experience over a number of years and is generally a sound guide. Logic always works – as long as the assumptions are valid and the process of logical deduction is correct. But logic can be difficult to confirm as correct. In mathematical proofs the danger point is when the argument uses the words "Clearly", or "Obviously". For when there is an error, that is where it will be found.

In this chapter we shall discuss various ways in which we can be led astray by common sense and by failing to be clear in our use of logic. When these two, common sense and logic, go wrong we can go badly astray because it never occurs to us that they *are* wrong.

These are the main reasons for the apparent failure of logic and common sense:

1 The evidence presented is an unfair sample.
2 The evidence is complete – everything is known exactly but intuition lets us down.
3 There is no exact knowledge, only probabilities, and using average values is misleading.
4 Quantities are assumed to be positively related. They always have been. But on occasion they can be inversely related.
5 Probabilities can be wrongly assessed but we never have a feedback which tells us how well we are estimating them.
6 We can be so attracted by the complex that we ignore the simple.

THE UNFAIR SAMPLE

In a military conflict it was decided that bombers and their crews should have armour protection from machine guns, cannon and flak. But where?

The more armour, the lower the bomb load. There was an absolute limit to the amount of armour a bomber could carry. The obvious step was to map the location of holes and damage in bombers returning from missions. When these maps were drawn it could be seen that in certain parts of the aircraft fuselage there was a higher density of damage than in others and the proposal was made to cover these parts in armour, for "obviously" there was a greater probability of strikes there than elsewhere. But second thoughts were better thoughts. It was pointed out that these were the bombers that had returned and the correct deduction was made that armour should be put in locations where there were fewer holes, or less damage, in the surviving aircraft.

THE PERILS OF INTUITION

Even in simple situations we can be misled by common sense and if we fail by common sense in the simple, what confidence can we have in the complex? Suppose we need to locate a depot to serve two customers and suppose (not unreasonably) that the cost of supplying a customer is the product of the amount being supplied and the distance travelled. Where should the depot be located?

For example, if A needs 50 units a day and B needs 100 units a day, then no matter what these demands actually are, the best location must always be on the line AB (Figure 3.1). (Those who doubt even this, can write out a formal proof). Let A and B be 100 km apart.

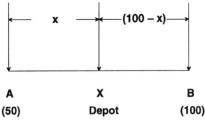

Figure 3.1 Depot location (1)

It is tempting to locate the depot at the centre of gravity of the two depots, 50 at A and 100 at B. That is to argue that in equity the distance from A to X should be $\frac{2}{3}$ of the way along from A to B. To do this is to fall into a trap caused by our intuition.

Let the cost of shipping 1 unit for 1 km be c. Put the depot at the customer who takes more product, i.e. at B. The total cost will now be $(50)(100)c$ = 5000c.

If we now move the depot one km towards A. The new cost will be $(50)(99)c + 100c = 5050c$.

Move a second km towards A and the cost will be $(50)(98)c + (100)(2)c = 5100c$.

As we move towards A the cost rises $50c$ every km, because for each km to A the cost of shipping to A reduces by $50c$ but the cost of shipping to B increases by $100c$, a net increase of $50c$. No matter how far apart A and B are, the optimal location is at the customer with the larger demand, and if both customers have the same demand then all positions between A and B have the same cost.

That was not surprising but now take this a stage further (Figure 3.2).

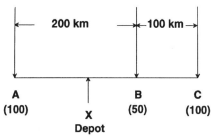

Figure 3.2 Depot location (2)

Suppose we now have three customers along a straight line (say a motorway). Again the depot must be on the line ABC. Suppose it is somewhere between A and B. If, wherever it is, we move it one km towards B, the cost of shipping to A will go up by 100 units, the cost to B will go down by 50 units and the cost to C down by 60 units. There is a net reduction in cost of 10 units per km for a movement of the depot in the direction of B. So if it is between A and B, it should be at B.

Now consider a depot between between B and C. The same argument gives a net reduction of 90 units per km for a movement towards B. So B must always be the best place. But notice, this argument has never used the distances between A and B (200 km) and B and C (100 km). A can be shifted 100 km, 1000 km, or 10 000 km to the left and B is still the best location for minimum cost.

This interesting result is a special case of a general statement. If the destinations are spread around a countryside a simple method will work. Put the destinations on a scale map with a firm backing. Bore smooth holes at the map positions. Take a piece of string for each destination, attach a weight proportional to the delivery quantity at one end, take the strings through the holes and knot them together (Figure 3.3).

Let the knot come to rest when the weights hang and it will be at the point of minimum transport cost. It is also the case that if X is where the

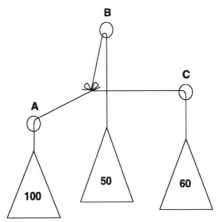

Figure 3.3 Getting knotted

knot comes to rest any of the holes can be moved away from X in the line of its string without affecting the point X. (This is also true if the points are in three or more dimensional space, although it is difficult to see an application of the result!) In Figure 3.4, D and E can each be moved along the dotted line without the depot having to move (and the same applies at A, B and C).

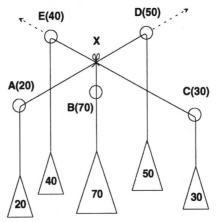

Figure 3.4 More knots

It is therefore always necessary to examine our assumptions when using common sense. Here it is once again the assumption of centre of gravity. It is plausible but it is wrong.

In the previous chapter we saw how logical thinking can reduce the number of alternative choices that we need to consider. This is one of the most powerful uses of logic and one of the few cases where we can work without data. Sometimes it is the data themselves which can lead us astray.

Example

A transport manager has to ship a product from three factories to three warehouses. A factory can ship to more than one warehouse and a warehouse receive from more than one factory. The cost of shipping on any route is the product of the amount transported and the cost per kilo. The amounts to be shipped out each day from each factory and required at each warehouse are:

Factory A	300	Warehouse X	600
Factory B	600	Warehouse Y	300
Factory C	500	Warehouse Z	500
Total	1400		1400

As can be seen, supply and demand are in balance. The costs per kilo for each of the nine routes involved are shown below. The problem is to decide how much should be shipped on each of these nine routes so that supply and demand are satisfied and total cost is minimised. As can be seen, Warehouse X is at Factory A.

Costs per kilo

From/To	X	Y	Z		Kilos leaving
A	(0)	(4)	(1)		300
B	(1)	(6)	(3)		600
C	(3)	(7)	(6)		500
Kilos arriving	600	300	500	Total =	1400

If we wish to, we can write the problem in mathematical language: Let the amount shipped from A to X be W(AX) etc.

Objective function: Minimise: $0.W(AX) + 4.W(AY) + 1.W(AZ) + ... + 6.W(CZ)$, subject to six constraints, one for each of A,B,C,X,Y,Z of the form $W(AX) + W(AY) + W(AZ) = 300$ = constraint for A etc.

But look at the data. The route A to X has zero cost, because warehouse X is at A, and the route C to Y has the highest cost. So we decide to send all of the product at A into its own warehouse, at zero cost, and also to send nothing along the most expensive route (C to Y). The rest of the seven routes can then be filled in, easily, by working down row by row and always choosing the cheapest alternative. Thus:

Common-sense solution (kilos)

	X	Y	Z	
A	300 (0)	0 (4)	0 (1)	300
B	300 (1)	300 (6)	0 (3)	600
C	0 (3)	0 (7)	500 (6)	500
	600	300	500	Total = 1400

Total cost = 5100

However, there are other solutions which are even cheaper, and the following can be shown to be the best possible, at a cost of 4000.

Amounts shipped

	X	Y	Z	
A	0 (0)	0 (4)	300 (1)	300
B	400 (1)	0 (6)	200 (3)	600
C	200 (3)	300 (7)	0 (6)	500
	600	300	500	Total = 1400

Total cost = 4000

Notice: In this solution *nothing* goes along the zero cost route – that is all the product at A goes to Z and the warehouse at X (i.e. at Factory A itself) is served by B and C. To add insult to injury, the most expensive route is used as much as possible.

How foolish can one get? But foolish is correct in this instance. Why? Our first argument overlooked the point that the whole set of nine decisions are not independent. They interact and it is not the case that if we take what appears to be the obvious solution for two of the routes then the others can fall into line. Such problems of supply and demand provide a minefield of sloppy logic.

PROBLEMS WITH VARIABILITY

One of the few cases where the mathematics illustrates a pitfall in practical management, is in what is known as queuing theory. Queuing theory concerns the interaction between the demand for service, arising in a random fashion and the supply of service, at a service point, where the service time varies from customer to customer. The basic problem is the random nature of the arrivals and the variability of the time taken to serve. Common everyday examples are queuing at post offices, bank counters, doctors' waiting rooms, or aircraft queuing to take off. Sometimes the service point is mobile and the customer static – as in maintenance crews serving machines or an ambulance service which goes to where the demand for service is located.

The basic relationships for which mathematical solutions can be provided are between the length of time spent in the system by those being served (i.e. their waiting time plus their own service time) and the amount of time that the service point is actually working. Two desires meet here. The customer wants minimum time in the system, even to the extent of always wanting no queue and immediate service. The person providing the service wants it to be used as fully as possible – to the extent of it always being in operation. These two extremes are mutually exclusive. The mathematics shows that the average time spent in the system depends, of course, on the nature of the variation in the interval between successive arrivals and on the variation in the service time. This average time spent in the system is indeed infinite if the interval between arrivals is on average less than the average service time. (In other words if the customers arrive faster than we can serve them they will wait for ever.) Why does this theoretical result never happen? It does not happen because no one will join a very long queue, let alone an infinite one and those in such a queue will become disenchanted and leave. In other words there was an assumption in the theory that the discipline of the queue and of its arrivals is so strong that they will never be put off. This assumption is false.

But what happens when the arrival interval is greater than the service time? Mathematically the average number in the system can be proved to be

$$A/(S-A) \qquad (3.1)$$

Where: S = Average number of people served per unit of time
A = Average number of arrivals per unit of time and S
must be greater than A

For example, if on average there are 10 arrivals each hour and 12 people can be served each hour, the average number of people in the system (being served or waiting) is 5.

The surprising thing is that when these two averages are the same, i.e. $A = S$, then the average queue length is theoretically *infinite*. That is if supply and demand are in balance the system is out of control. Indeed it is very sloppy logic to assume that if $A = S$ then supply and demand are in balance. If R is the ratio of the average time between successive arrivals and the average service time it must always be less than 1. It cannot equal 1 (Figure 3.5).

Why should this be so? The point we have missed in the "balance of supply and demand" argument is that the service point cannot do any work in anticipation if a customer is not there. This is illustrated by a taxi queue outside a railway station. If there are exactly 1000 parties to be picked up each day and if there are exactly 1000 arrivals of taxis each day, then the system will be in balance. Sometimes there will be a queue of people,

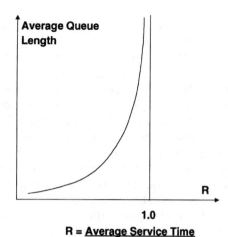

R = $\dfrac{\text{Average Service Time}}{\text{Average Arrival Interval}}$

Figure 3.5 Average queue length

sometimes there will be a queue of taxis, but at the day's end all people and all taxis will be dealt with. But if, when a taxi arrives and the driver finds no one waiting he goes away, then the number of "useful" taxi arrivals in the day will be reduced and the system will not be in balance.

In practice this can be manifest in a job shop, which receives different orders requiring different man hours of work. These orders arrive in a random pattern and no work can be performed unless the job order has been received. If the number of man hours of work available each week exactly equals the number of man hours of work needed on the jobs ordered, then overtime will be required. The system will in fact be unbalanced and management will be criticised for their apparent incompetence, whereas overtime is in the nature of operation and why this is so is shown by the theory.

Queuing theory is also an illustration of the seductiveness of techniques referred to on page 63. It is most attractive theoretically and does illustrate a parodox, but in any practical situation it fails completely because it is unable to deal with situations which do not comply with the very constrained and restrictive assumptions which it demands. In practice in these problems one would use simulation (refs 1 and 2).

ERRORS IN CAUSE–EFFECT RELATIONSHIPS

Our logic can let us down because, as we have noted, we have too easily made the statement "It is obvious that . . ." A familiar way of estimating sales results is share of market. There can be cases where a company can have its share of market increase in all its separate product groups from one year to the next, while overall its share of market decreases (see ref 3).

Marketing models generally assume that if price is increased, sales will decrease and economists introduce the concept of price elasticity (Figure 3.6).

Figure 3.6   Price elasticity

Such models all have a hidden agenda of assumptions. There are examples quoted (but rarely substantiated) of experiments where the same goods are offered for sale at different prices and sales decline at low prices because customers assume the product must be poor. Is the customer irrational? People may wish to express affection, not by the nature of a gift but by how much the gift has cost – and spending more becomes a virtue.

The theory of queuing, which has been quoted, has a variant in which potential customers do not join a queue when it is long and so the arrival pattern is reduced as a function of queue length. But in post offices where it is possible to queue in the warm (for example where the post office is inside a shop) old and lonely people arrive up to an hour before the post office opens *because* there is a queue and they can talk to other people. So the queue *attracts* more arrivals.

In marketing similar reversals of expectation can arise. Most advertising models are deeply depressing. Although the staff of agencies agonise over the words and pictures to be used in advertisements, the models themselves need not take account, in any measurable manner, of results of this agony, and express advertising effort solely in terms of money spent. The basic input is to assume that sales, however measured, will increase with advertising expenditure, although there will be a saturation level which must also be estimated.

Sometimes the product will sell without advertising and sometimes

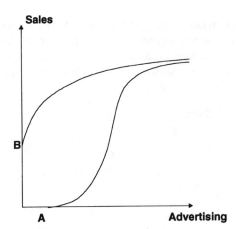

Figure 3.7   Typical advertising–sales relationships

advertising is necessary before any sales are achieved. In these cases the graph will go through A or B respectively, but this *type* of graph (Figure 3.7) is received doctrine. A study of the effect of advertising on the sale of beer is recorded in ref 4. The company concerned had a static level of advertising and static sales for some time (Figure 3.8).

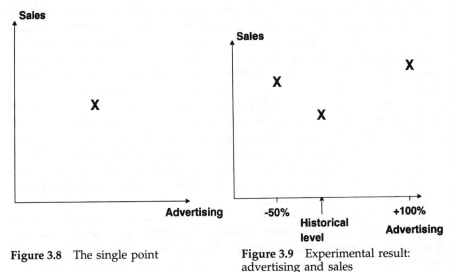

Figure 3.8   The single point

Figure 3.9   Experimental result: advertising and sales

Many curves could be drawn through the one point, and an experiment was carried out, in which advertising in some regions was increased by 50% and in others reduced by 50%. The sales in the first regions increased but the sales in the second region also increased (Figure 3.9). These results, checked thoroughly, are inconsistent with the hypothesis. Certainly in this case the experiment disposed of the models displayed in Figure 3.7.

The only possible conclusion is that, at the very least, we can no longer assume that sales never decrease as advertising increases. It could be that too much advertising causes a revulsion against the product (Figure 3.10).

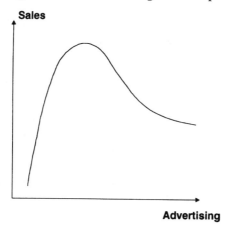

Figure 3.10   Advertising revulsion

Moreover, even such a relationship as this means that there must be more than one relationship in operation. Further experiments fleshed out the shape of the dotted curve and led to a hypothesis that the population divided into different groups each with its own response curve as in Figure 3.11. The conclusions and the moral are clear, always beware of the obvious and the self-evident. A final point is that in the analysis itself, the nature

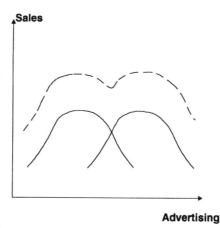

Figure 3.11   Mixed response rates

of the data, how we handle the data and the form of measurement, may hide the truth.

PITFALLS OF ASSUMING PROBABILITIES

It is fatally easy to guess a probability and it is often done with no sense of fear or shame, because there is no way, on a one-off basis, to check how well it has been done. We saw this in Chapter 2. Even bookmakers can fail. When, in 1961, President Kennedy stated that the USA would put a man on the moon in that decade, only one person in the UK had the nous to go to his local bookmaker and ask the odds. He was quoted 100–1 against and put on a modest £10. But we have no means of stating that the bookmaker was incompetent. If one estimates that the probability of Little Rock Braves winning the World Series baseball before the year 2000 is one in a million and Little Rock actually get into the major league and win the series in 1999 – was the probability wrong? And if one had bet against Little Rock would one have been foolish?

FALLING IN LOVE WITH COMPLEXITY

Logic is a game played by certain rules and follows from certain assumptions. Common sense also has embedded in it certain assumptions and sometimes these assumptions are never brought out into daylight. There can be a desire on the part of the decision modeller to go for the more sophisticated approach rather than a simple cutting through by logic and understanding to the heart of the problem.

Consider the following problem: A chocolate bar consists of a rectangle of 6 × 3 little squares of chocolate (Figure 3.12). It could be broken along the line AB and the larger piece could then be broken along CD (Figure 3.13). Eventually we could finish with 18 separate squares. What is the minimum number of breaks to get the ultimate 18 pieces?

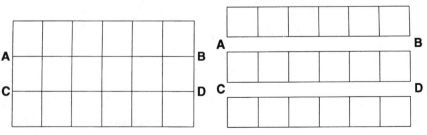

Figure 3.12   Figure 3.13

There are elegant mathematical methods to which one can turn – even, for the aficionados, dynamic programming. (Try it. But only after you have tried, turn to the end of the chapter.)

How did you get on?

Now for a parallel true story taken from Hastings (ref 5). At the height of his power Napoleon was invited to a chateau with a large estate. On enquiring what diversion the Emperor would enjoy most, it was determined that he would like to go out into the countryside and shoot rabbits. So the instructions went out to the staff, and one afternoon Napoleon and his courtiers went off in an elegant carriage, complete with guns and ammunition.

At the given spot keepers were waiting with a thousand rabbits. When the Emperor was ready, he advanced gun in hand and the keepers released the rabbits. To everyone's consternation all the rabbits swarmed towards Napoleon hopping around him and even jumping into his arms.

The keepers had collected a thousand tame rabbits who mistook Napoleon for the man who came to feed them lettuce each day. The keepers tried to drive them all off with horse whips, but the rabbits (as Hastings writes) were more expert in the principles of war than the keepers and outflanked them and followed Napoleon into his carriage. Napoleon was driven away without having harmed a single hair on a single rabbit. Napoleon wanted wild rabbits who would give him sport. Tame rabbits were of no use. They climbed all over him in great affection. He could not shoot them.

Moral of the Story

Often we want wild problems which will give us sport and can be disappointed when the problems turn out to be tame and friendly.

The Chocolate Bar Problem

Alas for the mathematics. Each break adds 1 to the number of pieces. You start with 1 and wish to finish with 18, so there are 17 breaks. Not one more, not one less. No matter how you do it.

Another example of this is the knock-out competition. If there are a number of competitors who will play off in pairs, the winner going through each time, the number of games to find the ultimate winner is one less than the number of competitors.

References

1 White, D.J. (1985). *Operational Research*, Wiley, Chichester.
2 Mitchell, G.H. (1972). *Operational Research*, English Universities Press, London.

3 Rivett, B.H.P. (1972). *Principles of Model Building*, Wiley, Chichester.
4 Ackoff, R.L. (1986). *Management in Small Doses*, Wiley, New York.
5 Hastings, M. (1985). *The Oxford Book of Military Anecdotes*, Oxford University Press, Oxford.

Berwyn Bank

The Third Principle: Think before embarking on analysis. Check whether the situation is sensitive or robust.

INTRODUCTION

Two Domestic Incidents

In the bathroom we are vividly aware that when we take a shower a small turn of the control changes the water temperature from icy cold to boiling hot. This is an illustration of a very sensitive decision.

In the kitchen we find that there are some joints of meat which, no matter how carefully they are cooked, turn out as tender as leather. These are robust in their response to what we do.

Management is faced with a control board. There are many dials giving measures, some accurate, others inaccurate or biased. Some dials are in meaningless units. The levers and switches on the control board are connected to the machinery in different ways. Some give rapid response which can be felt immediately, others have slow responses which are difficult to correct. But there are also those which are not connected to anything at all – and some of these are among the most used.

It behoves us all as analysts to know this, to expect it and to identify the sensitive factors and not to worry about the robust ones. It also reminds us to think before we plunge into a sea of data. The anecdote that follows illustrates this point.

Anecdote (True)

A major city which was connected to most of its suburbs by bridges and tunnels wished to reduce the number of cars driven by commuters. The

proposal was to charge a toll based on a levy for each car plus a fee for each passenger carried.

Sampling methods were used to collect information on the number of cars by bridge, by tunnel, by day of the week and by time of day. Comparisons were made with travel by bus or train and large-scale analyses were carried out to build a model of this whole activity.

The analysis was so immense that a consultant was asked to advise. The consultant pointed out that no analysis of this problem was necessary. The proposed fee structure would induce drivers to cut down the number of passengers and hence increase the number of cars. Logical thought showed that drivers should be charged for the number of empty seats. This would induce car pooling and reduce the size of cars. (*Note*: Cars carrying three or more passengers can now travel at no extra cost in the express lanes in San Francisco) (ref 1).

Moral of the Story

Think before embarking on data collection. And think again before starting the analysis. If it is lazy to sit and think, then be lazy. Time spent in thought is seldom wasted. But do remember that answers must be provided in time.

BERWYN BANK

Introduction

All the major UK banks have turned their attention to the inventory of cash held in the tills of their branches. It is easy to be over-stocked with cash. No branch manager is happy at the thought of running out of cash – it is not the sort of thing that customers like. It makes even the most placid feel nervous. But holding cash is expensive. A major clearing bank can hold as much as £200 000 000 in the tills of its branches. The opportunity cost of not being able to lend this money is considerable and, in the UK, the Bank of England leverage rules mean that lending is constrained as a multiple of liquid resources. But cash in tills does not count as liquid resources. There is a double penalty therefore in holding cash – it is not being lent and it is not part of the leverage formula.

All major clearers have reduced their holdings considerably as a result of statistical analysis of these cash holdings. This has led naturally, since the cost of delivering or collecting cash is a parameter in inventory studies, to studies of routing security vans. Berwyn Bank gives the flavour of this work. It introduces the problem of dealing with many alternative courses of action and the necessity to look at robustness before plunging into seas of arithmetic and data analysis.

That well-known research consultant, Tom Tryer, has received this letter from a former colleague who is a senior man in the Berwyn Bank. The letter starts with the usual chit-chat and a mention of some past history that Tom would prefer to be forgotten, and then goes on:

> I remember that at University we both had some lectures on systems analysis, as a result of which you decided to become an SA scientist and I decided not to. I have recently become responsible for a small group of our branches in the Brove area and can see that they have a problem where you could well be of help.
>
> In Brove we have four branches in a commercial area, which means they receive more cash on average than they pay out. It is our policy to hire security people to collect the cash at stated intervals and to take it to our money store. There seem to be two costs involved.
>
> Firstly, our branches cost us money (and that means *me*) for the cash they hold in tills. Such cash holdings do so, not least because under Bank of England rules although the amount of money we can lend is related to our liquid resources, cash does not count as a component of these resources. So there is an opportunity cost associated with holding cash, in addition to the loss of income by not lending it.
>
> I always find that there is a large subjective element in opportunity costs – we all know they are there but there is never any consensus as to how much they are. However, from my own point of view I don't care what they are in reality as Head Office charges me six pounds per day for every ten thousand pounds of cash in the tills at the end of business each day: (they do not count Saturdays and Sundays in their sums, so we get the cash for nothing over the weekend).
>
> From this point of view I would like the security vans to call every day on each branch, which I would have done were it not that I also have to pay for the vans. The security firm charges me two hundred pounds a day for hiring a van and a further one hundred pounds for each branch called on. (The money store is far enough away for it to be necessary for me to have a van for the whole day no matter how many branches are visited.)
>
> Obviously if it was not for the payment I make for cash stocks, I would have the van very rarely, even once a year.
>
> So there must be a point of balance between having the van once each day and once each year.
>
> Where is it? Table 1 shows the position of the four branches which for anonymity I have called A, B, C and D.

Table 1 Net cash receipts (£ per day)

Branch	A	B	C	D	Total
Average cash receipts	300 000	100 000	100 000	50 000	550 000
Average cash payments	230 000	60 000	80 000	40 000	410 000
Net average gain	70 000	40 000	20 000	10 000	140 000

There is an additional problem. The security company does not like a fixed schedule of regular visits, which they say leaves their guards open to ambush. They have written to say they want "an element of randomisation in the schedule". I do not know what randomisation is, but I have a working rule that anything described in a word of more than two syllables will be expensive.

Can you also comment on that aspect?

Yours sincerely,
Ivor Problum

Stage 1: Discussion

At a first look the problem seems to show a large number of alternative solutions. We could, for example, reduce the van costs by always calling on the four branches together. On the other hand, we could deal with each separately, and finally with all combinations in between.

Whatever we do we have the dilemma of costs:

	Cash cost	Van cost	Total cost
Frequent calls	Low	High	?
Infrequent calls	High	Low	?

As we have to start somewhere and because there are virtues in simplicity, we take first just one branch, selecting A because it is the biggest. To keep the arithmetic simple we shall take all cash flows in units of £10 000. At this measure the cost of holding cash is £6 per unit per day.

Stage 2: First Analysis of Branch A

The total cash held in the branch grows at £70 000 (i.e. 7 units) per day, and so the cost of holding cash grows at the following rate:

- In day 1 the cost is £42.
- In day 2 the cost is £84.
- And then the daily cost grows at £42 per day.

On the other hand the cost of collecting cash is 200 + 100 = £300 per collection. We can now see how the average total cost per day is made up (Table 2).

As can be seen in Table 2, the calling interval which minimises the average total cost per day is 4 days. The arithmetic thus far shows that for branch A, taken alone, the total cost per day is the sum of:

- The average transport cost per day:
  If there is a cycle of n days, then this average is $[300/n]$.
- The average cost of holding stock:

Table 2 Average costs for Branch A

Calling cycle (days) n	Total cost of holding cash	Average holding cost per day for cycle	Collection cost	Average collection cost per day for n day cycle	Average total cost per day for n day cycle
1	42	42	300	300	342
2	126	63	300	150	213
3	252	84	300	100	184
4	420	105	300	75	180
5	630	126	300	60	186
6	882	147	300	50	197
7	1176	168	300	43	211
8	1512	189	300	37	226

Note: From here on all costs will be in pounds and the pound sign will be omitted.

The cash held at the end of each successive day is 70 000; 140 000; 210 000 . . . 70 000n. The average cash held is $[7(n + 1)/2]$, and the average cost per day is therefore $21(n + 1)$.

The problem therefore is to minimise the sum of these two, that is, $21(n + 1) + [300/n]$ (Figure 1). Differentiation shows that the total cost is minimised when:

$$n = \sqrt{\frac{300}{21}} = 3.78 \text{ or } 4 \text{ days} \qquad (1)$$

This value of n is where the slopes of the line and the curve are equal and

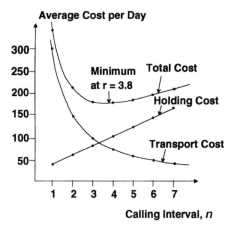

Average Cost per Day

Minimum at r = 3.8   Total Cost

Holding Cost

Transport Cost

Calling Interval, n

Figure 1 Cost functions

Table 3 Average holding cost per day for all n and r

r	$n = 1$	2	3	4	5	6	7	8	9
1	6	9	12	15	18	21	24	27	30
2	12	18	24	30	36	42	48	54	60
3	18	27	36	45	54	63	72	81	90
4	24	36	48	60	72	84	96	108	120
5	30	45	60	75	90	105	120	135	150
6	36	54	72	90	108	126	144	162	180
7	42	63	84	105	126	147	168	189	210
8	48	72	96	120	144	168	192	216	240
9	54	81	108	135	162	189	216	243	270
10	60	90	120	150	180	210	240	270	300
11	66	99	132	165	198	231	264	297	330
12	72	108	144	180	216	252	288	324	360
13	78	117	156	195	234	273	312	351	390
14	84	126	168	210	252	294	336	378	420

Table 4 Total daily costs

	$n = 1$	2	3	4	5	6	7
Average holding cost	42	63	84	105	126	147	168
Average calling cost	300	150	100	75	60	50	43
Average total	342	213	184	180	186	197	211

opposite (since the differential coefficient of their sum is zero). It now looks as though we are going to be in much arithmetic and so it is prudent to resort to algebra and obtain general costs.

So far as cash holding is concerned, cash is generated at a rate of r per day, where r is in units of 10 000. Over a period of n days the holding cost on each of successive days is $6r$; $12r$; $18r$; ... $6nr$. This sums to:

$$6r(1 + 2+ \ldots + n) = 3rn(n + 1)$$

The average holding cost per day over the n days is therefore $3r(n + 1)$. In tabular form (Table 3). For branch A, with $r = 7$, if we add the average cost of calling per day, $[300/n]$, we obtain the result shown in Table 4 (as indicated in Table 2).

The minimum is at $n = 4$, with an average cost of 180 per day. This differs from the answer given by elementary calculus (3.78) since we have to restrict n to integer (whole number) values.

Stage 3: Extension

Taking the other three branches in a similar way, we obtain the best n to minimise their total costs as:

	r	Best n	Cost per day
B	4	5	132
C	2	7 or 8	91
D	1	9, 10 or 11	63

We have calculated that for branch A the optimal calling interval is 4 days. For branches B, C, D the similar calculations are shown in Table 5.

Table 5 Costs for different cycles

		Cycle n (days)								
		4	5	6	7	8	9	10	11	12
B	Holding	60	72	84	96	108	120	132	144	156
$r = 4$	Calling	75	60	50	43	37	33	30	27	25
	Total	135	132	134	139	145	153	162	171	181
C	Holding	30	36	42	48	54	60	66	72	78
$r = 2$	Calling	75	60	50	43	37	33	30	27	25
	Total	105	96	92	91	91	93	96	99	103
D	Holding	15	18	21	24	27	30	33	36	39
$r = 1$	Calling	75	60	50	43	37	33	30	27	25
	Total	90	78	71	67	64	63	63	63	64

Stage 4: Alternative Schedules

1 Treat each branch separately, i.e. A, B, C and D have calling intervals of 4, 5, 8 and 10 days respectively. (We select 8 for C and 10 for D as there will be more combined transport days.) Because these combined transport days occur, the total cost is *not* the sum of the four separate minimal costs i.e. 180 + 132 + 91 + 63 = 466. There will be days when the transport cost will not be 300 for each branch, but 400 for two banks, or 500 or 600 for three or four branches. This will occur on days which are common multiples of 4, 5, 8 or 10. After a period of 40 days the cycle will repeat so:

- On day 20, branches A, B and C will be served.
- On days 8, 16, 24 and 32, branches A and C will be served.
- On days 10 and 30, branches B and D will be served.

- On day 40, branches A, B, C and D will be served.

It follows that over each 40-day period,

- There is one occasion when there will be a saving of 3(300) – 500 = 400 in transport cost.
- Four occasions with a saving of 2(300) – 400 = 200 each time.
- Two occasions with a saving of 2(300) – 400 = 200 each time.
- One occasion with a saving of 4(300) – 600 = 600 each time.

Over this 40-day period the total reduction in costs due to more than one delivery taking place in a day is 400 + 800 + 400 + 600 = 2200, i.e. 55 per day. The total cost calculated separately for the 4 branches i.e. 466 and is now reduced to 411 per day.

2 As another alternative, treat all branches together. In this case $r = 14$, $c = 600$, $n = [600/42] = 3.78$ or 4 days. This is confirmed arithmetically by taking the last row of Table 3 and adding to it the transport costs for four branches as shown in Table 6.

The figures in Table 6 correspond to cost = $3r(n + 1) + [c/n]$, where $r = 14$ and $c = 600$. As has been seen, the minimum of this cost is when $n = \sqrt{c/3r}$. Over the range $n = 2$ to 6 these are all less than the lowest possible cost (411) in case (1). That is over a wide range in case (2) it does not matter what you do, as it is still cheaper than case (1). How then does case (3) compare?

Finally we have case (3):

3 Involves taking the two big branches together (A and B) and the two small branches together (C and D). (Note: other combinations can be taken at will.)

In this case, for A and B, $r = 11$, $c = 400$, $n = \sqrt{[300/33]} = 3.48$. Reference to Table 3 gives the result shown in Table 7. We can take either $n = 3$ or $n = 4$ and cost = 265. For C and D, $r = 3$, $c = 400$, $n = [400/9] = 6.67$. The arithmetic is seen in Table 8.

Table 6 Total cost of all branches together

n	Holding $r = 14$	Transport (4 branches)	Total (per day)
1	84	600	684
2	126	300	426
3	168	200	368
4	210	150	360
5	252	120	372
6	294	100	394
7	336	86	422

Table 7 Total costs for A and B together

n	Holding r = 11	Transport (2 branches)	Total
1	66	400	466
2	99	200	299
3	132	133	265
4	165	100	265
5	198	80	278
6	231	67	298

Table 8 Total costs for C and D together

n	Holding r = 3	Transport (2 branches)	Total
1	18	400	418
2	27	200	227
3	36	133	169
4	45	100	145
5	54	80	134
6	63	67	130
7	72	57	129
8	81	50	131
9	90	44	134

So we take $n = 6$ and cost = 129. It appears that we should take 3 (or 4) and 7 as the two intervals and in that case we would select 3 and 7 as overlaps would be more frequent, the transport cost on the 21st day being diminished by 200 with a corresponding daily reduction of 10 per day.

However consider that if we take 3 and 6 as the intervals there will be more frequent overlaps. Each sixth day there will be a transport saving of £200, i.e. £33 per day. This gives a total cost of £362 which is the best solution.

Stage 5: Summing Up

For these three cases the costs are:
- Cost (1). Treat all branches separately. Cost £411 p.d.
- Case (2). Treat all branches together: Cost £360 p.d.
- Case (3). (A and B); (C and D). Cost £362 p.d.

Stage 6: Randomisation

Moving now to the problem of randomisation we examine the cost function:

$$\text{Cost} = 3r(n + 1) + \frac{c}{n} \qquad (2)$$

Let the value of n which minimises this be n'. Since

$$n' = \sqrt{\frac{c}{3r}} \qquad (3)$$

the cost function is:

$$\text{Cost (min)} = 3r + 2\sqrt{3rc} \qquad (4)$$

The ratio of (3)/(2) is the increase of cost if a value of n other than the optimal one is used. If we neglect the term $3r$ in both (2) and (3), then it can be shown that the ratio

$$\frac{\text{Cost } (n)}{\text{Cost (min)}} = \frac{1}{2}\left(\frac{n'}{n} + \frac{n}{n'}\right) \qquad (5)$$

Although it may be protested that we have omitted from both the numerator and denominator the addition of the term "3r", its incorporation in the following table would move the ratios listed even closer to unity.

Hence an approximation (and quite a good one) for the way in which costs increase if the value of n other than the real minimum is used:

$\dfrac{n^1}{n}$	Proportionate increase is less than
0.5	1.25
0.6	1.13
0.7	1.06
0.8	1.03
0.9	1.01
1.0	1.00
1.1	1.00
1.2	1.02
1.3	1.03
1.4	1.06
1.5	1.07

As can be seen considerable changes, from n' can be made without affecting the total cost very greatly. Referring back to Figure 1 one can see that we cheated the reader. The total curve is much flatter than shown and the picture is really (Figure 2).

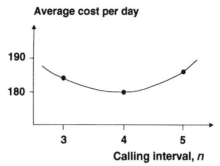

Figure 2   Deceptive robustness

It must be confessed that some texts on stock control persist in showing the total cost curve as being much steeper and so it appears more sensitive than it really is (see refs 2 and 3). So what is the cost effect of randomising the days on which the security van calls, in order that villains cannot plan ahead? If we have all branches visited on the same day, then it is easy to cost the effect of randomising.

At present the optimal interval is four days, when all branches are visited together. The cost is $[c/n] + 3r(n + 1)$.

Where $c = 600$, $r = 14$ and the relationship is:

n	Cost
2	426
3	368
4	360
5	372
6	394

As has been seen there is little difference (one pound per day) between cases (1) and (3) but if it is thought risky to have all banks visited on the same day then other alternatives can easily be calculated. In general the costs of moving from a theoretically optimal schedule are small (the student can confirm this) and we can conclude that the choice of a general routine will not bankrupt the bank.

Stage 7: Where Have We Got?

What we have gone through is a process that is mind bendingly boring. We have purposefully wallowed in all this arithmetic detail and after all this wallowing, some analysts will find the conclusion disappointing and feel their time has been wasted. Not so. Management has enough problems on its hands as it is and to show that one particular problem can be scratched off the list and ignored is useful. But the wallowing also makes a special point. Even when data analysis on a massive scale is easy, it is always worth while to test for robustness when faced with many alternatives that cannot be generalised algebraically. Try a few such alternatives and see whether there is much difference.

There is only one loose end. It has been assumed that the rate of accretion of cash is fixed day by day. In practice this will vary. It would be foolish to remove all the cash in hand when the van calls since immediately afterwards there could be a net outflow of cash. A statistical analysis could show what safety stock should be held but to do such an analysis would be silly. The cost of cash is only £6 per day per £10 000, so to hold a few thousand pounds in reserve stock would cost less than the manager's daily whisky and soda. The same would apply for branches which pay out cash. The vital statistics needed are:

1 The probability of running out of stock.
2 The cost of holding cash.
3 The cost of running out of cash – measured per pound, or per customer, or per hour?

The estimates of (2) and (3) are not easily made. Some textbooks assume they are known and then perform a simplistic analysis to determine the reserve cash to be held.

What then? If one asks a banker (who, like most bankers, may be innumerate) what probability in (1) is bearable, he will reply that it should never ever happen. For this to be the case the reserve stock is infinite and stock holding costs go through the roof. In real life these questions are solved by processes which some enthusiastic analysts refer to as an orderly search procedure but which in practice have all the characteristics of an oriental bazaar.

The lesson to be learned from this study is always to think before wallowing in arithmetic, even (or especially) when a nice seductive computer routine is to hand. And beware of assuming that because you have a formula your troubles are over. The two costs above (of holding and of running out of stock) are totally and completely at the discretion of everyone concerned.

Assumptions Made

What have we assumed in deriving the solution and conclusions? We have certainly assumed that:

- If the van calls at the end of the business day, it picks up all the cash in the tills. If it calls during business, it picks up all the cash accumulated by the end of the previous day.

- The amount of cash received each day is fixed.
- Variations in the rate of receipt of cash are dealt with separately by having a reserve cash which is always kept topped up.
- The cash holding charge is a daily charge in terms of the cash in the tills at the end of each day.

One should always write up a study for the private use of the research group. This will be different from the report which is produced and distributed. Both of these are now given.

NOTE FOR THE FILE

Introduction

A copy is attached of a letter from Mr Ivor Problum of Berwyn Bank in which he asks for help on a project to schedule the operations of security vans collecting cash from four branches in Brove. There is also an enquiry about the security aspects of rigid schedules and the possibility of randomisation of schedules.

Information Available

The letter gives the costs of vans calling on the branches. This is in terms of the number of branches called on in any one circuit – the rate is £200 for the daily van hire and £100 per branch called on. The other relevant cost is that of holding cash in stock, which is taken as £6 per day per £10 000 of stock. The objective given is to minimise the total costs of the operation, which has been taken as the sum of the cost of transporting cash and the cost of holding stock. The decision variable is the interval between calls.

Basic Arithmetic

It is useful to have a master table, or data bank, to which quick reference can be made to cost various alternatives. The variables are the interval in days between van calls (n), the rate at which cash is received in units of £10 000 per day (r), and the cost of calling (c).

Cost analysis. 1 The total cost of treating A, B, C and D separately is as shown in Table 01. However this total overestimates the cost since there will be savings in transport cost when schedules overlap (Table 02). The cycle of calls is 40 days (the LCM of 4, 5, 8 and 10) but within this cycle:

Table 01* Average holding costs per day for all n and r

r	$n = 1$	2	3	4	5	6	7	8	9
1	6	9	12	15	18	21	24	27	30
2	12	18	24	30	36	42	48	54	60
3	18	27	36	45	54	63	72	81	90
4	24	36	48	60	72	84	96	108	120
5	30	45	60	75	90	105	120	135	150
6	36	54	72	90	108	126	144	162	180
7	42	63	84	105	126	147	168	189	210
8	48	72	96	120	144	168	192	216	240
9	54	81	108	135	162	189	216	243	270
10	60	90	120	150	180	210	240	270	300
11	66	99	132	165	198	231	264	297	330
12	72	108	144	180	216	252	288	324	360
13	78	117	156	195	234	273	312	351	390
14	84	126	168	210	252	294	336	378	420

Table 02 Costs for A, B, C and D separately per day

Branch	Optimal n	Cost £
A	4	180
B	5	132
C	8	91
D	10	63
Total		466

Savings in transport cost

- Day 20. Three branches served (A, B, C). Cost £500, not £900. Saving £400.
- Days 8, 16, 24, 32. Two branches served (A and C). Cost £400, not £600, each time. Total saving £800.
- Days 10, 30. Two branches (B and D). Cost £400, not £600. Total saving £400.
- Day 40. All four served. Cost £600 not £1200. Saving £600.
  Over 40 days the saving is £2200 i.e. £55 p.d.
  Hence the net cost per day of this regime is £411 p.d.

---

* Throughout the 'Lives' table and figure numbers in the 'Notes for the File' and the 'Reports' are prefixed by a zero to distinguish them from other tables in the text.

2   Similarly the total cost of treating all branches together is minimised when $n = 14$ at a cost of £360 p.d. (see Table 03).

Table 03   Total cost of treating all branches together

n	Holding $r = 14$	Transport (4 branches)	Total (per day)
1	84	600	684
2	126	300	426
3	168	200	368
4	210	150	360
5	252	120	372
6	294	100	394
7	336	86	422

3   Take (A and B), (C and D) together. Reference to the master Table 01 gives for (A and B) the result shown in Table 04. We use $n = 4$ for combinatorial advantage at a cost of £265. See Table 05 for C, D.

Table 04   Cost per day for A and B together

n	Holding (£) $r = 11$	Transport (£)	Total (£)
1	66	400	466
2	99	200	299
3	132	133	265
4	165	100	265
5	198	80	278
6	231	67	298

We will not take $n = 7$ which apparently has the lowest cost of £129 per day. If $n = 6$ there will be extra overlaps with (AB) which more than compensate for the small increase of £1 per day. The cycle is 6 days and the transport saving is £200 per cycle, i.e. £33 per day.

Summary of Alternatives

1   All branches separately: £411 p.d.
2   All branches together: £360 p.d.
3   (A and B), (C and D): £362 p.d.

Table 05 Cost per day for C and D together

n	Holding (£) $r = 3$	Transport (£)	Total (£)
1	18	400	418
2	27	200	227
3	36	133	169
4	45	100	145
5	54	80	134
6	63	67	130
7	72	57	129
8	81	50	131
9	90	44	134

Randomisation and Robustness

We note that over the range $n = 2$ to 6, (2) and (3) are less than £411 (the optimum for (1)); and for $n = 3$ or 4, (2) is less than £362 (the optimum for (3)) but the difference is negligible. The robustness of the improvement of (2) and (3) over (1) gives scope for using either of them and randomising. If it is felt that there is a security risk because (2) involves all branches being always visited on the same day, and (3) has pairs of branches linked, it is straightforward to use the master table to evaluate the increase in costs due to any form of randomisation. A simple computer program would take care of this aspect, including the reduction in transport costs when collections overlap.

Reserve Stock

Given that the actual daily deposits will vary about the average then it is clearly prudent to incorporate a reserve cash store at each branch. This is drawn on whenever withdrawals exhaust the cash in the tills. Data are not presently available for hourly flow rates of cash flow. But the cost of holding half a day's extra supply of cash to meet unexpected withdrawals, i.e. a reserve of 35 000; 20 000; 10 000; 5000; at A, B, C, and D is £42 a day. This is a standard fixed charge which can easily be incorporated. It could be made even less by a statistical analysis which would give the risk probabilities involved.

THE TRANSPORT AND HOLDING OF CASH

A REPORT TO BERWYN BANK

BY T. TRYER

1. Introduction

The work reported here was carried out at the invitation of Mr I. Problum, a group manager of Berwyn Bank. It concerns the optimal schedule for collecting cash from a group of four branches in the town of Brove. The task was to determine how frequently the cash should be collected. (Please note that in this report all costs and cash figures are in pounds.)

2. Description of the Problem

There are two aspects to this task. The first concerns cost and the second concerns security. The costs involved fall into two categories. The first is the cost of holding cash in branches. At the end of each day head office records the cash held in each branch and the group manager's account is debited for this cash at the rate of 6 for every 10 000 of cash held.

The other cost is that of collecting the cash and transferring it to safe storage in the bank's money store. This is carried out by a security company who have to dedicate a van for a whole day for this operation no matter whether one, two, three or four branches are called on. They charge a fixed cost of £200 to which is added £100 for each branch.

It can be seen that frequent calls will minimise the cost of holding cash at the expense of increasing the van cost and vice versa. The actual minimum total cost can be obtained by analysing the range of alternatives. In this case the whole range does not need to be examined.

The second aspect is security. If a fixed schedule of regular predictable deliveries is undertaken then there is an open invitation to bandits to ambush the van. For this reason the security firm involved wished to introduce variability into the scheduling. This can be achieved without any serious cost effect.

3. Availability of Data

We have been able to obtain all the relevant data on costs, delivery schedules, traffic conditions, thanks to the ready cooperation of all the officials and employees of the bank and the security company.

4. Assumptions Made

In a study of costs and effectiveness the analyst has to make assumptions to enable the study to lead to a solution. (Real life complexity in its infinite variety is otherwise too much to cope with.) It is the task of the analyst to ensure that even so the solution is valid.

In this case we have assumed that:

1   If the van calls it will be during business hours and it will pick up only the cash which was in the tills at the end of the previous day. If it calls after business hours it will collect all the cash then in the tills.
2   The amount of cash received each day in a branch is constant.
3   The variations in rate of cash receipt are dealt with separately by having a reserve of cash which is always topped up.
4   The cash holding charge is levied daily in terms of the cash in the tills. If the van calls during opening hours this will be the cash held at the end of the previous day. Otherwise it is the cash held at the close of business that day.

5. Data Analysis

The structure of the problem is clear. If a branch, or branches are called on at a regular interval of days we can determine the average cost per day as the average daily cost of holding cash and of the calling cost.

That is, Average Total Cost per day for a given calling interval in days =

$$\frac{\text{Cost of holding cash between calls} + \text{Cost of call}}{\text{Calling Interval (days)}} \qquad (6)$$

The average daily rate of generating net cash at the four branches is:

A	70 000
B	40 000
C	20 000
D	10 000
Total	140 000 per day.

Three separate routines have been examined

1   Call on all four branches together.
2   Call separately on the four branches.
3   Call on (A and B) together and (C and D) together at their best intervals.

In some of the above there will be hidden transport cost reductions. For example (A, B) have their own optimal interval of 3 days and (C, D) have their own optimal interval of 7 days. So if A and B are called on together and C and D are also called on together at these different intervals then every 21 days all four will be called on simultaneously at a cost of 600 rather than 800. This saving has been incorporated into the results.

Taking account of these transport savings, the optimal schedules for the four routines listed above are:

1 All four branches together: Best interval 4 days. Cost 360 per day.
2 All branches separately: Best intervals:
   A   4 days
   B   5 days
   C   8 days
   D   10 days
   Cost 411 per day.
3 (A and B) together. (C and D) together. Best intervals:
   A and B jointly every 3 days.
   C and D jointly every 6 days.
   Cost 362 per day.

6. Conclusion to Cost Exercise

It can be seen that in terms of cost alone the first of these, calling on all branches together, is the cheapest although the difference between (1) and (3) is very small. It is in fact significantly cheaper than (2) and it is important to note that even if the calling interval is anywhere between 3, 4 or 5 days, the cost for (1) and (3) are less than the best that can be achieved with (2).

7. Security and Randomising

Any mixture of (1) and (3) will give approximately the same costs. However, this means in practice that whenever A is called on then so is B and that whenever C is called on then so is D. If this is felt to be a security risk then occasionally the routine of visiting the branches separately should be followed. It is encouraging that the extra cost would average about £10 per day. This can be looked on as a form of insurance premium.

8. Recommendations

1 All four branches should in general be visited on the same day.
2 An element of randomness should be introduced by choosing a calling interval of either 3, 4 or 5 days by drawing lots.
3 Occasionally one of the other two routines should be followed. When

this is done, the increase in cost from the overall minimum of £360 would not be more than £10 per day on average.

Acknowledgements

We wish to thank all those we have met or corresponded with us during this study. All have been most helpful and friendly.

Reflections

There was an awful lot of messy arithmetic in this. The arithmetic is still messy even if a computer carries it out. However, it was put in purposely. Firstly, it all illustrated the structure of the problem. Secondly, behind the facade of numbers there was something very robust and so the results were all very similar. In more complicated examples, and most problems are much more complicated, have a quick rough and ready check on a few alternative cases and see whether there is much variation in the results.

1   When faced with many alternative courses of action from which an optimal choice has to be made, ask:
    (a)   Is it possible to generalise? Is there an algebraic solution? This is certainly the case when all the relationships between the variables are linear and when the objective function is expressed in linear terms, for linear programming will apply. But here our objective was *not* linear, being of the form $ax + [b/x]$. When relationships are all linear the optimal solution will always be at an extreme. When there is non linearity then the optimum will probably be in the middle of the range of alternatives.
    (b)   Does it really matter? Check on a selection of alternatives, take extreme courses of action (here it was all branches separately and all branches together) and one, or two, in the middle (A and B together and C and D together) and see what is the difference.
    (c)   Formulate the problem carefully and derive a table, or data bank, of core data to which reference can constantly be made (Table 3).

Remember also that in practice life is *never* like textbook examples. The reality of this present case is that there would be embargoes on parking the van on certain days, some branches would be unwilling to have collections on other days. Public holidays, occasional Saturday openings would all enter in. This is why (b) above is so important.

2   Robustness is certainly endemic in our everyday life. A typical (if rather boring) topic of conversation at dinner parties is the set of alternative routes people have in getting to the same destination, particu-

larly, for example to go from a suburb to a city centre location. The curious thing is that when one tries different routes they all seem to take roughly the same time.

The reason is that we all learn from experience. If one route turns out to be good, more people start to use it. If another route is poor, people start to abandon it. This feedback ensures that all routes take about the same time.

The point is, that journey time is the dominant criterion and not journey cost. In any choice situation there will be many alternatives yielding different payoffs. In a free market choice, with full information equilibrium will be determined by that payoff which is the most important. Robustness depends on the objective.

References

1   Ackoff, R.L. (1974). *Redesigning the Future*, Wiley, New York.
2   Gregory, G. (1983). *Mathematical Methods in Management*, Wiley, Chichester.
3   Mitchell, G. (1972). *Operational Research*, Wiley, Chichester.

Further Work

1   Suppose there were special effects in cash deposits or withdrawals, e.g. on Fridays or at the end of the month. How would you deal with this?
2   Suppose there are restrictions on times or days when the security van might call. What then?
3   How would you take account of the bank being charged for cash over a weekend when the van cannot call?
4   The problem as it stands is robust. Examine the effect on costs of different rates of charging for cash, and of different values of r and c. Can you find situations where the problem becomes sensitive?
5   Create a programme on your PC which would enable (say) six branches to be considered with a range of different calling and holding costs. Examine these for robustness. Are there particular combinations of these costs which cause the decisions to be sensitive. Experiment with your model programme in this way.
6   Suppose that there is a variability in the rates of cash deposit from day to day in any branch. How would you decide on the reserve stock to be held?

Chapter 4

Describing a Problem

Those things which we loosely call problems are contained within a living system. What is a system and what are the characteristics of a living system?

A system is something of which we are all subconsciously aware in every-day life, for we are a part of many systems. (Lenin once remarked that he could not change any single thing in Russia without it affecting everything else.) A system is a collection of entities each of which affects at least one other entity in the system, each of which is affected by at least one other entity in the system and, finally, is such that such effects connect all entities to each other (see Figure 4.1).

We have sketched (Figure 4.1) some closed sets – that is there are no external (or exogenous) forces operating. Everything can be comprised in one diagram. But difficulties in real life systems are threefold:

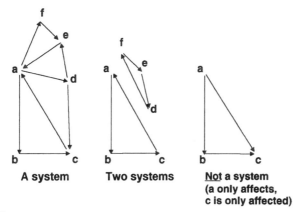

| A system | Two systems | Not a system (a only affects, c is only affected) |

Figure 4.1 Systems

1   Because of their nature, we cannot carry out the classic experiments usual in physics or engineering. In such laboratory experiments, the environment is held at bay (indeed a laboratory is a machine for isolating an experiment from the environment), and all factors involved are held constant, apart from one which is varied. In this way the effect of any factor acting on its own can be determined, and also the combined effects of a number of factors can be seen.

2   We can *induce* a logic of cause and effect but we cannot *deduce* it from observations.

Consider a shepherd, and his dog(s) and a flock of sheep (Figure 4.2).

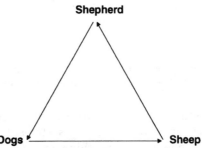

Figure 4.2   Shepherd and sheep (as the shepherd sees it)

We know that the shepherd observes where the sheep are, their direction of motion, where the dog(s) are and where he wants the sheep to go. The dog(s) can understand four whistled signals and by them the shepherd controls the system. (*Note*: These three entities do form a system as defined since each one affects and is affected.)

But to a man from Mars seeing this system for the first time, and for the reader observing the system (see Figure 4.3), there is no way of telling who is in charge. Intelligent sheep could get the shepherd to sound any noise they liked and the dogs could do the same if they were in charge. Evidence through our eyes and ears alone cannot determine who is dominant – i.e. who is the prime cause. This creates an important distinction between these types of analysis and the mainstream science.

3   Since the whole world is a system, where do we create the boundary? We know that if the reader walks across a room, the centre of gravity of the earth is changed and so the position of the sun moves. We can safely ignore this effect in astronomical calculations. But in our own life, where do we draw a boundary across which flow only the effects of exogenous variables which are affected by ourselves (see Figure 4.4)?

Such a diagram is typical of all living systems. They consume different kinds of input; a transformation process follows, which produces different

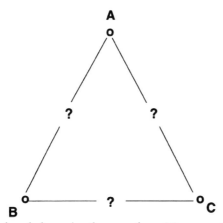

Figure 4.3 Shepherd and sheep (as the man from Mars sees it)

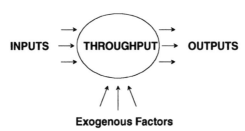

Figure 4.4 Simple living system

sorts of output. This is as true of an earthworm as it is of a modern hospital or an oil refinery. A hospital will consume:

People: Doctors, nurses, consultants, physiotherapists, cleaners, porters, patients
Equipment: Laboratories, emergency, surgical, etc.
Materials: Drugs, bed linen, food
Money: To fund, as a transfer function, everything else

It transforms those by a production process, into, for example:

People: Experienced and value added staff; employment; patient's discharge; value added patients
Knowledge: Papers, books, research
Materials: Waste products
Money: Taxes paid, profits on services, which can feed back into the system

The objectives and goals of such a system are difficult to ascertain. When a social system, such as a school, closes, the complaints which arise give an illustration of the objectives involved. It is not only the education of children. A school is an employer of staff. A school is a child minder, enabling parents to work. It provides a meal service. It monitors the health problems and social or home life of the children. To one part of society a school is simply a way of getting one's children into Oxbridge. It is also a way of establishing personal links which can be life lasting and life enhancing. For others it merely delays the time when the son or daughter will be unemployed.

So what is a school for? The above living systems all have three basic functions, the acquisition of input, the transformation of inputs, the provision of output. For each of these there is a variety of measurement available. In an industrial organisation they would include:

1 *Purchasing*
Raw material costs
Raw material quality
Raw material stocks
Costs compared with main competitors, or with best possible, or with averages
Security of delivery time

2 *Production*
Cost per unit produced
Proportion of orders produced on time
Capacity usage
In process stocks
Overtime
Accident and sickness rate
Production per employee
Production as function of labour costs
Added value

3 *Marketing*
Volume sold
Contribution to profit
Finished goods stocks
Share of the market
Stock turnover
Delivery delays
Customer satisfaction
Customer loyalty

There are also at least two control functions in all this. Human resources (personnel) and finance:

4 *Personnel*
   Dispute rates
   Labour turnover
   Absenteeism
   Sickness
   Accidents

5 *Finance*
   Return on assets
   Shareholder return
   P/E ratio
   Profits
   Profitability
   Cost per unit produced
   Current ratio
   Debtor days
   Creditor days
   Stock turnover
   Earnings per share

THE ANALYST

And into all this comes the analyst, most often invited because of symptoms and asked to "solve" a "problem". The difficulty is that problems do not exist in physical concrete terms. They are constructs in our minds. They are ideas. Ideas do not have owners.

They are also the product of a personal view and perspective. Each of us has a different view. No two people can look at an apple and see the same thing, since, to begin with, the two pairs of eyes are in different positions. Also we all bring to our observations psychological differences – we cannot even know whether we see an apple of the same colour. Added to this is our own set of biases, prejudices and experiences (no one is unbiased. For we cannot even define "unbiased" without reference to a subjective value system).

A problem may be regarded as a state of nature that inhibits us from moving from where we are, to where we would like to be.

All three of the concepts in the last sentence:

● where we are,
● where we would like to be,

- state of nature,

are subjective and personal.

This point is laboured so as to dispose of defining problems as is sometimes done, by reference to the technique used to tackle it. That is nonsense. Since problems cannot be absolutely defined and since there is a tendency to describe problems in such a way as to maximise our chances of solving them, we can see that there is no such thing as a queuing problem or a linear programming problem. There is no such thing as an operational research problem, no such thing even as a physics problem, a biology problem, an accounting problem or a political problem. All those lie in the biased prejudiced eye of the beholder.

There is an account of the story of a committee called to discuss the death of an old lady living alone at the top of a house, who had a heart attack (ref 1). The lady died while climbing the stairs to her third floor apartment after visiting a community health centre. The professor of community medicine said that this death would not have occurred had there been enough doctors to carry out home visits.

The professor of economics said there were enough doctors but the woman could not afford one. The cause of death was the failure of the welfare system.

The professor of architecture said the cause of death was a failure to have elevators and the bad design of the staircase.

Finally, the professor of social work said that the woman had an affluent son and had mother and son not been alienated she would have had no stairs to climb and been able to afford medical service.

In all of this, it becomes quickly forgotten that an old lady is dead. Her problem is taken by everyone as a symptom of something else. One person's problem is easily down-graded into just a symptom.

It is nearly always the case that the analyst will disagree with the problem as defined by the person who has asked for help. Sometimes this difference manifests itself in the treatment prescribed. A diesel engine factory requested help in its production line by means of a new production scheduling system. The problem was defined as the output of the line being only about 60% of designed capacity. A visit showed the problem immediately. Sales departments, so as to secure orders, were changing specifications and delivery dates and the knock-back effect of this was to reduce productivity; the present production control system was quite good enough for the job. But where now was the problem? Was it a problem of lost production due to sales force interference or was it a problem of lost sales due to production rigidity?

A problem can be re-stated simply by checking on the measurements used (this is why data should never be accepted without reservation when it is possible to confirm them by visiting the place where they arise). An engineering company suffered considerable complaints from (mainly overseas) customers at the lateness of orders being completed. A visit showed that there was a control system of a very elementary nature but that the greatest delay was caused by the fact that when an order was put in finished goods store, there was no trace of who had ordered it and the shipping manager had to wait until a letter of complaint was received matching an order in the store. But a study of orders – the specification, price and delivery date also showed that in many cases, even when the order was booked, it would be impossible for the delivery to be made on time. When the analyst asked why this was done, he was told that the order would not have been obtained had a later date been quoted. But, asked the analyst, does this annoy the customer? "No", came the answer – "they know from the start that we cannot meet the delivery date and we know that they do not need it by then anyway – we are both putting slack into our own separate systems".

So where is the problem?

To ask – where is the problem, is merely an overture to the next question – who is the client? In this we face the difficulty of dealing with other specialists all of whom have their own view. The following examples are verifiable:

1 At a British University, entry to the campus is through an attractive building which bears on it a medallion recording that the architect was awarded the Gold Medal of the Royal Institution of British Architects for the most outstanding building of the year. In practice no one wants to use the building. It fits no academic purpose so it is given to the students. They do not want it and press for their own purpose-built structure. One can receive the Gold Medal of the RIBA without reference to the people who use the building. So who was the architect's client – was it the university, the students, the passers by or was it the RIBA?

2 Awards for advertising campaigns often omit any reference to the effect of the campaign on product sales. For example, the *Sunday Times* award for the advertising campaign of the year award was won by a very punchy lively campaign for White Horse Whisky, based on the slogan "You can take a White Horse anywhere". The citation for the award did not refer to the effect of the campaign on the sales of White Horse Whisky. So who were the clients of the advertising agency?

3 In community care as many as 32 different agencies may be involved in the care of a single person. When a child is abused or battered a whole group of different specialists is involved – the courts, probation officer, social services, Department of Health, district nurses, doctors,

police, NSPCC. All of these have their own professional view and ethic. But no one is concerned solely with the well being of the child. So who has the child as a client?

In any situation the parts of an organisation will describe their own problems and perspective. As one moves up an organisation, perspective changes. We can often get the largest payoff for the organisation as a whole by changing one person's terms of reference or by resolving a problem at a higher level. This latter can be at the expense of the person offering his own problems for solution.

Important principles so often ignored in organisation planning include:

1 The optimisation of a whole does not necessarily coincide with the optimisation of the separate parts.
2 To set goals and objectives separately for different parts of an organisation may be inefficient and not optimal.
3 Such goals and objectives will build inevitable conflict within the organisation.
4 The potential range of a model is greater than the range of responsibility of a single manager.
5 A problem as first described to an analyst is probably too small and the constraints should be examined. In any event it will almost certainly change during the research.

The last has the very important rules for analysts:

1 A greater pay-off can often be obtained by relaxing constraints than by optimising within them and consequently
2 The person who invites the research may turn out to be an entry point to a larger problem to be solved at a higher level.

Problems can be redescribed because of a change of technical perspective – we all wear the blinkers of our expertise. The lifts at a polytechnic were constrained, and announced on ubiquitous notices, that they would not stop at floors 1, 3, 4, 6, 8, 10, 11, 13, 14, 16, 17 and 19. As Christmas fun, a problem was posed to the department of mathematics:
What is the next number in the series 2, 5, 7, 9, 12, 15? And why?

What was expected, was a recognition that these were the floors at which the lift *stopped*. The mathematicians, however, brought to bear on this a whole gallery of statistical and mathematical techniques. One mathematician realised the solution to the problem after 3 days, but no one else within a week. The problem was regarded as mathematical and mathematically it had no solution. Until the iron fetters of technical approach could be broken, *there was no solution*. Even though many times each day the set of numbers was observed.

A word on problem *definition*. Never use the word. Problem *description* is better, but always remember that the description will change ineluctably during the research. It may be politic not to keep changing the problem publicly, indeed sometimes it only changes subconsciously. But it does change continuously and inevitably (as will be seen in the Fifth Life).

One of the significant recognitions of the difficulty of problem description is the research which has been carried out in this area, particularly with regard to human dimension. There is a whole set of interlocking initiatives, loosely grouped with the label of "soft systems methodology". Soft systems are a counter balance to the classic hard systems of mathematical modelling and cause–effect modelling of main stream science.

It is fortunate that these latent concerns about problem description and problem management, which for some decades lay growling in the back of the mind of every analyst have now been recognised and formalised. The early pioneer in this was Checkland. As Checkland has pointed out (ref 2) the classical analytical approach in operational research, systems analysis and systems engineering seeks to help a decision maker to achieve desired objective(s), analyses alternative ways of achieving it (them) by formulating the costs and resources of the alternative ways and creates models showing the dependence of objects, systems, resources and environment. The assumptions of the three topics is common – that an important class of problems can be formulated as an orderly search for alternative ways of achieving objective(s) and that to do this models can be created and manipulated. There is agreement therefore on *what* constitutes a problem and the question is how to deal with it.

This is the approach of what might be termed hard systems science. Soft systems science, as part of its methodology takes definition of the problem not to be given but subject to discussion and logical analysis by mixed teams of researchers and managers.

The stages in the evolution of an agreed view of a system, together with an agreed set of objectives are established and formulated (refs 3 and 4). This will be discussed further in the closing section, but at this stage it is worth remarking on one particular point.

We deal with living systems, but life moves on at a rapid pace and when problems emerge there is in many cases, if not all, a deadline by which a solution must be proposed. But in the literature outlining the soft OR approach it is not often that one is brought up against this constraint. There can be a reflective contemplative approach, which assumes that the overall importance of the problem, the constraints, the objectives and the inter-relationships remain constant. But, we cannot enjoy the luxury of stopping the world turning, while we get off and discuss it.

The end point of soft systems approaches, is this understanding, but it is not enough for the analyst and his cooperative managers to understand what the world was like last year, rather what it would be like next year.

The argument therefore should not be cast in that depressing mode in which the hard system verses soft system is so often couched – "I am right and you are wrong". The stumbling block is the amalgamation of the quantitative and qualitative and the recognition that just as data are value impregnated as well as being subject to error, so words are appallingly bad instruments for conducting the process of soft systems analysis.

This has been discused now, so as to put the matter of problem description into a framework and a perspective. For the time being, however, and especially most of the Nine Lives, we act under the assumption that the problem has been formulated.

All this being taken as given – are there categories of problem type? Most people have tried their own categories including:

1 Financial models in which money is the only variable. Marketing models, production models and so on.
2 Classes of mathematical models.
3 Computer models.

Some years ago a text (ref 6) was written at a time when the majority of OR work was in industry. This suggested that most management problems were one of eight kinds: inventory, allocation, queuing, sequencing, routing, replacement, competition and search, and such a list betrays its age. It was a fair summary at that time. It obviously met a need and was taken up by many writers, in a manner which was intensely embarrassing to the authors. Indeed one standard management text stated (flatteringly, but wrongly) that there are only eight kinds of problems in management. As can be seen now, in the classification not a single mention of people was made, and yet the whole of life is personal.

Anyway, why should one bother with sets of standard definitions? The reason is that, underlying the surface flesh of complexity there may be networks of causes and effects and the identification of common structure may give an indication of possible methods of solution. What we are dealing with, therefore, is the distinction between form and content in describing a problem.

At a post office counter one is aware of the content of the problem, a relation between server and served. The server and the served have different goals. It is a far cry in content to observe planes landing at an airport – the change in content from little old ladies with plastic shopping bags at a post office counter to a machine weighing hundreds of tons, costing millions of pounds and packed with electronic equipment, unheard of when the little old lady was born. But the form is exactly the same – the little old lady and the jumbo jet, the Post Office counter and the apron at Heathrow, are identical paradigms of the queuing form.

The recognition, therefore, of the form, is the first stage towards a solution. But all classifications of problems are subjective and if they look likely to lead to a "solution", then the temptation to the analyst is to describe the problem in such a way that she can be a major contributor to its solution.

This temptation is as seductive to the hard analyst as to the soft analyst. One could only wish that it was more extensively recognised. It is recognised in the arts. Historians, particularly, realise that they cannot remain outside the process of history as mere observers. They are also interpreters. Hayakawa (ref 7) reminds us that words are not the same as reality. At best they only lead to an understanding of real meaning and at worst camouflage it. De Bono, whose research is under represented in the literature on problem formulation, reminds us forcibly of the flabbiness and misleading nature of verbal modelling (ref 8).

The constructs in our minds are personal and almost impossible to convey. Often words to express our thoughts do not seem to exist. The slant, the unconscious doctoring of experience to produce a thesis, can be lethal to communication. Which member of a research group, who has written a research report, has not cringed with embarrassment to hear it presented in public by the director of the group?

There is a strong aversion among many analysts to the reading of poetry. One hopes that the reader will study the following passage from *Mr Sludge. The Medium* by Robert Browning, as it represents in the view of the author something which should be constantly before anyone who is involved in our sort of activity.

> But why do I mount to poets? Take the plain prose-
> Dealers in common sense, set these at work,
> What can they do without their helpful lies?
> Each states the law and fact and face o' the thing
> Just as he'd have them, finds what he thinks fit,
> Is blind to what missuits him, just records
> What makes his case out, quite ignores the rest.
> It's a History of the World, the Lizard Age,
> The Early Indians, the Old Country War,
> Jerome Napoleon, whatsoever you please.
> All as the author wants it. Such a scribe
> You pay and praise for putting life in stones,
> Fire into fog, making the past your world.
> There's plenty of "How did you contrive to grasp
> The thread which led you through this labyrinth?
> How build such solid fabric out of air?
> How on so slight foundation found this tale,
> Biography, narrative?" or, in other words,

"How many lies did it require to make
The portly truth you here present us with?"

References

1 Ackoff, R.L. (1991). *Ackoff's Fables*, Wiley, Chichester.
2 Checkland, P. Chapters 4 (Soft Systems Methodology) and 5 (An Application of Soft Systems Methodology) in ref 5.
3 Bryant, J.W. (1989). *Problem Management*, Wiley, Chichester.
4 Patching, D. (1992). Seeking out the issues. *OR Insight*, 5, 1, 15–17. Operational Research Society, Birmingham.
5 Rosenhead, J. (1989). *Rational Analysis for a Problematic World*, Wiley, Chichester.
6 Rivett, B.H.P. and Ackoff, R.L. (1963). *Managers' Guide to Operational Research*, Wiley, Chichester.
7 Hayakawa, S.I. (1974). *Language in Thought and Action*, Allen & Unwin, London.
8 De Bono, E. (1990). *I Am Right. You Are Wrong*, Viking, New York.

The Happy Hamburger Company

The Fourth Principle: Just because the normal distribution is so endemic, it does not mean that it is always present.

The basis of all quantitative statistical theory is the normal distribution. This distribution has a logical self-justification and is mathematically pliable. When we obtain data, during a piece of research, which fall into a normal shape there are sighs of relief all round. Because of this expectancy, we may assume too easily that a distribution is normal. But sometimes our data, because of the way they are collected and classified, are only a part of a normal distribution. It can be fatal to take data from a truncated distribution and to calculate mean and variance as though they were from the whole distribution. Always plot the data before carrying out a statistical test.

Anecdote (True): The Rocket Attack on London

A crisis point in World War II was the attack on London in 1944 with pilotless aircraft (V1) and rockets (V2). Defence against V1 was possible. It involved using fighter aircraft, anti-aircraft guns, radar and ground spotters. But thousands of V1s and V2s got through and hundreds of people were being killed.

There was no defence against V2 except to capture or destroy the launching sites. Statistical analyses showed that the fall of these weapons was in the form of a two-dimensional normal distribution and that the centre of this distribution was accurately located over central London. At that time agents who had been sent to Britain during the war had been captured. Some had been executed but others, given the choice of working for the allies or being executed had chosen the former. They were given messages, some true but useless, some untrue, to send back by Morse code. (The agents had to send the messages themselves as there is a personal character to the key pressing rhythm.)

Statisticians took a subset of the actual locations of fall in such a way that the subset was a bivariate normal. It was a deliberately biased set which seemed to show that the centre of fall (the mean of the distribution) was to the north of its actual point. Information on these particular explosions was transmitted back by the captured spies. The deduction was made by the launchers that, because the information they received was consistent with a normal distribution, its mean was the true mean and the assumption was that the setting was too long and they were then altered. From then on, half of them fell in open country south of London.

Moral of the Story

Never assume that a sample is random. One has to be very careful in selection to produce a random sample. The fact that a sample is itself normal, does not mean it is a random sample from a normal distribution.

HAPPY HAMBURGER

Introduction

A large hamburger chain buys in approximately 42 000 kilos of raw beef substitute in each of its four-weekly accounting periods. This has always been the approximate amount needed and the raw material buyer, Mr Evans, makes the purchases by telephone.

The marketing managers of the four suppliers (the suppliers are Anstead, Benjamin, Carter and Davis) telephone Mr Evans, from time to time, offering a batch of substitute with a given weight in kilos at a given price in £ per kilo. Evans has a rough idea of the maximum price per kilo he should pay and if the offer price is not above this maximum then he accepts the offer. In this way, from experience, Evans knows that he can just about fill his quota. There is no bargaining over the telephone. If Mr Evans refuses the offer, the supplier tries elsewhere.

Having worked out this principle, taking advantage of the steady state market, Mr Evans is asked to see the managing director. He is told that Happy Hamburgers are contemplating a special promotion campaign designed to increase the sale of their product. It is estimated by the accountants that raw beef substitute to an extra amount of 3000 kilos per period will be needed in a campaign which will (apart from this extra amount of beef substitute) yield a net profit increase of £9000 a period. Obviously this will mean more purchases of substitute. Can Mr Evans buy this extra amount at less than this figure and so ensure a profit?

The managing director wants this advice in less than two hours and Mr Evans, for whom you work, tells you to report to him within an hour, on not more than a half page.

Apart from looking for another job, what would you do during the next hour, if all Mr Evans can give you is Table 1?

In Table 1, the four numbers for Anstead with weight 150 kilos, indicate that the separate lots were purchased from Anstead, each was 150 kilos and their prices were (per kilo) 170, 190, 210 and 220 pence. Similarly for all the other lots and suppliers.

Stage 1: A Rapid Reflection

Dr Johnson once remarked that the knowledge one is going to be hanged next morning concentrates the mind wonderfully. How much more is the mind concentrated if one is going to be hanged in two hours?

But do not panic.

Stage 2: Think

Ask: Is there a structure to the problem? And of course there will be if we *think*. The information in Table 1 gives *all* offers accepted, and moreover since the price break (which by inspection of Table 1 is at £220/per kilo) is such that all offers greater than it are rejected, then assuming that all offers made (whether or not they are accepted) are part of the same statistical distribution, it follows that, to buy more beef substitute, this maximum price has to be increased.

We now have to turn Table 1 around and examine price per kilo as the main variable. The following Table 2 reverses Table 1 and the student should confirm it personally. We can also present this in diagram form (Figure 1). We can now draw up our tactics and method of work.

Tactical Questions

1 *The suppliers*
    Are they offering at the same price? Does price/kilo depend on lot size?
2 *Mr Evans*
    How does the amount bought depend on his maximum price?

Stage 3: Method

1 Draw up a histogram, or distribution, of offers accepted.
2 Extend this to make a guess at rejected offers.

Table 1 Typical purchases in a four-week period (the actual weights will vary and the data here are to the nearest 25 kilos)

From Anstead

k	Prices	Total k	Lots
150	170, 190, 210, 220	600	4
200	160, 170, 180, 200, 210, 220, 220	1400	7
250	180, 190, 190, 200, 200, 210, 220, 220	2000	8
300	180, 190, 190, 200, 200, 200, 210, 220	2400	8
350	180, 190, 200, 200, 210, 210, 220	2450	7
400	170, 180, 190, 200, 200	2000	5
		10 850	39

From Benjamin

k	Prices	Total k	Lots
150	170, 180, 200, 220, 220	750	5
200	180, 190, 190, 190, 200, 200, 200, 210	1600	8
250	180, 180, 190, 190, 200, 210, 210	1750	7
300	160, 190, 190, 200, 200, 200, 210, 220	2400	8
350	190, 200, 210, 210, 210	1750	5
400	180, 200, 210	1200	3
450	170, 200, 220, 220	1800	4
		11 250	40

From Carter

k	Prices	Total k	Lots
150	170, 170, 190, 200, 210, 220	900	6
200	160, 170, 180, 180, 190, 190, 200, 200, 220	1800	9
250	190, 200, 210, 210, 220	1250	5
300	190, 200, 210, 210, 210, 220	1800	6
350	170, 190, 200, 220	1400	4
400	180, 190, 200	1200	3
450	180, 190, 200, 210	1800	4
		10 150	37

From Davis

k	Prices	Total k	Lots
150	170, 170, 190, 210, 210, 220, 220	1050	7
200	160, 190, 190, 200, 200, 210	1200	6
250	180, 190, 200, 200	1000	4
300	170, 180, 180, 200, 200, 210, 210	2100	7
350	190, 200, 220	1050	3
400	180, 190, 220	1200	3
450	180, 190, 200, 210, 210	2250	5
		9850	35

Table 2 Purchase prices

| Price | k Bought at different prices/k | | | | |
	A	B	C	D	Total k
160	200	300	200	200	900
170	750	600	850	600	2800
180	1500	1250	1250	1700	5700
190	2000	2050	2300	2000	8350
200	3100	3100	2300	2300	10 800
210	1600	2450	2000	2000	8050
220	1700	1500	1250	1050	5500
Total k	10 850	11 250	10 150	9850	42 100
Ave/k	197	198	196	196	197

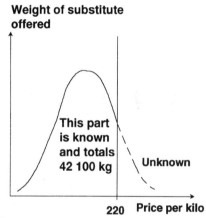

Figure 1 Price distribution

3 How far does the cut off at £220/kilo have to be raised to bring in an extra 3000 kilos?

4 What is the extra cost?

5 How does this compare with the estimate given of extra profit?

6 Report to Mr Evans and give him a ball-park estimate.

Then subsequently;

7 Does price/kilo depend on size?

8 Does the price vary with time?

9 Do suppliers differ in lot sizes or prices?

10 Extend the analysis to deduce the increase in cost for an extra 2000, 4000 and 5000 kilos.

Figure 2   Histogram of prices paid

11   Write a formal report to Mr Evans.

This whole analysis and report should be easily completed in half a day.

Stage 4: Analysis

1   Take all the bids in Table 2 irrespective of lot size or supplier and check whether the size of the lot is related to the price per kilo. The reader should now do this for each supplier and confirm, by inspection, that the lot size has no effect on price per kilo.
2   Draw a histogram (Figure 2) and add in a guess at the missing portion.
3   As an inspired guess we estimate the missing portions as:

Price per kilo	Kilos available
230	3300
240	1500
250	400

Since Mr Evans's first question is what would be the extra cost of an extra 3000 kilos, we can estimate this at £7590. Further extra costs would be read off in a similar way. (*Note*: this is a *guess* and you are not in error just because your guess is different.) And all this was done within the hour.

Stage 5: The Report

To Mr Evans, Raw Material Buyer.

You asked for an estimate of the cost of an extra 3000 kilos of beef substitute.

My full report will be with you tomorrow morning but as a result of a quick analysis, in the period of purchases covered by the data you gave me, the costs per kilo were:

Price per kilo	Total k
160	900
170	2800
180	5700
190	8350
200	10 800
210	8050
220	5500
Total	42 100

If we use this to deduce, by a graph, the offers which were rejected because they were over £220/kilo, my guess is as follows.

Price per k	Total k offered
£2.30	3300
£2.40	1500
£2.50	400

The answer to the question, "What is the extra cost of an extra 3000 kilos?", is 3000 x £2.30 = £6900.

Stage 6: More Analysis

Having survived the first hour of this project we must now answer the other questions:

1 Is there a relationship between price per kilo and the lot size?
2 Are the different suppliers the same as regards prices and lot sizes?
3 Does price per kilo depend on lot size?

Taking all the bids made – as in Table 1 – we calculate the average prices per kilo (for all suppliers) as shown in Table 3.

Table 3 Average price per kilo

		Supplier			
k	A	B	C	D	Average
150	198	198	193	199	197
200	194	195	188	192	192
250	201	194	206	193	198
300	199	196	207	193	199
350	201	204	195	203	201
400	198	197	190	197	195
450	NA	202	195	198	198
Average	198	198	196	196	197

1   Neither *t* test, Analysis of Variance, Correlation nor any other method is necessary to deduce that the price per kilo does not depend on the size of the batch.
2   Is there a difference between suppliers? Reference to Table 3 shows that the four suppliers sell at remarkably similar average costs. There is, also, no real difference between the average sizes of the lots offered by each supplier.

Stage 7: Conclusion

From the histogram of present prices accepted, together with the deduction of the shadowy upper portion as in Stage 3 above, we can deduce that the cost of purchasing extra amounts would be as shown in Table 4.

Table 4

Extra k	Contains	Total cost (£)
2000	2000 at 230/kilo	4600
3000	3000 at 230/kilo	6900
4000	3300 at 230/kilo plus 700 at 240/kilo	9270
5000	As for 4000 plus 800 at 240/kilo and 200 at 250/kilo	11 690

Assumptions Made

A number of heroic assumptions had to be made:

1   The data give prices to the nearest £25/kilo – we hope this is sufficient.
2   Prices are stationary and do not change during the week.
3   Since there is little surplus substitute available there is no point in favouring one supplier more than another.
4   The distribution of prices and the amounts available will be (roughly) constant.
5   That the buying process will remain the same. If Mr Evans himself goes out into the market then the price distribution may well change.
6   Our increased purchases will not change the shape of the distribution.
7   Our increased purchases of substitute will not force up the market price of real beef.

Final Stage

In this case the note for the file would consist partly of the above analysis and partly of back-up material.

NOTE FOR THE FILE

Beef Substitute Purchasing

Introduction

Purchasing department buys about 42 000 kilos of beef substitute per week from suppliers, Anstead, Benjamin, Carter and Davis. Total purchasing of substitute by us is approximately equally divided by these four.

Purchasing is by telephone. The four companies telephone Mr Evans, our purchasing manager, during each week as and when they have lots of substitute available. They quote the size of the lot and offer it at a price. Mr Evans decides whether or not to accept – so his response is a firm yes or no. For some time the market has been stable both as regards the amount of substitute they have available and the distribution of price. This has meant that by applying a cut off at £220/kilo Mr Evans can accept all offers at or below that level and buy his quota.

However, things are now changing. The MD has told Mr Evans that the company is planning a special promotion of its hamburgers and they estimate that for a few weeks we shall need an extra 3000 kilos of substitute each week.

The MD needed a rapid answer within an hour of the question: "Is the purchase of an extra 3000 kilos a week going to increase cost per kilo? If so, how much will an extra 3000 kilos cost compared with our present average price of £197/kilo?"

Data Available

The only data we were given are shown in Table 01 and are the purchases in a typical four-week period.

Data Analysis

The price per kilo appears to be part of a normal distribution of kilos offered and bought at different prices. Figure 01 below sketches in our hypothesis of the rest of the distribution, i.e. the rejected offers.

Estimation of extra cost. If extra kilos are needed, reference to the dotted portion shows that:

| Amount available (kilos) | 3300 | 1500 | 400 |
| Price (£ per kilo) | 230 | 240 | 250 |

Table 01   Typical purchases in a four-week period (the actual weights will vary and the data here are to the nearest 25 kilos)

From Anstead

k	Prices	Total k	Lots
150	170, 190, 210, 220	600	4
200	160, 170, 180, 200, 210, 220, 220	1400	7
250	180, 190, 190, 200, 200, 210, 220, 220	2000	8
300	180, 190, 190, 200, 200, 200, 210, 220	2400	8
350	180, 190, 200, 200, 210, 210, 220	2450	7
400	170, 180, 190, 200, 200	2000	5
		10 850	39

From Benjamin

k	Prices	Total k	Lots
150	170, 180, 200, 220, 220	750	5
200	180, 190, 190, 190, 200, 200, 200, 210	1600	8
250	180, 180, 190, 190, 200, 210, 210	1750	7
300	160, 190, 190, 200, 200, 200, 210, 220	2400	8
350	190, 200, 210, 210, 210	1750	5
400	180, 200, 210	1200	3
450	170, 200, 220, 220	1800	4
		11 250	40

From Carter

k	Prices	Total k	Lots
150	170, 170, 190, 200, 210, 220	900	6
200	160, 170, 180, 180, 190, 190, 200, 200, 220	1800	9
250	190, 200, 210, 210, 220	1250	5
300	190, 200, 210, 210, 210, 220	1800	6
350	170, 190, 200, 220	1400	4
400	180, 190, 200	1200	3
450	180, 190, 200, 210	1800	4
		10 150	37

From Davis

k	Prices	Total k	Lots
150	170, 170, 190, 210, 210, 220, 220	1050	7
200	160, 190, 190, 200, 200, 210	1200	6
250	180, 190, 200, 200	1000	4
300	170, 180, 180, 200, 200, 210, 210	2100	7
350	190, 200, 220	1050	3
400	180, 190, 220	1200	3
450	180, 190, 200, 210, 210	2250	5
		9850	35

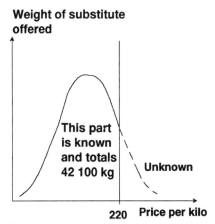

Figure 01   Price distribution

Breakdown of Data

Subsequent to reporting to Mr Evans on the above – the report is an appendix to this note – we analysed the data further as in the following table.

Table 3   Average price per kilo

k	Supplier A	B	C	D	Average
150	198	198	193	199	197
200	194	195	188	192	192
250	201	194	206	193	198
300	199	196	207	193	199
350	201	204	195	203	201
400	198	197	190	197	195
450	NA	202	195	198	198
Average	198	198	196	196	197

It can be readily seen that price per kilo does not depend on the lot size and all suppliers have very similar average prices and average lot sizes.

Further Work

It would in the future be useful to be forearmed and to study the availability of substitute if we wish to expand our business. There is no point of special promotions if the extra cost of substitute is more than the extra profit from the sales.

NOTE TO MR EVANS

Subject: Buying of Beef Substitute

Introduction

We have already sent you our report giving a quick answer to your question; how much extra will be the cost of an increase of beef substitute purchase of 3000 kilos a week? This note supplements that short report.

Further Analysis

We have split purchases by supplier and by price per kilo as in the following table:

Table 3 Average price per kilo

| k | Supplier | | | | |
	A	B	C	D	Average
150	198	198	193	199	197
200	194	195	188	192	192
250	201	194	206	193	198
300	199	196	207	193	199
350	201	204	195	203	201
400	198	197	190	197	195
450	NA	202	195	198	198
Average	198	198	196	196	197

As can be seen the average price offered per kilo depends neither on the size of the lot nor on the supplier.

Assumptions

In order to carry out this work we have had to make some sweeping assumptions and we list these for your comment.

[Note to the reader. Here would be the assumptions reproduced from p. 106]

Conclusions

1 We stand by our estimate that an extra 3000 kilos should be available at £2.30/kilo.

2   It would be helpful if you could take a log of all offers you reject as this would remove some of the guesswork now necessary.
3   Moving from one steady state of purchases (42 000 kilos a week) to another does produce uncertainty. It would be useful for the company to have a forward contingency plan rather than to have to rely on rapid back-of-the-envelope guesswork.
4   We emphasise that we have had to assume that our suppliers will not increase their prices if we need more substitute.

Note: The frank nature of the conclusions reflects the close relationship of the research team with Mr Evans. It would not do to write to the MD in this vein! Rather:

Revised Conclusions for the MD

1   We estimate that there is 3300 kilos a week available at £2.30 per kilo, a further 1500 kilos at £2.40 and 400 kilos at £2.50.
2   We have done our best in the limited time in which we appreciate you were forced to make a decision. It might be useful to have analyses of the relationship between purchasing, production, marketing and bottom-line profits in the form of a set of contingency plans which should enable top management to have better service and a wider horizon.

Reflections

We are always dealing with partial information. Sometimes what we are interested in is the part that is missing. How can this be estimated?

If we have truly random samples from the whole, then we can simply assume that what is missing is more of what we have got. But if our sample is not random we can still estimate the missing part if we know the way in which the non-randomness occurred.

So once again – go to the source of the data and find out how they were collected.

This study is based on an investigation into the production of lengths of steel bars in the UK steel industry.

Further Work

1   How would you deal with a rise (or fall) in prices during a week?
2   How would you monitor the steady state of the price distribution?
3   If prices varied according to demand for substitute how would you decide on the optimal blend of substitute and real beef?

4 If it was possible to take a forward contract for delivery of substitute in four weeks' time, what factors would influence you?
5 What would be the effect on your analysis if lot size and prices were correlated?
6 How would you check that the price per kilo was a stationary distribution?

Chapter 5

Uncertainty

It is probably the case that we are always uncertain. Determinism makes algebra easy and can give an air of versimilitude to an otherwise bald and unconvincing narrative. But there is nothing to be ashamed of in being uncertain. Indeed we can often harness uncertainty to our profit, by being able to measure it and put a value to it.

The reaction of each of us to uncertainty is a personal matter. We each have our own behaviour in the face of risk. This will depend not only on our psyche but also on our resources. Often, as the average reward we might expect increases, then so does the variability of what might happen. For example in a lottery the existence of a large prize always increases the chance of not getting any money back at all. This is why dull and boring investment in secure stock with lower interest rates is more attractive to those with less resources than to those with great resources who can afford to go for those opportunities which have a higher, but more risky, rate of return. Risk and reward go together.

Uncertainty is important in itself and important also is the reaction of people to it. Its influences on management behaviour are so often hidden. Clearly the first step is to measure it.

MEASUREMENT OF UNCERTAINTY

Uncertainty is measured by probability. If we are uncertain about what will be the price of a raw material in three months time we can express our uncertainty in terms of the probability that the price will lie in a given range. But how do we define probability itself?

The term "likely" or "probable" is often used of an event in relation to its relative frequency. We are used to estimating chances or probabilities, e.g. the chances of rain or of getting a seat on the next bus, and many people try to estimate the probability that a horse will win a race or a team a football match. We should be hard put to it in these cases to obtain an exact measure of the probability of the event concerned, though possibly prepared to make an intuitive attempt in the form of laying odds. In insurance of all kinds, precise calculations are made, on the basis of large masses of data concerning age at death, frequencies of fires and accidents, etc., to determine premiums. In the totalisator betting the odds against the various horses are precisely determined by the proportions in which money is laid on them; these proportions reflect the public's estimates of the horses' chances of winning on the basis of their past histories. It may be necessary to take into account a factor changing with time, such as the improving form of a horse or the effect of changing social conditions on the chances of dying before a certain age.

MEASUREMENT OF PROBABILITY

We must now therefore consider the problem of obtaining a numerical measure of probability. There are three separate cases.

Mathematical Probability

The mathematical theory of probability, which plays a large part in the development of statistical theory, originated in the consideration of the problems of games of chance. In the toss of a coin, the throw of a die or the spin of a roulette wheel, out of the number of possible events, one happens. In these examples, before the event, we can enumerate the possible events and describe them as 'equally likely' or 'equally probable'. For instance, the throw of a die may result in any of the numbers 1, 2, 3, 4, 5 and 6 as the score shown. Our reasons for regarding them as equally likely are that the die is (almost exactly) symmetrical and the conditions of its projection are presumed not to favour any one of the numbers rather than any other. When such considerations of symmetry give understandable significance to the phrase 'equally probable' in the class of events concerned, we may make the following rather formal definition.

Definition

If an aggregate of n equally probable occurrences includes m equally probable ways in which a particular event may occur, the probability of that event is m/n.

Thus when all possible occurrences, on an assumed basis of equality, have been enumerated, the probability of a particular event is the ratio of the number of occurrences favourable to that event, to the total number of occurrences. A probability so defined may be called a *mathematical* probability. Simple examples are: The probability of throwing a 4 with a die is 1/6, of drawing a card higher than a 5, ace counting high, from a pack, is 36/52; of throwing 'heads' twice in succession with a coin is 1/4, the equally probable occurrences being H,H; T,H; H,T; T,T.

It is usual to denote the probability of an event by p and to call the occurrence of an event "success". The probability of failure, i.e. of non-occurrence of the event, is denoted by q.

$$\text{Thus if } p = m/n = \text{the probability of success,} \tag{5.1}$$

$$\text{then } q = \frac{n-m}{n} = \text{the probability of failure.} \tag{5.2}$$

$$\text{and } p + q = 1. \tag{5.3}$$

The extreme values of p are 0 and 1, corresponding, *if n is finite*, to certain failure and certain success. When a probability is expressed in the form of odds, the ratio used is favourable to unfavourable occurrences or vice versa. To say that the odds against an event are 7 to 2 means the probability of its occurrence is 2/9.

Frequency in the Long Run

This method of measuring probability depends on our ability to structure a series of trials. When a trial, the result of which may be one of several different occurrences, is made, the observed occurrence is definite. It cannot happen a fractional number of times. We say that the probability of each of the possible scores resulting from the throw of a die is 1/6 and we certainly cannot obtain each score 1/6 of a time with a single throw. Can we then say that we shall obtain each score exactly once in six throws, or each exactly 100 times in 600 throws? The answer is clearly no, but we have a strong faith that if the die is thrown *many times* the six possible scores will occur "on the average" with practically equal frequencies. If this did not happen we should suspect that the die lacked symmetry or was what Damon Runyon described as "strictly phoney". We have, in fact, a strong underlying belief in *causality*. Symmetry, though capable in many instances of definition in a positive form, is essentially a negative fact, the fact of no known or observable difference. If the outcome of our experiment shows some consistent difference, such as one number being thrown more often than the others, we believe this must be due to a cause conducive to that result and conclude that the die lacks symmetry, or that there is a bias in its projection.

There is, however, much more in it than that checking of the assumptions made in a mathematical probability exploration. Often we do not know the causation, which we do when we have a die or a pack of cards. For example we may not know the causation of a disease or of an accident. But we do have historical data from which we can estimate the probability of more than, say, five admissions to hospital of a particular diagnostic complaint during one week simply as the long run historical frequency of the proportion of weeks in which there were more than five such admissions. Such estimates are termed long run, or historical, or posterior, probabilities.

Subjective or Prior Probabilities

In the foregoing we have dealt with situations that are repeatable. But what of the one off situations that are not repeatable and which do not have a clear cut mechanism? What of the one-off situation referred to earlier – the probability of a horse winning a race, a football team winning a match or of a research group discovering a specific drug before another group does?

In these cases it is natural and proper to estimate such a probability in terms of what might be called a degree of rational belief. These subjective probabilities will follow the laws of objective probability, in particular the certainty and impossibility of probabilities 1 and 0. They can also be tested by the same frequency tests as objective probabilities, namely that of all one-off events to which we have assigned a prior probability of 0.40, then 40% of them (approx.) did occur. Such validation has taken place in special (repeated) one-off events such as a forecast that the probability of rain is 0.40.

Probabilities of events for which there is no enumeration and no historical data, are estimated prior to the event taking place and so are called "prior probabilities" (or Bayesian probabilities; ref 1). This distinguishes them from the second case in which the probability could only be estimated historically. This particular estimation should not be undertaken as a simple light hearted guess. This is a skilled operation and there is an extensive literature on the proceedures which can be followed (see for example ref 1).

The basic and very important point which the previous argument illustrates is that all three classes of uncertainty are measured by the same metric – a probability – and that in all cases probabilities follow the same laws.

Problems of Measurement

It is important to remember that the first time we measure, even crudely, the probability of something happening we receive significant quantitative information and a payoff which can be very high.

It can be difficult to estimate probabilities with even moderate accuracy.

In practice over some years of experiment, by the author, with different groups of people, the probability estimates of the sticks forming a triangle (see Chapter 2, Appendix) was close to 0.50 although the correct answer is 0.25. In other words, the forecast was that it will happen twice as frequently as it does. In the birthday problem the probability estimates are nearly always less than one in ten, that is, only one-*fifth* of the actual frequency. Such errors in large scale planning could be catastrophic. The difficulty here is that in one-off situations we can never know how badly we have estimated probabilities. The effect of that error may be masked by many other effects, and anyway life moves on and we are too busy to look back. There is also a natural resistance to looking back, since it will never yield glory and only apportion blame.

Remember: The catastrophic mistakes of banks and insurance companies in recent years, involving the write off of billions of pounds, were all caused by appallingly bad probability estimates. They only came into public view because of their size. How many smaller errors (involving only millions of pounds) have gone unreported, or even unnoticed? No one will ever know.

Validation

Validation can be difficult where probabilities are involved. In the mathematical approaches to allocation in the following chapter, if the basic assumptions made are correct then the answer obtained is definitely the best. There is no argument. Suppose, however, that we are faced with an event which has a very low chance of occurring, say one chance in a hundred. We might then act on the basis that the event will not happen. Now suppose it *does* happen. Were we wrong to act as we did? Events which have chances of occurring of 1 in 100 do *sometimes* happen (on average 1 in 100 times). The question of whether an action which turns out to be disastrous was a wrong decision can be debated but our problem is this: when a single action is taken in a one-off situation and an unexpected result occurs there is no way of either validating or invalidating our calculations in general and of the probability estimates in particular. The single act of validation which is not uncommon is really, in cases of uncertainty, useless and dangerous. If, however, it is persisted in and does not confirm the analysis, no amount of protesting will change the minds of some managers that a one-off trial is useless where probabilities are concerned. If the analyst estimates that the probability of an event is 80% and then it fails to occur, he will be derided as incompetent. All the analyst can do, if by chance the cookie crumbles in his favour, is to be impassive. Take the credit and leave in glory.

There is a desperately serious point here. Popper (ref 2) maintains that a statement which is not capable of validation is meaningless. If we cannot validate a probability, or a set of probabilities, does that not render them void of meaning?

Perils of Averaging

Anyone who takes out insurance does so, not because he expects to gain, but rather because he is willing to pay for a certainty to replace an uncertainty. Commodity markets and futures exchanges (when used for prudent trading and not for gambling) are places where uncertainties and certainties are traded. Suppose the reader was offered the following uncertain choice situation. It is a nice situation in which the reader cannot lose:

First Choice

Take part in a lottery in which you can

- Win zero with probability 1/2
- Win £1m with probability 1/4
- Win £2m with probability 1/8
- Win £4m with probability 1/16
- Win £8m with probability 1/32 etc. etc. etc.

Second Choice

Receive £2m for certain.

Most readers would take the second choice of the £2m. (*Note*: those who would not, but would take the gamble, are not wrong. There is no right or wrong in the following argument – only an appeal to internal consistency.)

In averaging terms the gamble is worth:

$$0(\tfrac{1}{2}) + 1(\tfrac{1}{4}) + 2(\tfrac{1}{8}) + 4 \left(\tfrac{1}{16}\right) \tag{5.4}$$

$$= \tfrac{1}{4} + \tfrac{1}{4} + \tfrac{1}{4} \ldots = \text{infinity} \tag{5.5}$$

In this case a decision based on average return would mean taking the first choice. Those who take the second choice are willing to trade some of the higher average return for a reduction in the uncertainty. This is the same reason why people take out insurance. Insurance companies make a profit out of their customers, so on average alone it is better not to take out an insurance policy. But we do so and pay the insurance company to take the uncertainty so that we can have the certainty of not losing money.

Many such examples can be selected and they all reflect our approach to uncertainty and our behaviour when faced with it.

Rationality and Consistency

We have seen, therefore, that behaviour in the face of uncertainty is very personal. There are no "correct" answers, only consistent answers. Even where consistency is concerned, some people reject the idea that consistency is a virtue. Utility theory is a valiant attempt to grapple with uncertainty and it is essential to understand it and the implications of the manner in which it uses probability (see refs 3, 4 and 5).

There are difficulties associated with using utility. One problem is that there is in all of us what may be called an irrationality. The process of establishing a utility involves contemplating hypothetical gambles and many have a blank spot on probability. This is sometimes dealt with by using only 50/50 gambles. Of more severe nature are the acceptability of the axioms necessary for the existence of a utility function (ref 2).

In our three classes of probabilities – those which are confirmable in an experimental manner, those which can be deduced from assumptions and those which are prior estimates – all use the same measure even though its firmness may well depend on the class. The trouble is that $p = 0.75$ *looks* equally firm no matter which way it has been derived. Attitudes to risk (however measured) will change as resources increase. This is illustrated by the following (true) case study.

A very large international company, with at least 50 large subsidiaries had a rule that investment propositions acceptable to a subsidiary but involving more than a certain sum, had to be sent to the main board for acceptance. In a period of three years in which a well-known analyst acted as secretary to this main board committee, not a single proposal was rejected. The reason of course was that, based on resources available, the subsidiary is more risk averse than the main company and any proposal that gets through the filter of the subsidiary will certainly pass the board. What should have happened was that the main board was also presented with proposals rejected as too risky by the subsidiaries.

It is important that organisations should have an internally consistent attitude to risk. One of the reasons why banks are notoriously reluctant to support new ventures is not only because one black mark associated with a branch manager whose lending goes bad on one occasion, counts more adversely in career prospects than many loans which go well, it is also because of this filtering process and because so many problems involving risk are dealt with by a gust of emotion or by "taking a view".

After the event we can excoriate these people, all of whom are known for their caution. However, prior to the event, what should they have done?

Basic to probability is an assessment of how well risks can be estimated and robustness must always be examined. That is, how badly wrong can we be in assessing risk before the validity of the decisions is affected? Even without any prior assessment of probability it is still essential to have such sensitivity analyses carried out.

References

1 Lindley, D. (1990). The present position in Bayesian statistics, *Statistical Science*, **5**, 1, 44–89.
2 Popper, K. (1974). *The Logic of Scientific Discovery*, p. 191, Hutchinson, London.
3 Rivett, B.H.P. (1971). *Principles of Model Building*, Wiley, Chichester.
4 Fishburn, P. and Tversky, A. (1977). In Bell, P., Keeney, R. and Raiffa, H. (eds), *Conflicting Objectives in Decisions*, Wiley, Chichester.
5 White, D. and Bowen, K. (1975). *Theories of Decision in Practice*, Hodder and Stoughton, London.

Getting a Lift Up

The Fifth Principle: Expect the objectives to change during a study.

Objectives and goals constantly change. First the explicit goals of various parts of an organisation will be different, often because of the performance criteria by which they are judged. Second, individuals and groups have their own hidden agenda which have to be teased out. A useful approach to deduce the hidden agenda is to analyse the decisions and choices which are actually made.

However, there is also a third part to all this. An analyst is a change agent. As a result of the analysis the organisation will change in some way. The process of analysis will focus on the question, "Why are we doing so and so?" The answer will frequently involve a recasting of objectives, goals and performance criteria. One must therefore expect objectives to change during a study.

Anecdote (True)

A bishop in the Church of England requested the OR group of his local university to advise him on the optimal size of the unit of management, the parish. This would involve the closing of churches and the amalgamation of some parishes. Taking this optimal size as the objective the OR team approached the problem in the form of choosing between two extremes

Parishes	Total costs	Availability for worshippers
Many	High	High
Few	Low	Low

There seemed to be the well-known problem in distribution of resolving conflicting effects (ref 1). Clearly one stage was to estimate the probability of church attendance in terms of the distance of travel to the church. This is a common problem and one expected something like an inverse square law.

Not so. To the surprise of the team the analysis showed that over half the worshippers did not attend their nearest church, indeed many travelled great distances. The reason was that distance was not nearly as important as the style of the service and of the vicar. Some wanted low church, some anglo catholic, some liberal, many evangelical and so on. The objective therefore was not to optimise in some sense the conflict between attendance and costs. This became subsumed in the larger objective of ensuring a mixed menu of styles of churchmanship in a given area. Given this recognition the problem resolved itself.

Moral of the Story

The bishop was concerned with a standard measurement problem – how many outlets, how many factories, how many warehouses. But the performance depended on people, the people who had to feel a desire to go to a church. They were the market. The important factor was not the cost of "purchasing" the product but the nature of the product.

GETTING A LIFT UP

Introduction

Patrick House is a 22-floor office block in which approximately 2000 people work. It is a prestige development with high rents but in the present economic climate the owner's agents are concerned that when the present tenancies expire they should be renewed for further periods, even if this means a reduction in the rent. Consequently they are in the invidious position of being sensitive to complaints without being able to spend much money in dealing with them. The floors are occupied as shown in Table 1.

Most of the complaints deal with such things as decor, maintenance, heating, condition of the washrooms and so on. However, there is a persistent undertone of dissatisfaction with the lift service and complaints at the length of time occupants have to wait for the lift. The agents, who have a student on work experience from the local university, decide to have a look at the problem of giving a better lift service and what alternative would be the best.

Stage 1: Listen

Before any set of alternatives is listed it is wise to examine the extent and the nature of the complaints. We must get behind the very high degree of emotion that obviously exists and see who is complaining about what. A

Table 1

Floor	Organisation	Business
21	Berwyn Services	Bar, restaurant, executive club
20 19	Thomas, Richard & Henry	Solicitors
18 17 16 15	Inland Revenue	Tax
14 12 11	MGR & Co.	Advertising agency
10 9 8 7	Regional Health Authority	Health care
6 5	MGR & Co.	Advertising agency
4 3 2	Gessit, Prayhard & Sine	Chartered Accountants
1 Ground	Berwyn Malls	Shops, cafes, fast food

short questionnaire is sent to each tenant asking for their impressions of the service and the occasions when they are conscious of delays. They are asked to assess the service in three categories: Good, Medium, Bad. Table 2 summarises the responses.

When the responses are discussed with the agents they are particularly concerned at the complaints from Thomas and MGR since their leases will

Table 2 Service impressions

Floor(s)	Tenant	On arrival	Delays to these floors	From these floors	Leaving building
20 & 19	Thomas	M	B	M	B
18 to 15	IR	G	B	M	B
14	MGR	M	B	B	B
12 to 7	RHA	M	B	M	B
6 & 5	MGR	G	B	B	M
4 to 2	Gessit	G	G	M	G

be up for renewal next year. Between them they occupy a quarter of the building and the nature of their businesses means that they have many visitors. If they quit, the consequences will be serious, not only for the owners but also for the agents themselves, who will be fired by the owners.

Stage 2: First Thoughts

All tenants except Gessit are discontented with the interfloor service. Those who assess the service to and from the top floor as bad are those who in the nature of their business do a great deal of expense account hospitality on the top floor, that is, the advertising agency and the accountants. In addition the advertising agency personnel have to make the longest journey between floors.

It is a sad comment on human nature that complaints about slowness when leaving the building are much more than those about slowness when arriving. The only tenant who is happy with the service when leaving is the one nearest street level.

The agents feel therefore that the heart of the problem lies in giving a better service, first for interfloor and second for those leaving the building.

Stage 3: Review the Alternatives

What are the alternatives? The agents list:

1 Increase the power of the lift motors. This should increase the acceleration of the lifts and the speed between floors.
2 Stagger the arrival and departure time so that peak loading is reduced.
3 Limit the stopping places of some of the lifts so that less time is spent in loading and unloading.

At this stage the work experience student tells the agent that she has an idea of a fourth alternative but is told to be quiet and to get on with sorting invoices. Which she does.

Stage 4: Analyse the Alternatives

The agents now get down to the task of going through these alternatives one by one and start with the possibility of replacing the motors. Checking with the tenants, the agents find that the tenants are in favour of this. However, the tenants are less in favour when they realise that the heavy cost would mean a rise in rents. There is total loss of preference for this alternative when they also realise that for some months at least one of the lifts will always be out of action.

So they move on to the next alternative (2) above. As they start to think about it the student again raises her hand and offers an immediate solution. She is told to go out and bring in some sandwiches for lunch. Which she does.

However the agents do go so far as to ask her to make some calculations. The student points out that the main problem is interfloor movement and journeys to and from the top floor. None of these is likely to be affected by staggering arrival times but it is thought that the tenants should be asked about it if only to reassure them that the agents are doing their best. The reaction is anger. Most of the tenants work to flexi-time for lower and middle grade staff and these people resent being asked to work to a fixed time rota. In addition, the senior staff say firmly that the building and its services are made for the tenants and not the other way round. The agents retire from the battlefield in some disarray.

Stage 6: Listen (Again)

By now things look desperate as there is only one possibility left. The agents look at this with a heavy heart until they realise that there is at last something they can give the student to do. She is asked to log the journeys made by people in the lift. Where do they get on and where do they get off? Before she starts she mentions that maybe the analysis is not necessary after all as she has an idea. By now the patience of the agents is getting exhausted and they tell her sharply to get on with the job. Which she does.

It takes some time to collect the data which she does by riding up and down in the lift for hours on end. Eventually she produces a sort of input–output table which shows the number of people moving between each pair of floors. Everyone looks at this table with great seriousness but it turns out to be not of great help. In fact it is of zero help.

Most of the interfloor movement is between the floors occupied by particular tenants but there is the hope that each tenant could be restricted to one stopping place only. This would mean that lifts would only serve, for example, floors 3, 5, 10, 14, 17, 19, 21. This looks very attractive as it reduces, at a stroke, the number of stopping floors from 19 to 7. However, this again causes great concern with the tenants. They say, correctly, that most of their staff go on and off at adjacent floors and if the lifts did not stop at all their floors the staff would leave.

By now the agents are in despair. So dismayed are they that when the student now says "I have a comment to make", they give in and ask her to make it, which she does:

"On my course, the professor is very keen on setting objectives carefully and on checking whether we have got the problem in perspective, so can I ask you gentlemen, what will be the way in which you will check the effectiveness of your solution, whatever it is?"

"That's obvious. It is to give a service which cuts down waiting time for the lifts", they answer.

"How will you know when the waiting time is short enough?"

"When the complaints stop", they reply.

"Exactly," says the student. "That is why your objective is not to give a better service. It is to stop the complaints. As my professor would say, giving a better service is not the end, it is the means to the end. You have been concerned with the means to an end without defining the end. The end is to stop the complaints. When you look at it that way we have to ask what other means there are to achieve that end."

By now the agents are enthralled by this student. "Go on," they implore.

"Our professor has been teaching about the perception of time and how difficult it is is to estimate the passage of time. When people are occupied then time seems to pass very quickly."

"That's true," they all cry. "But we cannot give people things to do while they wait for the lift."

"No. But you can get them to occupy themselves. The landings by the lifts are pretty bare and bleak places. They could be brightened up by a display of pictures but, as, my professor says" (by now the agents were getting fed up with hearing about this professor, but they held their breath as the student continued) "My professor says that self-regard is the greatest occupation in which we all partake, so why not put a series of large mirrors on each landing. I am sure that most people will be happy to study themselves in the mirrors and from what I have seen, the men, especially those in the accounting firm, will be happy to look in the mirrors to see the girls. Once they do that they will not notice how long the lift is taking."

The agents were doubtful about this solution but as it did not cost much they went ahead. At the tenants' meeting one month later the agents enquired of the tenants whether they could spot any improvement in the lift service. All round the table the reaction was "We do not know what you have done but it seems greatly improved. How did you do it?"

One agent looked sheepishly at the student and replied "Just something we worked out for ourselves." A tenant turned to the student and said "You really must be learning a lot by working with practical managers and seeing how things should really be done. Just think what you have learnt from them."

Which she did.

Reflections

Do not let either the brevity or the levity of this happy tale diminish its importance. In many years of experience the writer has never found any piece of work in which the objectives as originally envisaged have remained static.

In many cases there are no stated objectives when the work begins. There can be anything from a vague disquiet to a recognition that something is badly wrong. All that one has is a symptom.

Working on a problem, involving others in it, is an excellent way to tease out hidden objectives. In some cases no one knows what they are or even whether there is any objective at all.

One of the most common faults is to treat symptoms rather than the underlying cause. Another is to confuse ends with means. In some places indeed there is a deliberate, if unacknowledged inversion of means and ends. This is not uncommon in voluntary organisations.

For example a number of people may recognise a human need suffered by a group of people in society. They set themselves to form a charity to alleviate that need, and work diligently, organising and collecting money. The group being helped are the ends and the people who have responded to that need are the means.

There can then occur a subtle and ineluctable inversion. The helpers begin to enjoy what they are doing and the *ends* for these people can now be to have a warm feeling of being involved and caring (this is not a cynical remark). The disadvantaged group now becomes the *means* to that end. Studies of the efficiency and effectiveness of charities come up again and again to this problem of inversion.

However, this is not confined to voluntary organisations. It can happen in government, commerce and industry. It is present in some family organisations where running the business can become a hobby and they become reluctant to face brutal facts.

This is also common where people are engaged in a process or product which they love. It is noteworthy that men who are ardent football fans and who have built up businesses by hard work, careful cash control and great prudence throw all caution to the winds when they become directors of their local football club.

One can only reflect that if people want a hobby they should buy a train set. It is much less expensive and certainly much easier to run successfully than is a business.

Reference

1   Gregory, G. (1983). *Mathematical Methods in Management*, Wiley, Chichester.

Further Work

Have a look at some of the service functions in your own institution. What are the objectives of:

• The student union?
• The refectory?
• The library?

● The bookshop?

For those who are not in education what are the objectives of schools, transport systems, public libraries? What performance criteria are relevant?

What symptoms would you expect to find if any of these were not doing its job effectively? What is meant by "effectively"?

What are the ends and what are the means for all of these?

Discuss these problems with others and see how the perception of the objectives changes over time and by the subgroups considered.

Chapter 6

Deterministic Problems

We have seen that there are three elements in any management analysis, as indeed there are in any process of management control: Unit(s) of quantitative measurement, probability and the effect of time. In this respect the problems of finance and banking are examples: only one unit (money), risk and the discounting effect of time.

The previous chapter established that uncertainty is always present and it may now seem perverse to describe deterministic problems as those where probability, chance, risk do not operate. However, there are many cases where the uncertainty is small and we can effectively act on the assumption that once a decision is taken, then, in all important aspects of its consequence, one knows exactly what will happen. In some texts such problems (deterministic) are discussed before problems involving variability. This is because the deterministic problem can be "solved" more easily. We reverse the order, since variability is the natural state of the world; there is at the basis of our world a fundamental indeterminacy. Sometimes the impression can be given that the "clean" problem is deterministic and that when variability does exist then this is because we are incompetent.

But the opposite is the case. Variability always exists and where determinism is used it is because of special circumstances or special assumptions made in order to solve a problem. We shall now review both the deterministic problem where there is no time effect (the one-off problem) and those where there are sequences of decisions interacting with each other – but in both cases it is assumed that one knows full well the exact consequence of any decision. The difficulty is that there are so many possible decisions.

The first example which follows is the simplest case where the relationships between the variables are known, where there is a single objective which can be expressed in terms of the outputs and where the resources are also expressed in the terms of the inputs and outputs.

Problems can become complex in many ways. The second example introduces complexity by way of an increase in the number of factors.

The third example: In many cases one is aware that factors such as raw materials cost, product pricing, share of market, which have been used as though they are fixed and known, are in fact subject to variability. This can be analysed by risk analysis. All these three are one-off problems.

The fourth example: Another complication is when the problem is no longer one off. Today's solution will affect what we can do tomorrow. This is the final type of problem in a development from the simplest one with which we started.

THE SIMPLEST PROBLEM

The simplest form of deterministic one-off problem is that where the relationships between what is put in and what is brought out are all linear and where the objective function is a linear relationship of the outputs. Consider for example a factory workshop where:

1   The cost of the various inputs, raw materials, labour, are all proportional to their amounts.
2   The cost of the transformation from inputs to outputs is a linear function of these two sets (e.g. fixed and variable costs per unit of time).
3   The value, or contribution to profits, of the outputs is proportional to their amounts.
4   Any constraints on what can be input, what is transformed and what can be output are all linear functions of these amounts, (e.g. availability of raw materials, capacity of production processes, limiting factors in the market).

In this case every relationship can be expressed in linear form. We saw in the diet mix problem in Chapter 2, Appendix, that the optimal diet would be on the boundary of the feasible zone. This is important in this present situation. The melding together of many linear relationships will give a total relationship which is linear. No matter how many dimensions we are working in, we shall have a feasible zone (or space) and the optimal course of action, as measured by the linear objective function, will be on the linear boundary of the feasible zone – that is the optimal result will be prevented from being even better by at least two of the constraints which will be acting as brakes. The consequence of this is that one should therefore be very careful about constraints and not treat them lightly. They literally are constraints, not only on what we are permitted to do but also on how well we can do it. Clearly therefore, in deterministic problems, whether linear or non-linear, the constraints must be examined carefully and incorporated into the problem (refs 1 and 2).

COMPLEXITY

Linear problems are not uncommon (although less common than teaching programmes at some universities would lead one to think). They deal with very complex situations in an elegant and easy manner.

A research team investigated the costs of transporting coal in the north of England. In this case coal from each mine was shipped by road or by rail to cleaning plants where stone and impurities were removed and from there by road or by rail to coke ovens where coal gas was produced and the coke used for steel production (Figure 6.1).

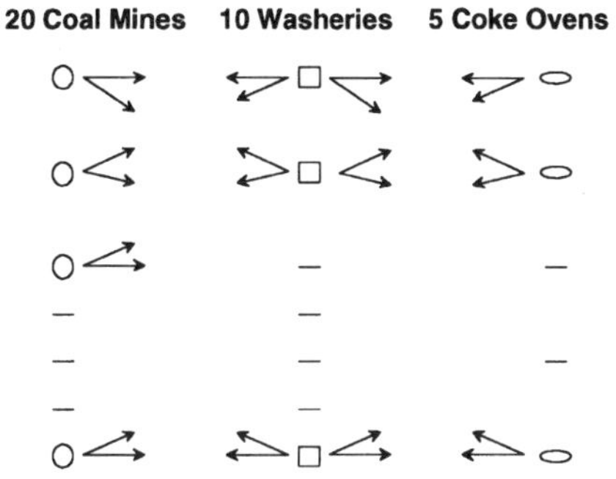

Figure 6.1   Coal transport network

By road there were 200 links from each mine to each cleaning plant and 50 links from each plant to each coke oven making 250 road links in all. There were also another 250 rail links. Along each of these 500 links there was a different cost per ton of carrying coal. The problem was to decide how much coal should go by road and/or by rail from each mine to cleaning plant to coke oven so as to minimise the transport cost, without violating any of the constraints. What are these constraints?

1 The production at each of the 20 mines: (20 constraints)*
2 The maximum amount that could be
   shipped out of each mine
      by road: (20 constraints)
      by rail: (20 constraints)
3 The maximum amount that could be taken
   by road or by rail along each of the 500
   links: (500 constraints)

4 The maximum amount that could be
   received at, and also sent from each
   cleaning plant by road and by rail: (40 constraints)
5 The throughput capacity at each of the
   cleaning plants: (10 constraints)
6 The maximum amount that could be
   received by road and by rail at each of the
   coke ovens: (10 constraints)
7 The demand at each coke oven: (5 constraints)*

Those constraints marked with an asterisk are in the form of equalities while the remainder are inequalities. The problem therefore was to minimise an objective function of 500 variables subject to 625 constraints of which 25 are equalities and 600 are inequalities.

It is interesting to note that such a solution in earlier days was achieved by hand calculation – it would now take a few seconds on a small computer – and would involve many days of data collection. It is also interesting that the saving in cost was only about 5% from the previous solution, which was achieved by an unskilled clerk who had been doing the job for years. One should always remember that given full information, a single objective and a rapid feedback that tells how well one is doing, there is a learning mechanism and people do rather well. However, even if the payoff is only 5%, in large high cost industry, 5% of a very large figure is itself a large figure and is worth achieving.

In such problems, particularly in the oil industry where models with thousands of variables and constraints are not uncommon, the important task is to formulate the problem correctly and also to be aware of the assumptions being made. A researcher in an oil company once remarked that in 20 years spent in formulating such problems to be solved by linear programming (LP) he had never met one in which all the assumptions of linearity and continuity were clearly correct.

Continuity itself can be a problem. The examples so far have not been constrained so that the inputs or the solution had to be in whole numbers. This can be the case, however. In vehicle production one cannot produce a fraction of a vehicle even if this is the theoretical optimum. Integer programming is an adaptation of LP which deals with this; but throughout this book we shall become aware that powerful methods of optimising can only be used at great expense. This expense is *not* necessarily the cost; indeed in today's terms much computing is dirt cheap. The expense is in the strong assumption necessary to use powerful methods; these are the danegeld which have to be paid.

Almost without exception, whenever deterministic assumptions are made there is a nagging feeling that one has been over simplistic, that uncertainty and variability will creep in. It is, however, always possible to carry out some form of sensitivity analysis, to see what effect there is on the result obtained, when some of the parameters or estimates used, are allowed to vary. In special cases formal statistical theory can obtain this effect in the form of the mean, variance and statistical distribution of the resultant effect. But even where this is the case it is preferable, because of that intimate "hands on" effect of playing with data, to obtain the result experimentally. This is by means of the Monte Carlo experiments mentioned in the next section.

RISK ANALYSIS: THE INTRODUCTION OF VARIABILITY

Risk analysis is a first step of introducing the effect of variability into a deterministic problem. Suppose a new factory is to be constructed. In a formal, accounting type statement, the return on the investment will take into the arithmetic all the relevant factors including construction costs, time to complete, raw material costs, processing costs, labour costs, selling price, market size, advertising and promotion costs and sales. Given each of these there is a unique figure for the return on the investment.

But much is concealed by this analysis. Each figure used is a guess, uncertainty is endemic. Risk analysis replaces each of the fixed numbers assigned to the relevant factors by a range of alternatives with assumed probabilities. A Monte Carlo method takes a random sample of one from each of these alternatives and then evaluates what the return on the investment, would be if these had been the values of the factors as previously, in terms of a single number. This is repeated a large number of times, generating a different random number for each alternative each time (in practice this is very rapidly done) and replaces the fixed return by a variable return. For example the fixed return might be 26% and the results of the Monte Carlo could be as shown in Table 6.1.

For example if in 100 runs of a Monte Carlo, on 10 occasions the single figure of return was in the range 26% to 30%, then the estimate of the probability of the return actually being in the range of 26% to 30%, would be 0.10. This process is very powerful and illustrates how the answer changes if the assumptions are altered, (this is termed how "robust" the answer is). It also highlights which of the quantitative assumptions are the most sensitive in their effect on the single parameter answer. Care should be observed in taking the answer beyond this. One can too easily assume that the distributions assumed for the variability of the input parameter, such as cost of construction, raw material price etc. are correct. These are

Table 6.1

Range of return	Frequency of return in the range
30% +	0.05
26% to 30%	0.10
22% to 26%	0.20
18% to 22%	0.30
14% to 18%	0.18
10% to 14%	0.11
6% to 10%	0.06
Average 20% (approx.)	

inspired guesses and no more than that, but the use of risk analysis to examine sensitivity and robustness is prudent.

The perils of dealing with variable factors as though they are fixed is illustrated by one OR analyst who observed a company in the oil rig business which ran such an analysis just once and used the single result it gave as an input to design criteria. This is like turning a roulette wheel just once and assuming that because it came up with Red 30 on that occasion, then Red 30 is what it will always produce.

There is an interesting extrapolation. In practice it seems to be the fact that in major investment decisions, the input assumptions made turn out to be far too optimistic. Actual costs, actual construction times, actual returns so often turn out to be badly wrong, in the negative direction. The questions have to be asked: is this due to over optimism, is it due to incompetence, are the data deliberately doctored by those who want the project to be accepted?

Or is it a consequence of using "best" estimates of the input parameters? A number of risk analysis examples do show that the average value of a return calculated by a number of Monte Carlo runs is significantly less than the initial single value return based on the set of single "best" estimates of the input assumptions. There does seem something embedded in the statistical evaluation which makes the best estimate, single number calculations a highly biased estimator. It appears that the optimism is not due to incompetence or dishonesty but is buried in the statistical algebra.

But beyond this as in all situations where probabilities are guessed we have to use it with caution especially when the underlying probabilities are informed guesses (refs 3, 4 and 5).

SEQUENCES OF DECISIONS AND CONTINUOUS TIME

Thus far we have taken the single one-off decision. But often what we do today has a knock-on effect. There can be a need to identify what must be done today as distinct from those actions which can wait.

These problems can be approached by a critical path network analysis. Take a trivial problem to make the illustration: A total task can be separated into a number of elements. Each element needs a given number of hows to complete and the elements interlock so that their start and completion times depend on what has already been done. The logic can be expressed graphically (Figure 6.2).

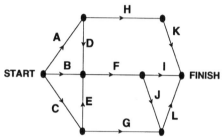

Figure 6.2 Simple network

Such a diagram shows that there are 12 elements A to L. A, B and C can start together, L can only start when G and J are completed and so on. That is the logic. The quantitative data are the hours needed to complete each of the eleven tasks.

Task	A	B	C	D	E	F	G	H	I	J	K	L
Hours	3	2	4	5	5	2	3	3	8	7	5	6

Critical Path Analysis (refs 5 and 6) will identify that sequence of elements, following each other immediately, which have to be strictly controlled for the whole job to be completed in minimum total time. In this case it is B, F, J, L, totalling 17 hours. This is the fastest time for the whole job and the 8 elements excluded have some slack time: i.e. they do not have to start immediately. On the other hand the amount of permissible delay can be identified.

Critical path studies can encompass thousands of elements and are powerful – but no better than the input data. They can be adapted where the fixed time inputs are replaced by statistical probability distributions (i.e. variability can be encompassed) but the same warning note has to be sounded as with risk analysis.

All methods for sequencing decisions and analysing them rely on identifying points of decision and making appropriate choices at each stage. For example a decision tree (refs 2, 3 and 5) will take a forward chain of decisions in which, after each decision there is a result and once that result is known the next decision can be taken.

What we then have is a step-by-step progress into the future with each step realising more information. The problem is to decide the first step and then, stage by stage, take successive steps. The method is illustrated in refs 3 and 5. It is elegant and powerful but like all powerful methods it requires strong assumptions and care should always be taken to ensure that these assumptions are justified.

CONTINUOUS TIME

The introduction of time into the picture can come in many ways, including, as we have seen, taking a set of interlocking decisions one by one en route to a single goal and also those cases in which what we decided today, has an influence on what happens tomorrow. We now take this latter situation.

Problems in finance are of a special purity (using pure in its mathematical sense and not necessarily in a normal, or theological, sense.) At this stage in our argument we introduce the topic in terms of basic assumptions. A standard problem in investment analysis is to find an index which assesses the "value", or the "attractiveness", of a flow of money which will arise in the future (ref 3). For example, if these are annual returns in pounds (Table 6.2), each over a ten-year period, which is the most attractive?

Table 6.2

(a)	(b)	(c)
1000	1900	1500
1100	1800	1500
1200	1700	1500
1300	1600	1500
1400	1500	1500
1500	1400	1500
1600	1300	1500
1700	1200	1500
1800	1100	1500
1900	1000	1500

Looked at intuitively, (a) seems very attractive since it might continue to rise after 10 years, (b) will not look very attractive 10 years from now while (c) is the sort to gladden the heart of a traditional banker. No nonsense here with variability. We have a nice steady earner.

Table 6.3

(a)	(b)	(c)
1000	1900	1500
2100	3700	3000
4300	5400	4500
4600	7000	6000
etc.	etc.	etc.

But what about the effect of time? If we are uncertain about the future and have a suspicion that the future figures might not be as certain as we wish, we could cumulate the returns as shown in Table 6.3.

In this case (b) will give us our money back sooner but over the 10 years all will give the same total return. Are they equally as 'good'? Does the order in which we get our money back matter? A way out of this dilemma is by means of using a discount rate. The following argument has to involve some mathematics but this can be omitted without any great loss by those who are unable to cope with it.

Algebraically, if the return in each year is a_1, a_2, a_3, ... etc. and if the interest rate is r, then a sum of money "a" today will be worth

$$a(1+r) \quad \text{in one year} \tag{6.1}$$

$$a(1+r)^2 \quad \text{in two years} \tag{6.2}$$

$$a(1+r)^3 \quad \text{in three years} \tag{6.3}$$

Inverting this, a sum of

$$a_1 \quad \text{in one year's time is now worth } \frac{a_1}{1+r} \tag{6.4}$$

$$a_2 \quad \text{in two years' time is worth now } \frac{a_2}{(1+r)} \text{ etc.} \tag{6.5}$$

and so a cash flow of a_1, a_2, a_3, ... a_{10} in the next 10 years is worth today

$$\sum_{r=1}^{10} \frac{a_i}{(1+r)^i} \tag{6.6}$$

This is termed the present value of the cash flow.

And it all looks very pretty, even to the extent that a writer of an expository article in an accounting journal once claimed that now that the whole thing has been put on a scientific basis the problem of assessing cash flow has been solved. But it has not been so put, unless one question is answered. How do we estimate r? Is it the rate:

1 We ourselves have to pay to borrow money from the bank?
2 We ourselves have to pay to our shareholders?
3 The general rate of return from other capital investments we make within the company, investments with which this one is in competition for resources (the opportunity cost)?

There is no scientific basis at all, in the *scientific* sense that the specific gravity of mercury is uniquely defined and measured. The important question, as is so often the case, is not what shall we do, but how important are the assumptions? There is another problem. Often the accountants do not tell us how they define a discount (interest) rate. It emerges silently from the financial equivalent of a Quaker meeting and will be influenced by an emotional feel. It can be seen that in evaluating the present value by the sum $\Sigma\ [a_n/(1 + r)^n]$ the contribution to the present value of years further ahead diminishes by the proportion of $[1/(1 + r)]$ each year and if the project looks uncertain in future years (and our degree of certainty will be less as time moves on) then taking a larger value of r has a severe damping effect and reduces the contribution of future years to the present value. For example the factor $[1/(1 + r)^n]$ for $n = 3, 5, 7, 10$ and $r = 0.05, 0.10, 0.15, 0.20$ is shown in Table 6.4.

Table 6.4 Discount factor

r	$n = 3$	$n = 5$	$n = 7$	$n = 10$
0.05	0.86	0.78	0.71	0.61
0.10	0.75	0.62	0.51	0.38
0.15	0.66	0.50	0.38	0.25
0.20	0.58	0.40	0.28	0.16

It does make sense to use such a damping factor but in so doing the problem has been turned from one in which there is a rational determinism to one in which the very sensitive and dominating uncertainty is which value of r to take. It may be the case that in considering alternative investments, different values of r may be used according to their "soundness".

If the initial investment which gives rise to the cash flow is I, then $I - \Sigma\ [a_n/(1 + r)^n]$ is termed the net present value of the cash flow. If this is negative then one would be better advised to find some other place to invest I at the rate r (which is just what GEC did in building up its cash mountain in the 1980s).

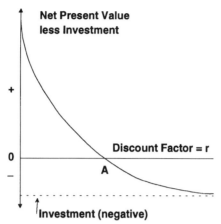

Figure 6.3   Net return

The effect of different values of r can be shown (Figure 6.3). The value of r at which the NPV is damped to zero (point A in Figure 6.3) is termed (for no particular reason) the internal rate of return (IRR) and clearly the greater the IRR the more attractive the investment. This has the advantage that it takes away from the analyst the opportunity of bringing in prejudice by the selection of r in NPV calculations, but the disadvantage that there is no way of expressing a view as to the soundness of the figures.

In all this we see therefore the need to identify the hidden subconscious assumptions and then to question the assumptions. It must be confessed that it is rare indeed, outside of soft systems methodology, to carry out a public and comprehensive analysis of assumptions. These assumptions must be consciously stated and their sensitivity tested. To treat any problem as deterministic does not terminate the argument. It opens up a close examination. It is essential here, as in all OR, that the analyst is totally open regarding his assumptions and the sensitivity of what is being assumed.

References

1   Williams, H.P. (1985). *Model Building in Mathematical Programming*, Wiley, Chichester.
2   Gregory, G. (1984). *Mathematical Methods in Management*, Wiley, Chichester.
3   Ansell, J. and Wharton, F. (Ed.) (1992). *Risk: Analysis, Assessment and Management*, Wiley, Chichester.
4   White, D.J. (1985). *Operational Research*, Wiley, Chichester.
5   Waters, C.D.J. (1989). *A Practical Introduction to Management Science*, Addison-Wesley.
6   Morris, C. (1993). *Quantitative Approaches to Business Studies*, Pitman, London.

Tattie Fabrix

The Sixth Principle: Forecasts should always make plain their assumptions. Assess the accuracy needed before using a forecast. Remember that the most dangerous piece of input data is a probability that can neither be refuted nor confirmed (p. 117).

INTRODUCTION

It is time to move on from the determinism of the early lives and to introduce concepts involving probabilities. In those previous studies, even when probability was present, it was treated as though it was yet another parameter. It was noted in the Third Life (Berwyns Bank), that removal of the assumption of fixed cash movements was dealt with by having a reserve stock and then to go on as before. With the Fourth Life (Happy Hamburger), there was a statistical distribution but it was used simply to show there was a reservoir of meat available at a higher price.

Probabilities always have underlying assumptions and have to be guessed. Where the probability is determined mathematically, the assumption made is that all alternatives are equally likely. Where there are historical data, we can use them to estimate probabilities, but it is still an estimate. We know with greater certainty the number of atoms in a molecule which we have never seen, than we do the probability of an event we have seen many times.

However, a guessed probability can be used to great effectiveness in forecasting, especially where it can be shown that the forecast result is robust against errors in the probability estimates. One such is Tattie Fabrix, based on actual studies in the textile industry in New England, USA, and in Lancashire, UK.

Anecdote (True)

The Week was a four-page duplicated weekly news letter written and edited in the 1930s by a leading Communist writer, Claude Cockburn. It gave a commentary on the politics of the day from a left wing viewpoint and also had a City column on financial matters. It was published in London with a limited circulation.

The news letter was produced on a shoe string; Cockburn did all the writing and a typist produced it. Cockburn had a running battle with his typist because every edition was full of misspellings and typing errors. One morning there was yet another row and Cockburn stormed out to a City lunch in London's Guildhall leaving his typist in tears. Cockburn found that his neighbour at lunch was a leading stockbroker. Asking him where he got his information he was told that it was partly from gossip, partly by reading newspapers and company reports but also from reading "that Communist rag *The Week*". This surprised Cockburn because he never gave tips, but on being pressed was told that the tips were in the City News column of *The Week*. Keeping his identity still a secret, he questioned "But I thought there were no tips in *The Week*, as it was anti-capitalist?"

"That's so", said his neighbour, "but you have to know the code."

Cockburn's head began to swim. What code? he thought.

"I did not know there was a code – how does it work?" he queried.

"Obviously there has to be a code, otherwise everyone would get in on it and no one would make money. So the code is very very cleverly done. The City column discusses different companies and their affairs. If the paragraph on a company has no typing errors then leave it alone. But if it has errors, then buy the shares; and the more typing errors, the more shares you should buy", said the stockbroker.

"Good Heavens", (or words to that effect) replied Cockburn.

"Does it work – does it make money?"

"It is the best tip around", came the response. "And as for making money, its made me thousands." (See ref 1.)

Moral of the Story

A good forecast is one that works. If the tealeaves are infallible, drink lots of tea, and remember that if forecasts are more likely to be accurate simply because of their technical content, then mathematicians and statisticians would be wealthy.

Mathematicians and statisticians, in fact, are not at all wealthy. The point about technically based forecasts is that one knows how they are based and can experiment with them. This means their usefulness, their assumptions and their performance can be assessed without going bankrupt in the process.

TATTIE FABRIX

Dinkie Fabrix is a major manufacturer of a wide range of fabrics used in making up cloth for the rag trade. It has a small subdivision, Tattie Fabrix, which markets a limited range of fabrics in a sector of the fashion market. These fabric sales are seasonal in nature, all starting and finishing at the same time. The seasons are 20 weeks in duration. The fabrics are designed in house some months before the season begins. Samples made by the manufacturing arm of Dinkie Fabrix are distributed to trade buyers. In the light of their response before the season begins, Dinkie makes up a basic supply of stock of each of the lines which will be on offer during the season.

When the season opens orders are received week by week. The first set of orders arrive in the week preceding the season, and in the light of these orders Tattie requests Dinkie each week to manufacture given amounts of each of the lines. As the season progresses, the manufacturing lines come under pressure from the other parts of Dinkie Fabrix and it is the firm policy only to allow Tattie Fabrix to place orders up to the 12th week of the 20-week season. After then the manufacturing side will switch to products for other parts of Dinkie Fabrix.

The sales manager of Tattie, Mr Markup, is judged by the contribution to profits of his operation. He purchases each line from the production arm, at a given price per 100 pieces (100 pieces is the unit of production). There is a price fixed for selling each of these lines but any goods left over at the end of the season are debited to Mr Markup at given figures.

For example, Mr Markup is charged for line 1 at the rate of £100 per 100 pieces. He can sell them for £200 per 100 pieces but any pieces not sold are taken back by the company for re-sale at a distress price and only allows him the rate of £70 per 100 pieces. Effectively for Mr Markup this means that his gain when he sells line 1 is £100 per 100 pieces and his loss for what he fails to sell is £30 per 100 pieces.

Mr Markup is anxious about this whole process and approaches the firm's accountants, Messrs Gessit, Prayhard and Sine for advice.

You are Caroline Addup, an analyst with G, P & S and the partner in charge of management consulting asks you to see Mr Markup and formulate a work plan.

GESSIT, PRAYHARD AND SINE

Memorandum for the File

(Conversation with Tattie Fabrix)

Yesterday I visited Mr Markup of Tattie Fabrix who outlined to me his problem. (Here the analyst lists the points made in the summary above.)

I was told by him that orders received for each line start slowly, then increase week by week to about the tenth week and then decline. It is the policy of the company to meet all orders immediately which implies that the stocks of any line should not reach zero. I pointed out that if one does not allow for zero stocks then the odds are that there will be stock left over at the end of the season and a penalty cost will have to be paid. Mr Markup said that this was of course so, but that all hell would break loose (his words, not mine) if a customer's order was not met immediately. He did not make it clear whether hell would be released by the customer or by his bosses in Dinkie Fabrix.

Mr Markup said that before the season began he would ensure that his stock of each line was at least 1000 pieces, as once the buying season got under way the rate of receipt of orders could outstrip production. He also said that his feeling was that roughly the same pattern of build-up was repeated each year. Within a few weeks he knew what were going to be the hot cats and what were going to be the dogs. (His words, which apparently mean the high sellers and the low sellers respectively.) He had learned, he said, from bitter experience not to concentrate on the hot cats without taking into account the profit margin involved. Some lines have high sales because they are priced too low.

Mr Markup reflected that we were just over half way through the current season. For each of his lines he knows the residual stock in hand and the orders so far received (all of which have been met). He is uneasy about having to guess what should be made week by week and he knows that in week 12 he has to put in his final orders for manufacture for this season. I tried to get Mr Markup to say what it is that he wants us to do. After a lot of general discussion and hand waving we agreed that it should be to take his situation at the 12th week of the season and to tell him how he should decide what to have made, to maximise the expected profit from the manufacture. As we are now in week 10 we have two weeks to do this.

I have managed to get the week by week sales orders for the last season and they are attached as Table 1. Both last season and this season there were ten lines, numbered 1 to 10, but there is no necessary relation, between two different lines with the same number, in the two seasons.

I also list in Table 2 the profit and loss position for each of this year's lines, the sales achieved during the first 10 weeks for each of these lines and the present stocks in hand.

For the next week Mr Markup will order in the same way as usual but in 2 weeks' time (week 12) we shall have to give him a quick method for putting in his final order.

Table 1 Orders received each week last season (in pieces)

Week no.	Line										Total
	1	2	3	4	5	6	7	8	9	10	
1	84	326	359	461	412	193	329	212	307	451	3134
2	90	109	200	178	238	269	118	210	237	143	1792
3	86	222	209	335	269	377	53	203	370	199	2323
4	106	218	389	211	497	459	220	338	730	528	3696
5	176	263	336	291	552	679	435	468	644	158	4002
6	367	384	450	276	611	377	547	349	427	661	4449
7	277	375	369	908	545	690	342	373	887	888	5654
8	305	467	354	1047	758	1152	629	822	1194	605	7333
9	117	754	683	1158	711	510	634	720	1419	237	6943
10	751	579	328	408	1144	1327	624	930	928	1543	8562
11	118	419	397	648	1046	683	610	999	439	1123	6482
12	330	472	640	687	642	740	408	805	587	1016	6327
13	174	706	701	720	921	984	806	582	550	620	6764
14	350	210	674	875	327	547	460	529	835	607	5414
15	427	262	664	897	520	486	315	508	948	427	5454
16	245	228	223	420	617	813	180	523	1006	207	4462
17	108	231	291	141	330	665	205	265	318	59	2613
18	127	123	227	252	308	161	228	99	424	229	2178
19	117	54	168	11	125	140	129	152	413	197	1506
20	258	244	331	317	480	480	304	141	694	464	3713
Total:	4613	6646	7993	10241	11053	11732	7576	9228	13357	10362	92701

Note: The data record the orders received up to the beginning of the week in question.

Table 2 This season's lines: week 10; stock remaining; orders to date; profit and loss (in £ per 100 pieces)

	1	2	3	4	5	6	7	8	9	10
Remaining stock	2000	1000	1900	4100	1200	2100	1800	4400	3700	2600
Total Sales to date	3800	2500	3500	7000	1900	3200	3200	6800	5400	4800
Profit (+)	100	200	150	180	300	300	150	140	100	175
Loss (−)	(30)	(50)	(40)	(55)	(150)	(100)	(55)	(40)	(35)	(55)

In Table 2, the profit figure is what accrues to Mr Markup's account for every one hundred pieces made and sold. For example in Line 1, he pays Dinkie Fabrix £100 for every 100 pieces, receives £200 for them if they are sold (net profit £100) and £70 if they are not sold (net loss £30).

Caroline Addup

Stage 1: How Did Sales Build Up Last Season, Week By Week?

Always look first at the wood before you look at the trees – go for the overall pattern. But always then look at the trees.

Think about the Problem

It looks like a matter of balance. If we produce nothing at all, then there is no contribution to profit (or loss), but we shall have overheads to pay for. If we produce too much, we shall lose money. Somewhere in between there should be an optimum – but we still do not know whether it will be a profitable optimum. The possible profit is shrouded in uncertainty and we shall have to measure that uncertainty – which means getting probabilities. Whenever we make something it will have a financial potential. If we make 100 pieces of a line and they sell, there will be a gain of P and if they do not sell there will be a loss of L. If the probability of them selling is p, then the expected profit is $pP + (1 - p)L$ (where L is negative). We shall therefore try to find p at a given time period.

On reflection it can be seen that if at a given time we already have stock in hand of a given amount, then an extra 100 pieces will only sell if the stock in hand is also first sold. So p will depend on the stock in hand.

But we can go one stage further. Selling the stock in hand (and the extra 100 pieces also) will only happen if the total season's sales on that line exceed the sales already made (S), plus the stock in hand (H) plus the 100 pieces. Therefore the chance of the 100 pieces being sold is the chance of the total season's sales exceeding a given amount – this given amount being

($S + H + 100$). Our strategy is to to take the data given and see whether we can estimate this probability (Tables 3 and 4). These data are plotted in Figure 1.

Table 3 The total sales week by week last season (in hundreds of pieces)

Week	1	2	3	4	5	6	7	8	9	10
Sales	31	18	23	37	40	44	57	73	69	86
Cumulative	31	49	72	109	149	193	250	323	392	478
Week	11	12	13	14	15	16	17	18	19	20
Sales	65	63	68	54	55	45	26	22	15	37
Cumulative	543	606	674	728	783	828	854	876	891	927

Note: Differences from Table 2 are due to rounding off.

Table 4 In cumulative terms, taking a percentage of the ultimate total of 92 701

Week	1	2	3	4	5	6	7	8	9	10
Cumulative as % of total	3.4	5.3	7.8	12	16	21	27	35	42	52
Week	11	12	13	14	15	16	17	18	19	20
Cumulative as % of total	59	65	73	78	84	89	92	94	96	100

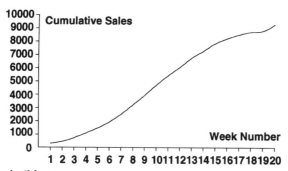

Figure 1 Sales build up

Stage 2: Think of What We Need for a Solution

This means that we now have a rough guide for estimating the total season's sales over all lines provided that this season builds up approximately like the last. For example, if the sales after 8 weeks total 36 000, then our estimate of the total is (36 000) (100/35.0) since we expect by the 8th week to have achieved about 35% of the total. This estimate is 103 000.

However, it is useful to look ahead to what we need to answer the problem. Suppose for a given line, by the 12th week, we have received orders for 5000 and a stock in hand remaining of 3000. As we have seen, this stock will only be sold at full price if the total season's sales for this line are more than 8100. If we order another 100, then this order will only be sold if the total season's sales are more than 8100/5000 = 1.62 times the orders received after 12 weeks.

Let the probability (i.e. of sales achieving more than 1.62 times the 12 week total) be p. In our first thinking we realised that, if we can determine p, then the expected profit of this batch of 100 will be $E(P) = pP - (1 - p)L$, where P is the net profit if the 100 are sold and L is the net loss if they are not sold.

Tactics: find p. To find p we have to introduce the concept of variability. Table 4 is of no use for this. But if we replace Table 4 by a table for each of the 10 lines last year we can see how the separate lines vary week by week. So we return to Table 1.

Stage 3: Hunting p

When we go to Table 1 we could replace each cumulative figure in it by its ratio to the ultimate sale for that line at the end of the season. But this is not the best thing to do, because we were thinking above of multiples, not percentage ratios. So take Table 1 and first go down each column cumulating and calculate by how much this cumulative has to be multiplied to be the total.

For example, line 1 starts with weekly sales 84, 90, 86, 106, 176, 367 etc. Their cumulatives are 84, 174, 260, 366, 542, 909 etc. In order to obtain the ultimate total seasons sales of 4613 for line 1, these weekly cumulatives must be multiplied respectively by 54.9, 26.5, 18.7, 12.6, 8.51, 5.07 etc. (All this is quick and easy on a PC.) For all lines for the 20 weeks see Table 5.

But how do we obtain probabilities? We shall do this by a very crude method which may bring a blush to the cheeks of those of a delicate nature. Take the row for week 12 as follows.

Multipliers (week 12)

Line	1	2	3	4	5	6	7	8	9	10
	1.64	1.45	1.70	1.55	1.49	1.57	1.53	1.44	1.64	1.37

The lowest is 1.37 and so we can say that at week 12 the probability of achieving by the season's end at least 1.37 times the sales already achieved, is 10/10. What is the chance of achieving at least 1.5 times the 12-week

Table 5 Weekly multipliers

Week/line	1	2	3	4	5	6	7	8	9	10	Total
1	54.9	20.4	22.3	22.2	26.8	60.8	23.0	43.5	43.5	23.0	34.0
2	26.5	15.3	14.3	16.0	17.0	25.4	17.0	21.9	24.5	17.4	19.5
3	17.7	10.1	10.4	10.5	12.0	14.0	15.1	14.8	14.6	13.1	13.2
4	12.6	7.60	6.91	8.64	7.81	9.04	10.5	9.58	8.12	7.84	8.87
5	8.51	5.84	5.35	6.94	5.62	5.93	6.56	6.45	5.84	7.01	6.40
6	5.07	4.37	4.11	5.85	4.29	4.98	4.45	5.18	4.92	4.84	4.81
7	3.89	3.50	3.46	3.85	3.54	3.85	3.71	4.29	3.71	3.42	3.72
8	3.09	2.81	3.00	2.76	2.85	2.80	2.83	3.10	2.79	2.85	2.89
9	2.87	2.13	2.39	2.11	2.41	2.49	2.29	2.50	2.15	2.68	2.40
10	1.96	1.80	2.17	1.94	1.93	1.94	1.93	2.00	1.87	1.91	1.94
11	1.86	1.61	1.96	1.73	1.63	1.75	1.67	1.64	1.76	1.59	1.72
12	1.64	1.45	1.70	1.55	1.49	1.57	1.53	1.44	1.64	1.37	1.54
13	1.55	1.26	1.48	1.40	1.32	1.39	1.32	1.32	1.53	1.27	1.38
14	1.38	1.21	1.31	1.25	1.27	1.31	1.22	1.22	1.40	1.18	1.28
15	1.23	1.15	1.18	1.13	1.20	1.24	1.16	1.15	1.27	1.13	1.18
16	1.15	1.11	1.15	1.08	1.13	1.14	1.13	1.08	1.16	1.10	1.12
17	1.12	1.07	1.10	1.06	1.10	1.07	1.10	1.04	1.13	1.09	1.09
18	1.09	1.05	1.07	1.06	1.06	1.06	1.06	1.03	1.09	1.07	1.06
19	1.06	1.04	1.04	1.03	1.05	1.04	1.04	1.02	1.06	1.05	1.04
20	1.00	1.00	1.00	1.00	1.00	1.00	1.00	1.00	1.00	1.00	1.00

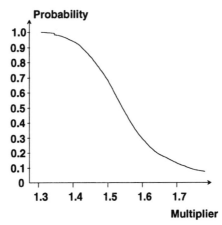

Figure 2 Estimated curve for *p*

figure? Since 7 of the 10 multipliers are more than 1.5, we could say that this probability is 7/10 = 70%.

Stage 4: Capturing *p*

Carry out this operation and graph the result (smoothing out the points). These points are as follows.

Probability	10/10	9/10	8/10	7/10	6/10	5/10	4/10	3/10	2/10	1/10
Multiplier	1.37	1.44	1.45	1.50	1.53	1.55	1.57	1.64	1.64	1.70

Note: do this. Plot the points and obtain your curve to compare with Figure 2. Reading off Figure 2, the values are as shown in Table 6. The probability,

Table 6 Week 12

M	p%	M	p%	M	p%	M	p%
1.30	100	1.40	95	1.50	68	1.60	30
1.31	100	1.41	94	1.51	65	1.61	27
1.32	100	1.42	93	1.52	60	1.62	25
1.33	99	1.43	90	1.53	56	1.63	24
1.34	99	1.44	87	1.54	52	1.64	22
1.35	98	1.45	85	1.55	47	1.65	20
1.36	98	1.46	82	1.56	43	1.66	19
1.37	97	1.47	78	1.57	40	1.67	18
1.38	97	1.48	75	1.58	36	1.68	16
1.39	96	1.49	72	1.59	32	1.69	15

Note: You may well have different numbers. This is because one is drawing a curve by eye. There is no single correct answer, even if you use a package.

$p\%$, of the ultimate seasons sales being at least the multiple M of the sales after twelve weeks.

Stage 5: Using p

Using Table 6, we can, for any line, take the sales at week 12 and estimate the expected profit of manufacturing various amounts of the line. For example, suppose the remaining stock total and sales at week 12 for each line are as shown in Table 7.

Table 7 An example at week 12

Line	1	2	3	4	5	6	7	8	9	10	Total
Remaining stock	2000	1000	1500	3400	1500	2000	1800	3900	3200	1700	22 000
Total sales	5000	3000	4700	8800	3000	4000	4200	7200	5900	3500	49 300
$P(\pounds)$	100	200	150	180	300	300	150	140	400	175	
$L(\pounds)$	(30)	(50)	(40)	(55)	(150)	(100)	(55)	(40)	(120)	(55)	

Take line 1. The total sales to date are 5000, an extra 100 pieces produced will be sold if the total season's sales exceed 7100 (remember there are already 2000 pieces as yet unused in stock). These 100 pieces will be sold if the total season's sales are more than 7100/5000 times the 12-week figure, i.e. more than 1.42 times. Reference to Table 6 shows that the probability of the season's sales achieving a multiplier of 1.42, is 0.93 and so the expected contribution to profit of an extra 100 pieces of line 1 is $pP + (1-p)L = 91$ (using Table 2).

The next 100 after that will be sold if M is at least $(7200)/(5000) = 1.44$. For $M = 1.44$, $p = 0.87$ and $E(P) = 83$. The third 100 will be sold if M exceeds $(7300)/(5000) = 1.46$ and then 0.82 and $E(P) = 77$. Repeating this process for successive increments of 100 pieces we obtain Table 8. This same calculation may be made for the other nine lines giving the results shown in Table 9.

Remember, Table 9 should be cumulated to give the total expected yield, e.g. 400 pieces of line 3 will yield expected profit of $148 + 146 + 144 + 140 = 578$.

Stage 6: Further Use of p

Scheduling production is now possible. If we are only allowed to produce 100 pieces, then the best selection is line 2. If it is 500 pieces then the best selection is:

Line 2:	300 pieces
Line 3:	200 pieces

Table 8 Line 1: expected profit of further production; increments of further production of 100 pieces

Increments of 100 pieces	M	p	Expected profit
1	1.42	0.93	91
2	1.44	0.87	83
3	1.46	0.82	77
4	1.48	0.75	67
5	1.50	0.68	58
6	1.52	0.60	48
7	1.54	0.52	38
8	1.56	0.43	26
9	1.58	0.36	17
10	1.60	0.30	9
11	1.62	0.25	2

Table 9 Expected profit increments of further production per 100 pieces, as at week 12

Increment/line	1	2	3	4	5	6	7	8	9	10
1	91	192	148	168	102	140	119	37	104	94
2	83	187	146	166	30	88	99	32	67	65
3	77	175	144	163	Neg.	60	84	25	46	37
4	67	145	140	156		20	68	14	20	14
5	58	120	131	149		0	41	9	5	0
6	48	90	121	145		Neg.	27	5	Neg.	Neg.
7	38	50	108	128			6	Neg.		
8	26	25	97	121			Neg.			
9	17	10	83	114						
10	9	Neg.	66	105						
11	Neg.		49	98						
12			36	86						
13			17	77						
14			7	55						
15			2	46						
16			Neg.	39						
17				30						
18				20						
19				15						
20				8						
21				2						
22				Neg.						

Larger amounts can be scheduled using the same common sense approach. For example 3000 pieces could be scheduled to maximise their expected profit by taking:

Line	1	2	3	4	5	6	7	8	9	10	Total
Produce	0	500	800	1100	100	100	200	0	100	100	3000
Profit expected	0	819	1035	1513	102	140	218	0	104	94	4025

The profit expected is calculated as follows: For line 2 there are five tranches each of 100 pieces yielding successive expected profits shown in Table 9 as 192, 187, 175, 145, 120. These total 819 as shown above. Similarly for the other lines. The whole process linking together all the data and calculations is easily put on a PC. The computer literate should do this.

Stage 7: Beware of Seduction

It all does look very neat and elegant, but before one gets carried away there is some thinking to do.

At the heart of the problem is the validity of the logic which leads to M and its use. It could also be protested that the argument leading to the value of p for any M is thin. It is. But what are the alternatives? If we had a basic well-tested theory of the relationship between the season's total sales and the weekly sales and knew its algebraic form, then curves could be fitted by usual methods. But we do not have such a theory so we have to do the best with what we have. It is encouraging that from week 5 onwards the multiples in Table 5 do cohere so well and by the time the critical week 12 is reached they range from 1.37 to 1.70. We have only produced one of the cumulative graphs of M against p (Figure 1) but if we had drawn the graphs for weeks 9, 10, 11, 12 and 13 (as on Figure 1, the student should do this now) it can be seen that they form a family of curves. Curve fitting to the points can now be achieved by fitting each curve not only to its own set of points but also to the rest of the family (rather like a between and within analysis of variance). It is useful for those who are computer literate to carry out such curve fitting.

The critical question is – does it matter? The reader should attempt to draw, by pencil and graph paper or by computer graphics, alternative forms of curves to fit the data. Table 10 gives readings from three possible relationships (a, b and c) and compares their expectations of profit with the previous relationship used in Table 6. These are all plausible relationships between M and p and hence with $E(p)$. The reader is invited to test other possibilities.

There are some differences but it must be remembered that the object is to rank different lines in order of the values of $E(p)$ for successive increments. Hence it is probably the case that using consistently any one

Table 10 Possible relationships for line 1 at week 12

	As in Table 6		(a)		Alternative (b)		(c)	
M	p	E(P)	p	E(P)	p	E(P)	p	E(P)
1.30	1.00	100	1.00	100	1.00	100	1.00	100
1.35	0.98	97	1.00	100	0.96	95	0.95	93
1.40	0.95	93	0.96	95	0.90	87	0.89	84
1.45	0.85	80	0.85	80	0.77	70	0.79	73
1.50	0.68	58	0.72	64	0.67	57	0.65	54
1.55	0.47	31	0.49	34	0.53	39	0.48	32
1.60	0.30	9	0.28	6	0.35	15	0.32	12
1.65	0.20	(Neg.)	0.17	(Neg.)	0.28	6	0.22	(Neg.)
					0.15	(Neg.)		

of the four alternatives will not affect which particular line has the greatest potential, that is the greatest $E(p)$.

As a general rule, when deciding at what level of precision one should operate one must always remember the provenance of the raw material, i.e. the data. In this case the approach has been rough and ready and given the sweeping assumptions which have been brought into play it is not really necessary to be concerned at the different values of $E(p)$ which have been obtained. When a meat axe has been used there is no great value in switching to a surgeon's scalpel.

Assumptions

The assumptions made in this approach can be brought together:

1 The cost and profit figures are mutually consistent.
   Note: There is no such thing as "correct" cost and profit figures since they depend on the particular accounting conventions used.
2 The build-up of sales week by week is similar year by year and homogeneous from line to line.
3 The logic of the build-up of M against p is acceptable.

These are considerable assumptions and their implications should be explored with management.

There is a statistical argument that has to be ventilated. This involves the use of $E(p) = pP + (1 - p)L$. It is tempting to argue that a particular 100 pieces scheduled for production will only be sold if its predecessors are all sold first and hence we should use some form of conditional probability. This would be valid if we were scheduling in the light of knowledge that the predecessors have been sold. But it is true and valid to argue on increment, i.e. a particular 100 pieces will be sold if all its predecessors have been sold as well as itself and the probability of this being p as defined is correct as long as we apply it just to the increment. It would be incorrect to take the whole cumulative amounts of 100 pieces and apply the value of p to the whole lot since it is not a question of the whole lot being sold or not being sold, but only of this last tranche of 100 pieces.

REPORT TO TATTIE FABRIX FROM G, P & S

THE SCHEDULING OF PRODUCTION OF FASHION LINES

Introduction

We were invited by Mr Markup to derive a method to improve the scheduling of the production of fashion lines. The problem arises because of the transient nature of sales orders for these lines and because, although the season extends for 20 weeks, it is not possible to schedule more production after 12 weeks. Hence stocks have to be built up at the 12-week point with 8 weeks of (unknown) sales remaining. This report gives the basic data used. It shows how the schedule is calculated, the assumptions made and how the schedule should be used. We also make suggestions for improving the present process.

Data Availability

There are two sets of data used. The first are sales statistics for the last year showing how the orders received increase week by week. In the first week of the season there is an initial surge, as this week includes orders previously received. Sales increase for about 10 weeks and then, week by week, the orders decline, with a final surge in the last week.

The second set of data are the cost figures. Tattie Fabrix pays a (different) fixed amount per 100 pieces to Dinkie Fabrics for each of the 10 lines in question and receives another, fixed, amount when they are sold. If goods are not sold Tattie receives a lower amount for them, which is less than their purchase price from Dinkie.

Before the season begins Tattie creates a basic stock of each of the lines and week by week orders replenishments from Dinkie which are delivered immediately. Tattie delivers to its customers directly from stock but cannot order more stock from Dinkie after the 12th week.

Strategy of Research for the Schedule

The basic problem is to be able to estimate the probability that a given tranche of 100 pieces (the unit of production) will be sold. For example, if at week 12 a given line has already received, and satisfied, orders for 5000 pieces and there are 2000 pieces further in stock, we need to determine the chance that if we schedule 100 pieces more to be produced, they will actually be sold. In other words, if we have sold 5000 pieces by week 12, what is the chance that by the end of the season we shall have sold more than 7100 pieces (that is 5000 + 2000 + 100)? If these chances can be estimated then the problem can be solved and a schedule derived. We shall show how this can be done.

Analysis of Data

The build-up of sales last year is shown for the 10 lines produced (which are different this year from last) in Table 01. From Table 01 it can be seen how sales orders build up to a peak around week 10. If we take the cumulative of all orders, week by week, for all the lines we shall find that they build up to their ultimate total week by week like this (Figure 01).

Of course different lines will vary. Our problem is to estimate the chances of different totals being achieved given the ultimate total sales at 12 weeks. These multiples, of the total compared with the cumulative sales achieved at the end of each week, last year, are shown in Table 02. It is important to note that the pattern is approximately the same no matter what is the ultimate total.

For example, for line 4, the ultimate season sale achieved was 1.55 times the total orders received at 12 weeks, and for the other lines at 12 weeks, their respective multiples were as follows:

Sales multiples at 12 weeks

Line	1	2	3	4	5	6	7	8	9	10	All lines
Multiple	1.64	1.45	1.70	1.55	1.49	1.57	1.53	1.44	1.64	1.37	53

If a given line had achieved orders of 8000 at 12 weeks then we would expect the ultimate total certainly to be more than 10 000, since this is only 1.25 times the 12-week figure and last year every line did better than that. On the other hand no line achieved a multiplier of 1.8 and so we would not expect that sales would reach 1.8 x 8000 = 14 400. The sales therefore will be in the range 10 000 to 14 400.

As the total sales we might expect increases, the chance of achieving it will fall off. Sales of at least 10 000 for the given line are almost certain and sales of more than 14 400 are very highly unlikely. The way the chance falls off depends on the chance of the appropriate multiplier being achieved and these are shown in Figure 02. For example, if the sales at 12 weeks are 8000 the chance of the ultimate exceeding 12 000 is the chance of the multiple exceeding 1.5 which is 0.60.

Deriving a Schedule

We can more usefully take the Figure 02 above in the form of a table to give for any multiplier (M), the chance, p, that the ultimate season's sales will be more than M times the 12-week figure (see Table 03).

Table 01 Orders received each week last season (in pieces)

Week no.	Line										Total
	1	2	3	4	5	6	7	8	9	10	
1	84	326	359	461	412	193	329	212	307	451	3134
2	90	109	200	178	238	269	118	210	237	143	1792
3	86	222	209	335	269	377	53	203	370	199	2323
4	106	218	389	211	497	459	220	338	730	528	3696
5	176	263	336	291	552	679	435	468	644	158	4002
6	367	384	450	276	611	377	547	349	427	661	4449
7	277	375	369	908	545	690	342	373	887	888	5654
8	305	467	354	1047	758	1152	629	822	1194	605	7333
9	117	754	683	1158	711	510	634	720	1419	237	6943
10	751	579	328	408	1144	1327	624	930	928	1543	8562
11	118	419	397	648	1046	683	610	999	439	1123	6482
12	330	472	640	687	642	740	408	805	587	1016	6327
13	174	706	701	720	921	984	806	582	550	620	6764
14	350	210	674	875	327	547	460	529	835	607	5414
15	427	262	664	897	520	486	315	508	948	427	5454
16	245	228	223	420	617	813	180	523	1006	207	4462
17	108	231	291	141	330	665	205	265	318	59	2613
18	127	123	227	252	308	161	228	99	424	229	2178
19	117	54	168	11	125	140	129	152	413	197	1506
20	258	244	331	317	480	480	304	141	694	464	3713
Total:	4613	6646	7993	10241	11053	11732	7576	9228	13357	10362	92701

Note: The data record the orders received up to the beginning of the week in question.

Figure 01 Sales build up

Table 02 In cumulative terms, taking a percentage of the ultimate total of 92 701 (or 928 in the units of Table 3)

Week	1	2	3	4	5	6	7	8	9	10
Cumulative as % of total	3.4	5.3	7.8	11.8	16.1	20.9	27.1	35.0	42.4	51.7
Week	11	12	13	14	15	16	17	18	19	20
Cumulative as % of total	58.7	65.5	72.8	78.6	84.6	89.4	92.2	94.6	96.2	100

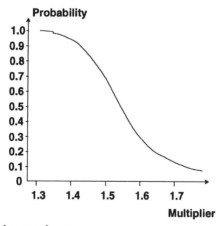

Figure 02 Estimated curve for p

For a particular line, suppose that at 12 weeks there are total orders so far supplied of 6000, with a further 2500 remaining in stock. Then the probability of an extra 100 pieces, which might be scheduled, being sold, is the probability that the season's sales will be more than 8600, i.e. a multiplier of $(8600)/(6000) = 1.43$. This chance as above is 0.90.

Table 03 Week 12: probability, p%, of the ultimate season's sales being at least the multiple M of the sales after 12 weeks

M	p%	M	p%	M	p%	M	p%
1.30	100	1.40	95	1.50	68	1.60	30
1.31	100	1.41	94	1.51	65	1.61	27
1.32	100	1.42	93	1.52	60	1.62	25
1.33	99	1.43	90	1.53	56	1.63	24
1.34	99	1.44	87	1.54	52	1.64	22
1.35	98	1.45	85	1.55	47	1.65	20
1.36	98	1.46	82	1.56	43	1.66	19
1.37	97	1.47	78	1.57	40	1.67	18
1.38	97	1.48	75	1.58	36	1.68	16
1.39	96	1.49	72	1.59	32	1.69	15

If the profit on a sale is £200 and the loss of no sale is £100, then the expected profit is $200 \times (0.9) - 100 \times (0.1) = 190$, since the chance of a sale is 0.90 and of a no sale is 0.10.

The next 100 pieces will only be sold if the total season's sales are more than 8700, a multiplier of 1.45, with the probability which is now reduced to 0.85 and an expected profit of:

$$200 \times 85 - 100 \times 15 = 155 \tag{1}$$

This is lower than the previous tranche because there is less chance of it being sold and hence more chance of it being sold at the distress price.

Example of the Schedule

For the present 10 lines this season we show the actual profit (P) and loss (L) in the following table. Suppose also that at 12 weeks the total orders and remaining stocks would be as shown in Table 04.

Table 04 Stock, sales and cost data

Line	1	2	3	4	5	6	7	8	9	10	Total
Remaining stock	2000	1000	1500	3400	1500	2000	1800	3900	3200	1700	22 000
Total sales	5000	3000	4700	8800	3000	4000	4200	7200	5900	3500	49 300
P(£)	100	200	150	180	300	300	150	140	400	175	
$-L$(£)	(30)	(50)	(40)	(55)	(150)	(100)	(55)	(40)	(120)	(55)	

For line 1, in order to sell the first 100 pieces which might now be produced, there is required a multiplier of $(7100)/(5000) = 1.42$ and Table 03 shows that the probability of this 100 being sold is, therefore 0.93. The expected profit of this is 100 (0.93) − 30 (0.07) = 91.

The next 100 will have a multiplier of 1.44, a chance of 0.87 and an expected profit of 83 which as we would expect is less than the 91 expected for the first 100 pieces. This can be done for all 10 lines as shown in Table 05.

Table 05 Expected profit increments of further production per 100 pieces, as at week 12

Increment/line	1	2	3	4	5	6	7	8	9	10
1	91	192	148	168	102	140	119	37	104	94
2	83	187	146	166	30	88	99	32	67	65
3	77	175	144	163	Neg.	60	84	25	46	37
4	67	145	140	156		20	68	14	20	14
5	58	120	131	149		0	41	9	5	0
6	48	90	121	145		Neg.	27	5	Neg.	Neg.
7	38	50	108	128			6	Neg.		
8	26	25	97	121			Neg.			
9	17	10	83	114						
10	9	Neg.	66	105						
11	Neg.		49	98						
12			36	86						
13			17	77						
14			7	55						
15			2	46						
16			Neg.	39						
17				30						
18				20						
19				15						
20				8						
21				2						
22				Neg.						

If at week 12 there is a limit of 3000 pieces for the final production run, we would cream off the above figures and take the 3000 which give the highest profit. This would be as follows

Line	1	2	3	4	5	6	7	8	9	10	Total
Produce	0	500	800	1100	100	100	200	0	100	100	3000
Profit expected	0	819	1035	1513	102	140	218	0	104	94	4025

The above profit figures are obtained by totalling the relevant separate increments. For example the profit of 819 for line 2 is the total (see Table 04 above) of 192 + 187 + 175 + 145 + 120 = 819.

Conclusions

The method proposed is not perfect and should not be treated as the last word. It is important to understand the assumptions that have had to be made, but nevertheless the scheduling process should be an improvement on the present method.

Assumptions Made

In order to approach a solution we had to assume:

1 The probability distributions of M are (roughly) valid, (note the solution is quite robust against this).
2 The build-up of this season will be like the last.
3 The cost and profit data are valid.
4 Prices do not change during the season.
5 There is no cost involved in running out of stock.
6 The limitation of an arbitrary amount of manufacture at week 12 is sensible.
7 There is no cost of setting up to produce a line.
8 There is nothing we can do about the long lead time for the final weeks.

Suggested Improvements

We are most worried about (5) above. Although nothing explicit has been said, it is implicit that the only costs involved are those of making the pieces and the only revenue is selling them at two prices. Hence we have not taken any account of the costs of being out of stock.

The present situation, of not taking any quantitative analysis until week 12 could be improved in two ways. First, we could carry out a similar cautionary analysis at weeks 10 and 11. Second, the logic behind the arbitrary restriction of manufacturing at week 12 could be reviewed. It is a question of the bottom line profit and the profitability to Dinkie of what Tattie Fabrix can produce, compared with other manufacture which is at present squeezing out the TF production. This should be reviewed.

Acknowledgements

All the staff of Dinkie Fabrics and of TF have been helpful both in outlining the present production processes and in making available all the necessary data and to them all we express our sincere thanks.

NOTE FOR THE FILE

The student is invited to compose this as an exercise. Remember its purpose is to allow easy reference to the work by other members of G, P & S and so it must be completely honest and accurate. It must also highlight imperfections, faults, mistakes and outline how further work might be carried out.

Reflections

This is a common problem in statistics, the newsboy problem. At its heart lie costs which may be difficult to estimate, not only production costs, but also the cost of being out of stock, which in this case was avoided (ref 2).

However, no formal statistical method has been used. Instead of a surgeon's knife we have used an axe – and without any anaesthetic. The purists may avert their eyes, but it is reassuring that the robustness of alternative solutions seems high. Remembering the warning in Chapter 5, it is this robustness that enables us to use probabilities that are not firmly based. So maybe we do not need to be so pure. But the professional statistician may like to look at alternative basic models of build-up of sales and use them in a newsboy type analysis.

Finally, we can see the way in which arbitrary parameters, which may not have been chosen with total care, can have a leverage effect. What is the validity for the parent company of the cost Dinkie pays for the fabrics, for the prices it receives, whether full or distress, the cut-off at 12 weeks and the amount of final manufacture allowed? Both in practice and in textbook examples these can too easily be accepted as given on tablets of stone. They are never carved on stone and are often freely negotiable. They can be the most sensitive parameters of all.

This study is based on investigations by the author in textile industries in the USA and in the UK.

References

1   Cockburn, P. (1971). *The Years of the Week*, Penguin Books, London.
2   Gregory, G. (1983). *Mathematical Methods in Management*, Wiley, Chichester.

Further Work

1   Where does the cost of stock out come in?
2   How would you estimate the probability of running out of stock, line by line, in weeks 13 to 20?

3 How would you estimate the amount of unfilled orders at the season's end?
4 Comment on the method for obtaining the probability distributions of M for different weeks.

If You Are Computer Literate

5 Derive a program for smoothing each set of weekly curves, from Table 05, in such a way that the whole set is smooth between the curves as well as along each curve.
6 Produce a package that takes the order input data and produces the weekly production schedule.

_____ Chapter 7

Forecasting

The model and the objective function both consist of a mixture of variables, controllable and uncontrollable, but there is also a shading of controllability. It is dangerous to treat variables as being either totally controllable or totally uncontrollable. One of the problems of dealing with uncontrollable variables, both in the model and in the objective function, is that of devising forecasts for them. In some cases these forecasts are point estimates about which we may, by some Bayesian approach, form a probability distribution. These are the static variables, within the terms of which we solve the model against the objective function. We can regard them as being constant over time. For example, in linear programming we may well have to estimate a number of such static variables and the introduction of probability in this case is simply in order to test the solution of the linear programme for sensitivity.

There are, however, other categories of uncontrollable variables where we are concerned with a series of point estimates over a period of time, such as, for example, a time series. In these cases we are generally provided with historical data, say commodity prices, from which our task is to try to forecast the value of the variables at specific instants or over a period of time.

THE SIMPLISTIC CASE

The easiest approach to this problem is the simplistic one, which is very tempting to the statistician. This is to assume that because the analyst himself knows nothing about the structure, then nobody else knows anything about it either, and that what has to be done is to take numbers and analyse them for underlying relationships. The basic problem then divides into what are loosely called the "the long term" and "the short term" forecasting problems.

In the long term forecasting problem (it must be emphasised that long term and short term are purely relative concepts) we analyse the series for the two basic components of trend and cycle. By trend we mean the tendency of the long term moving average to change, and by cycle the property of the series to oscillate about a basic trend. In these analyses we first extract from the historical data an estimate of trend. This is frequently carried out by some form of regression analysis which is linear in nature. If we are concerned with a non-linear trend, we are often content to estimate it over a long term period by means of a series of successive straight lines, although the trend may be a well-tabulated function which can be better to use. A short term trend of a non-linear nature can be approximated to by a form of cyclic effect. Having then, by means of regression analysis, extracted from the data any basic trend, the residual historical variations from this trend are analysed for cyclic effects. There are many methods of dealing with this problem and clearly it is sensible to test for common effects such as weekly or monthly cycles (ref 1).

Generally one is content to extract trend and cycle, and, having done so the residual variations about the combined trend and cycle are analysed on an historical basis for short term variations. In forecasting, one extrapolates forward the trend and cycles and the divergence from this trend and cycle is taken as a residual variation from the mean of a distribution. The residual problem in short term forecasting is based on the hypothesis that we now have a static situation in which the variables with which we are dealing can be regarded as independent samples from some statistical distribution, whose mean is given at any moment by the combination of trend and cycle. Once again there are methods of dealing with this. The mean of this distribution can be estimated from the moving average of the residual variations over a period of past time. Alternatively one may recognise that more weight should be given to recent data from the mean than long past data and develop some form such as an exponentially weighted moving average. For these methods standard computer programs are available (ref 1).

MANY VARIABLES

So far we have been dealing with the problem of one single variable in a time series. It may be the case, however, that two separate variables are linked by some means of lag relationship. For example, the sales of the particular product in one country at a moment of time may be shown to be related to the sales of another product in another country at a later moment in time. Here we see a lag-related variable.

Reference has already been made to the provision of computer programs for analysing such series of related data. This presents the analyst with an awkward dilemma. It will be understood that the underlying theme of this book is the necessity to start model construction from a hypothesis which is explanatory in nature, and from this to deduce logically those features which are going to be helpful in decision making. The dilemma is that because there are easy data processing procedures for correlation and for the analysis of correlated data, then one should simply take the data and subject them to a whole series of essentially random tests of association. In doing this it may well be that certain factors of trend or cycle, or of relations with a lag-variable, will be thrown up by the analysis. It may, in fact, be much quicker to analyse rapidly a whole batch of data in what may be termed a random meaningless manner and to derive significant relationships, than to go through the laborious process of understanding the real situation and formulating hypotheses which represent it.

Notwithstanding the seductive ease of data analysis, one should only carry out such unthinking analyses when one is resigned to the fact that it may be too difficult to formulate a prior hypothesis. The reason is that even when we have, by the unthinking approach, derived a basic 'model' (it will be noted that this is hardly a model at all within the terms used in this book) there is still the task of explaining it. Basic to our craft of modelling is the need to explain relationships. It is after all the task of the executive to manipulate systems which he does not understand and it is the task of the analyst to try to understand the system. The "why" question is always much more important than the "how".

STRUCTURE

We emphasise the need, therefore, to start, wherever possible, from a basic structure which we induce before any analysis is undertaken. This means that in estimating cycle and trend we will induce such processes as are explicable and then test whether what we have achieved is significant. In the same way, in studying the relationship between certain variables we should start with the logical relationship which can be explained, and then test their significance.

Another method of forecasting is to form a hypothesis whereby the variable which is being forecast can be shown logically to derive from the conjunction of a number of subsidiary variables. The relationships between these subsidiary variables may be adducible and the individual variables themselves may be subject to some form of control. In this case, what is apparently an uncontrollable random variable may be partly controllable and it can be possible to forecast one partly by means of the conjunctive structure. An example of this is the study of forecasting sales of a particular brand of beer over a period of time (ref 2). In summary form the equation suggested was:

Sales of brand = Total population
    × Proportion of potential beer drinkers.
    × Average net disposable income per capita of beer drinkers.
    × Proportion of NDI spent on food.
    × Proportion of food expenditure spent on beverages.
    × Proportion of beverages which are alcoholic.
    × Proportion of alcohol which is beer.
    × Proportion of beer sales which are for the brand in question.

As can be seen, the multiplying factors above are partly controllable and partly uncontrollable. In addition the sensitivity of the result to the multiplying factors is such that the less one can control, the greater the sensitivity of the factor. For example, if one could do any one thing to increase the sales of a particular brand of beer in this situation, the logical deduction is that one should try to increase the population. There is, however, a limited amount that one person can do in this regard. Consequently the analysts will concentrate attention on the less sensitive but more controllable features. In fact, there is an important problem in comparing sensitivity and controllability and seeing where the focus of management's attention should be made.

ACCURACY AND SCOPE

There remain two important questions which have to be answered in every forecasting problem. The first is that of accuracy of forecasts and the second is how far ahead one should attempt to forecast. In considering the accuracy with which we wish to forecast, we have to remember that the only thing that is certain about any forecast is that it will be wrong. The question at issue is how wrong can we afford to be? Hence whenever forecasts are suggested and incorporated into a model one should test the solution of the model for sensitivity against the errors in the forecast.

These errors in the forecast will stem from two causes. There will be errors stemming from the fact that we have stated a wrong value of a variable and there are those errors which stem from the basic distribution which we have assumed. In a problem where we must consider a series of variables over a period of time, each of which has its own static distribution appropriate to that particular time, we will have to examine the consequences of assuming at any one time these variables to be distributed normally, or in a triangular fashion, or any other way. In some cases the optimal answer to the problem will remain the same even though the form of the distributions are taken to be quite different.

For example, forecasts of commodity prices can be cast in terms of the ranges in which prices might fall, month by month, over the next two years. Because we are less and less certain as the future extends further ahead, these ranges will increase in width as the months become further ahead. The methods for deciding how much to buy now at today's price, can use a well-established technique known as dynamic programming (ref 3). Using this technique the ranges of possible prices must be transformed into probability distributions and there will be many such distributions which are plausible (including normal, triangular, rectangular etc.) but the answer to the question of what do we do today, do we buy and if so how much, may be very similar for a range of different assumed distributions. This is a robust assumption.

RELEVANCE

In analysing the relevance of a forecast we need first the effect of errors in the prior distributions that have been used, and second, the effect on the consequences of the decision, of errors in the forecasts themselves. There are two approaches by which this can be done. One can take the forecasts which are derived and see what the effect is on the optimal course of action, of errors in this forecast, how robust the course of action is to errors in the forecast of changes in the basic distributions. This gives an estimate of how much we should be committed to a particular course of action, which may be regarded in some way as optimal. The second approach is to take a given course of action and study how the pay-off stemming from it is likely to change against errors in the inputs and forecasts. Both of these approaches should be tried before any decisions are made about any specific course of action which should be followed.

For example if, in deriving an optimal solution in a linear programming problem we have made forecasts of certain variables, this approach would mean two sorts of test. One would be to take the optimal course of action as given by the linear programme, and to see how the pay-off from it varies as the input parameters are allowed to vary. The second is to take the optimal course of action and examine how much the input parameters have to vary for this course of action to be non-optimal and to estimate the loss in pay-off which will occur because the new optimal course of action is no longer taken (ref 4).

The second question is how far ahead one should forecast. This naturally links with the problem of the accuracy of forecasting but there is one important difference. Analogies are dangerous things, but if we may take one, consider the case of a large oil tanker which cannot be stopped or have its course significantly changed within the next ten miles. It is, then, prudent to be able to see at least ten miles ahead. Consequently, when we consider the period ahead for which we should forecast, we have to ask two questions. The first of these is over what period of time are the actions which are now taking place going to have an effect? Second, to what extent can we change decisions which have already been taken?

In consequence of this, in the heavy expenditure for providing energy, such as in building a nuclear power station, because the investment is going to pay off over a period of at least twenty years, one has to forecast at least twenty years ahead. In other situations with a very fluid, flexible decision-making problem, where it is possible to change one's mind and not be committed far ahead, then one works to a much shorter time period. We can observe the effects of this politically. It is rare for a government which is going to face a general election, at the maximum of five years ahead, to plan for more than this period, unless it is forced to. It will always seek to extract what credit it can from current situations by means of short term planning and short term forecasts.

A CAUTIONARY TALE

Perhaps one can conclude this section with a cautionary tale. Reference has been made above to the problem of forecasting energy consumption. Some years ago the author was concerned with a problem which arose in the UK mining industry. For many years there was no problem in marketing coal. One had only to allocate coal to eager customers. It then became difficult to sell small-sized coal, this being the coal which is always the least attractive to the customer and the most difficult to sell. The response to this situation was a considerable research and development plan aimed at producing more large-sized coal. What was not seen at that time was that the increasing difficulty of selling small coal was a symptom of a forthcoming difficulty of selling even the more attractive large coal. The problem was treated as one of product mix and not of total sales. At that time coal sales were 200m tons a year, and the forecasts which were then made of coal sales for 20 years ahead, were of the order of 320m tons a year. When that time was reached, the industry was struggling to maintain sales of even one-third of that amount. The forecasters did not even get the sign right.

The cautionary note is not that the forecasters and planners were incompetent, but that there was the very human error of seeing in a situation what one wants to see. In forecasting, the temptation is always to tell people what they want to hear and to be optimistic. Industries, governments, institutions of all kinds, in surveying the future will generally tend to see what they want to see and hear what they want to hear.

References

1 Makridakis, S.K. and Wheelwright, S.C. (1989). *Forecasting Methods for Management*, Wiley, Chichester.
2 Ackoff, R.L. and Emshoff, J.R. (1975). Advertising research at Anheuser Busch Inc., *Sloan Management Review*, Spring, **16**, 3, 1–16.
3 Norman, J. (1975). *Dynamic Programming*, Arnold, London.
4 Buffa, E.S. and Dyer, J.S. (1977). *Management Science/Operations Research*, Wiley, Chichester.

Nirvana Residential Homes

The Seventh Principle: Examine carefully the boundaries set on a problem. A model can deal with a greater span than can the brain of any manager. Management boundaries do not coincide with model boundaries.

INTRODUCTION

As has been said previously, the type of analysis which is the subject of this book is called by various names. The "official" descriptions are operational (operations) research or management science. It can appear in other subjects such as management accounting or cybernetics. However, the cement which binds any group of subjects together into a coherent whole, are either a similar subject matter, or a similar methodology, or unifying laws.

It is in this aspect that all guises of management analysis are weak. We lack unifying laws and hence the subject can become a series of case studies and even, at the extreme, a collection of anecdotes.

One law, or hypothesis, is the law of the boundary conditions. This states:

1 That for any management problem where there are constraints on what is permissible, then the optimal course of action will not be made worse by removing the constraints. This much is obvious. But there is an extension.

2 There will be certain key constraints which if they are relaxed will yield a wide range of new solutions which will not only be better but also for which a randomly selected solution within the new range will still be better than the old.

It is not unusual for a study carried out in a commercial environment to yield a solution which, while "correct" for the problem as stated, has to be altered, or even abandoned, because of the dominating effect of tax laws. By proper tax planning, any other solution will be an improvement on the "correct" one previously devised.

Anecdote (True)

A food manufacturing company divided its activities into three parts: raw material buying, production scheduling and marketing. Its forward planning was based on two major reviews each year complemented by monthly reviews. During December, marketing produced its forward plan of advertising, special offers and price discounts month by month for the 12 months. These were passed to production who had the responsibility of ensuring that finished goods stocks were always sufficient to meet demand and production then formulated its monthly plan which was passed to purchasing. Purchasing were responsible for ensuring that raw material stocks were always sufficient to meet the needs of production and in the light of this they entered into forward contracts. During the next 5 months, month by month, marketing made marginal changes to their plans, each time passing them to production, who did the same and purchasing updated their plans to the end of the year.

However, 6 months into the year, the horizon was put forward by an extra 6 months, which meant that the forward plan once again encompassed 12 montths. The company was very strong in its fundamental divisions and the two stockpiles (finished goods and raw materials) effectively ensured that the directors of marketing, production and purchasing did not speak to each other – and they did not.

This process fitted in with the span of the human mind but not the span of the model. The OR group of the company took the total problem of purchasing, production and marketing and formulated a total plan month by month which tore down departmental boundaries. The effect was to reduce inventories by 50% and to increase the return on assets by 2%.

Moral of the Story

With the aid of computers and modelling a man's reach need not exceed his grasp. Imagination, however, must always be present.

NIRVANA RESIDENTIAL HOMES

Nirvana Residential Homes (NRH) owns and operates throughout the UK a very large chain of homes for the elderly. This chain is non-profit making and the residents pay an economic rent to the management. The homes consist of separate units for single people or couples, each unit containing at a minimum a living room, a bedroom, a kitchen, a bathroom. A home may have between 10 and 300 units, often in private grounds, there may be a warden living in but the actual quality of the home will be extremely variable.

The policy of the board of directors of NRH is to devolve management of the homes to local trustees, indeed the charity deeds of many of the homes require local management of the homes on site. In general, trustees are diligent and caring, but inevitably, some are lazy and indifferent. One feature they share is that each home is fiercely independent and will not cooperate with others, even though they may be only 20 miles away.

The board have for some time been concerned at the level of quality in a number of the homes and have invited an OR analyst from a local university to survey a sample of homes and to make recommendations for raising the general level.

The following is an extract from the analyst's report:

> The quality of the Homes is certainly variable. At their best they are quite excellent. The units are bright and clean, attractive bathrooms with showers, separate lavatories, well-equipped kitchens with refrigerators, freezers, microwaves, central heating, attractive gardens, warden(s) living on site.
>
> At their worst they can be quite dreadful. Coal fires, bath in the kitchen, poorly equipped and with a communal lavatory outside. At one such home the senior Trustee told me "They [the residents] love their coal fires, they love going out to collect their coal in buckets and the outside lavatories enable them to meet each other and have a gossip."
>
> No Trustees purposely do a bad job. But there is a need for an assessment of all Homes so that the Trustees know how they are doing.
>
> I suggest that I visit all the Homes and discuss this with the Trustees. There are 212 homes and if I visit two a week the whole task could be done in only two years.

The board receives the report and agree with the need for an assessment but are horrified at the proposal of the analyst to visit each home. The less charitable of the board think the analyst wants to pad out her private consulting and suggest instead that she writes to each home to determine what the trustees feel are the most important criteria for a home to satisfy.

Stage 1: Question: What Do You Think Are the Possible Criteria?

List them and compare with the following set which the analyst produced.

Possible criteria

- Central heating
- Indoor lavatory
- Separate bathroom and lavatory
- Constant hot water
- Private grounds
- Security from outsiders

- On-site warden
- Proximity to shops
- Proximity to church
- Buses near by
- Chiropodist visits
- Hairdresser visits
- Communal lounge
- Meals provided
- Mini buses available
- Trustees visit regularly

Stage 2: Question: How Would You Decide the Important Criteria?

In this case the analyst sends a list to each home and asks the trustees to select what in their opinion are the five most important factors.

The response is as follows, 130 homes respond and the numbers of votes for each criteria (at 5 per home) is as follows (Table 1).

Table 1

			Score
1	Central heating	95	15
2	Indoor lavatory	50	8
3	Separate bathroom and lavatory	50	8
4	Constant hot water	70	11
5	Private grounds	115	17
6	Security from outsiders	15	2
7	On site warden	40	6
8	Proximity to shops	20	3
9	Proximity to church	10	2
10	Buses near by	50	8
11	Chiropodist visits	10	1
12	Hairdresser visits	15	2
13	Communal lounge	10	1
14	Meals provided	10	1
15	Mini buses available	20	3
16	Trustees visit regularly	70	11
		650	100

The analyst then prepares a check list so that each trustee can compare how their own home matches good standards.

Stage 3: Question: How Would You Do This?

There is no "correct" answer. Discuss various methods and write a short essay on it.

In this case the analyst decides to take a total score of 100 points and divides them between the categories in proportion to the votes cast, giving the second column in Table 1. (This column has been adjusted to give a total of 100.) As a rough guide the analyst having noted that 6 of the list account for 70 points, suggests that 75 points should be the minimum acceptable standard.

The trustees are now all given this as a self-checking device and the analyst collects her fee and goes on to other things. Unfortunately for her, and for everyone else, the following letter comes in to the board from a home and it is typical of a number of complaints received:

> We have a committee of residents and have put before them your scoring list. Although we come out at a score of 75, our residents are still dissatisfied and say that this scoring method is "ill judged".

Who is right? (Actually the phrase "ill judged" was not the earthy expression used by the residents.)

State 4: Question: Who Is Right? Why Is the List Not Acceptable?

The point is that the list is what the trustees think is important and not what the residents think. It is the residents who are concerned as they are the ones who live in the homes.

Stage 5: Question: What Next?

What is not next is to give the same list to the residents – the list of criteria came from the analyst who had only spoken to trustees. If the list is used, it should be supplemented with a category of "Any other? Please state."

This is done and the revised list is given below. It will be seen that the priorities are different. We have converted votes into points score (Table 2).

However, what was most interesting was the response to the enquiry regarding other criteria. What emerged was a universal concern about what happened if they became ill.

Stage 6: Enter the Real Problem: What Does Happen?

The policy of the homes is to keep residents as long as possible in their own residences but if residential nursing care is needed they then have to be put in a local authority special unit. The view of residents is that on transfer to a special unit they are written off and left to die. As one

Table 2

	Category	Trustees	Residents
1	Central heating	15	15
2	Indoor lavatory	8	20
3	Separate bathroom and lavatory	8	4
4	Constant hot water	11	10
5	Private grounds	17	3
6	Security from outsiders	2	8
7	On site warden	6	8
8	Proximity to shops	3	12
9	Proximity to church	2	3
10	Buses near by	8	2
11	Chiropodist visits	1	1
12	Hairdresser visits	2	5
13	Communal lounge	1	0
14	Meals provided	1	0
15	Mini buses available	3	7
16	Trustees visit regularly	11	2
		100	100

geriatrician put it "They turn to face the wall and quietly die without causing any trouble."

The analyst questions national demographic data and discovers that in the whole population people in the age range at which they first enter a Home have a 12% chance of needing special residential care before they die. Life expectancy is less in a local authority unit than for the population at large even when there is a full back-up of care. This is to be expected but what is of concern is that of those admitted to special residential care, over half die within six months. The view of the medical experts is that removal is looked on as a sentence of death and this combined with the shock of removal has a significant life threatening effect.

Stage 7: Two Questions

Why not have such a unit at a home where the shock of removal would be greatly lessened?

The subsidiary question is, what factors affect the financial viability of a home unit?

Stage 8: Some Cost Data to Be Collected

The analyst now collects the following data (Table 3).

Table 3 Unit costing (legal fees, planning approval, site preparation: £10 000)

Size	Construction (£)	Medical/nursing (£)	Materials (£)
5 beds	60 000	50 000 p.a.	10 000 p.a.
10 beds	90 000	65 000 p.a.	20 000 p.a.
15 beds	120 000	80 000 p.a.	30 000 p.a.
20 beds	150 000	95 000 p.a.	40 000 p.a.

Note: Materials include medicines, laundry, food, power etc.

The analyst is told that the cost of repaying a mortgage, based on an interest charge of 10% in terms of the term of the mortgage is shown in Table 4.

Table 4 Annual mortgate repayments per £10 000 borrowed

Term in years	10	15	20
Payment p.a. (£)	1500	1150	1000

Stage 9: Build a Model for the Cost Per Year of Building and Operating a Unit

The reader should try this. Take first the case of a five-bed unit and from Tables 3 and 4 cost out the annual payments on the mortgage and the nursing and materials cost. Confirm the following figures (Table 5).

Table 5 Annual costs (£'000s)

Loan period	Number of patients			
	5	10	15	20
10	71	100	130	159
15	68	96	125	153
20	67	95	123	151

Note: Those who wish can express all the above in algebra.

There follows a long and acrimonious debate at board level between those who hate being in debt and wish for a short loan period and those who want low annual payments so as to cater for more patients. After an exhausting discussion the inevitable compromise is reached and they settle for a 15-year period.

Stage 10: But What of the Income to Meet These Costs?

The analyst discovers that because of the low incomes of the patients, the Home will receive from Social Security a payment of £200 p.w., or £10 000 p.a. for each patient. This income, set against the expenditure can be studied best in graphical terms (Figure 1).

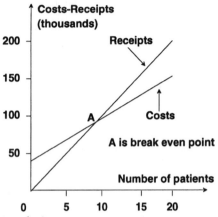

Figure 1 Break even analysis

It can be seen that for less than nine patients there will not be sufficient income to support the unit and that nine is the critical mass of patients.

However, this does not mean that a home with nine residents will be viable since not all of them will be in receipt of the extra grant of £200 p.w. As mentioned above, only about 12% of the population will eventually need this and so the critical mass of residents to produce on average nine patients is 75.

The analyst is happy with such a clear-cut answer, although slightly uneasy at the sweeping assumptions (*Note*: list them) and also uneasy at the very rough data she has had to use. But time is pressing and all she needs now is to check how many homes can take advantage of this result. The distribution of the size of homes is as follows:

Number of residents	1–10	11–20	21–30	31–41	41–50	51–60	61–70	70+
Number of homes	4	10	15	18	25	30	50	30

It can be seen that at most 30 homes can build a special unit. In terms of this problem as described, however, this is the best that can be done.

The reader should now write a report to the board of NRH covering the whole of this study, including self assessment by trustees and leading to the calculations and conclusions for a special care unit and the critical size of 75. The assumptions made should be listed carefully. Which assumption is it that restricts the number of homes to at most 30? This question, and its answer, leads us to the theme of the "reflections" which now follow.

Reflections

The Break Point

The reader should by now be familiar with two important points. The first is that the problem as initially defined will almost always ineluctably change during a study, often because a different perception of goals and objectives has been obtained. The second point is that every investigation is carried within a set of constraints. Some of these are technical, for example the capacity of a hospital or the maximum capacity of a transport system or the physical properties of materials.

There are also constraints imposed by the market, for example the saturation sales of a product. There are social and attitudinal constraints, such as the reluctance of single parents to work overtime.

In this study we have met the most difficult of all to break, that is the organisational constraint. Such a constraint, if broken, can often lead to a gain which outweighs anything else we can do. A particular example is when we can persuade an organisation to work in a new way by linking together parts of the system which have been kept apart.

How then does this apply in NRH? It applies in the boundaries within which the homes operate. The income the special care residents receive comes from the Department of Social Security (DSS). When a patient is transferred to a local authority hospital the cost to the Department of Health is about £450 p.w. Overall therefore it is in the interests of the community, let alone those of the patient, for patients to stay in their home.

Reference to Table 4 shows that if the DSS grant were to be increased to £260 p.w. (£13 000 p.a.), then the break even number of patients is five, with an equivalent number of residents of 40. This means that most of the homes could have a special unit.

The release of potential from breaking organisation constraints is familiar to all seasoned analysts. This has been for them the golden thread which stretches across the years and across all styles of management and all government, commerce, trades, social groupings. The impact of the IT revolution which widens the grasp of a manager will be an important catalyst in yielding significant returns from restraint breaking. However, size and the conquest of complexity are not all. The human dynamism which is released by allowing the individual more responsibility in human sized organisations is also powerful and we must be careful not to follow a Gadarene rush to size just for the sake of integration. It is this possibility of reconciling the initiative which stems from the free information possibility, with the returns from breaking down organisation barriers which is one of the most exciting prospects for the future.

The most important thing is to break out of the shackles where we believe that something *is so* because it has always *been so*. So much of what we find has been frozen out of history.

Further Work

Identify further constraints in this problem.

What would be the consequence of allowing a Homes' Special Unit to be used by the general public for long or short stays?

Chapter 8

The Analyst

Rather late in this discussion of "problems" and our approach to them we now mention what is, perhaps, the most important factor of all, namely the analyst himself (or herself). Even in the traditional sciences the analyst is not some pure being, making observations and guided by the light of reason. Research is an emotional business. The story of the double helix research is the story of emotional rivalry as well as pure science. The researcher gets deeply involved: involved with the problem and involved (often in a competitive way) with other researchers. He will be prejudiced and biased and concerned with the prestige that will follow success. Hence he will define "problems" in such a way that he can "solve" them. We have seen that problems can be stated in many different ways. Analysts have an impressive capacity to ignore problems, however defined, which currently have no chance of solution. Most current areas of interest and management research are into classes of problems which have *always* existed. It is not that researchers have listed them and acknowledged them and have them put on one side as being intractable. They have not even been listed or acknowledged. They have been invisible. However, it is not only in problem recognition or definition that we have been prejudiced, it can also be in the methods of analysis and this can, and does, happen in the most established and pure sciences.

In the UK, both the BBC and the ITV employ professional statisticians to analyse audience viewing figures. But when there is a difference in audience estimates, the BBC figures for their own viewing are always greater than the ITV figures for BBC viewing and vice versa. There is no conscious cheating. It may be that there can be introduced into the sampling process on which such analyses are based some form of unconscious bias, but the important factor is not only *how* it is done but that it exists despite the efforts of qualified statisticians.

Even in such dispassionate areas as chemical analysis similar effects may be manifest. There are attested cases where both a supplier and a customer have teams of chemists analysing the same material. The supplier's own chemists analysed the same material on despatch and the customer's own chemists analysed the material when it was received. Whenever there was a disagreement, the supplier's estimate of quality, from these standard objective tests was better than that of the customer's chemists as it arrived. There was no possibility of any change in quality during transit.

So What Is Truth?

We, the researcher and analyst, can be subject to the temptation to enrich the data to produce a desired result. With apologies for the age of the following true story we recount an early experience in the life of the author. This was a study of the performance of 17 pounder solid steel shot (3.7″), a British anti-tank ammunition in World War II. Such shot was produced in batches at many different workshops and in order to test the quality of the shot from each workshop, samples were sent for proof to Woolwich Arsenal. Shot was fired at standard steel plate and the damage done to the plate was measured. In this way the shot was related to the damage done to the plate by a reference set of standard performance shot. But when, in innocence, the question was asked "How does one standardise the plate?" the response was "By firing standard shot at it". The whole process was circular, shot is standardised by firing it at standard plate and plate is standardised by firing standard shot at it. The circularity was ignored as otherwise we could have neither standard shot nor standard plate.

This process of testing was obviously time consuming. Some weeks could elapse between the production of the ammunition in a factory and its testing at Woolwich, so other means were sought. The first step was to correlate the hardness of the steel in the shot with its performance at Woolwich. This involved slicing the shot across at the shoulder and taking hardness readings of the metal section. This showed a good relation but suffered from the defect that it was destructive and was also time consuming. There was still a time lag in which some thousands of shot could be produced before the test results were made known. This led to the final stage in what was becoming an emotionally charged saga.

In the headquarters of the Ministry was a man who passionately felt that the hardness of the metal at the shoulder of the shot should be related to the electrical resistance of the metal at the shoulder while the man for whom the author worked felt quite passionately that this was nonsense. (All this feeling on both sides was in the absence of any data.) Each week the author went to a group of different factories and collected sample data of the hardness of the shot and the electrical resistance in terms of the steel works which had originally produced the steel used in the shot. At regular intervals graphs were produced such as the following for the 12 manufacturers, A to L (Figure 8.1).

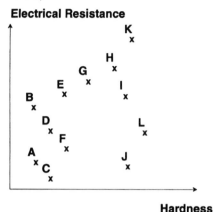

Figure 8.1 Original data

Together, the two researchers went to HQ and produced their graphs which were always received (even when as inconclusive as that above) with cries of delight. The standard questions were posed by Mr X with answers by the author:

X: "Where did the steel at point B come from?"
Author: "Jenkins Works."
X: "They produce steel that is rubbish. Delete the point B. Where did the steel at C come from?"
Author: "Berwyn Plant"
X: "It is well known that their baking is suspect. Delete C."

Same comments, and so on, until the author and his eraser had removed from the graph all the points B, C, F, I, J, L, and we had a plot (Figure 8.2).

At this point the HQ man would put a ruler along the sheet in the direction of the relationship and cry "Eureka" (or words to that effect), "There is the relationship." The author's senior would then cry "Not quite correct" (or words to that effect) and would sweep the ruler on to the floor. (The author's weekly task in this discussion was to pick up the ruler.) These discussions took us through many months and were never resolved. The point was that all the parties had a vision, and the HQ man in particular did not feel *he* was biased in removing points from the graph. Even Einstein is reported to have said "If your experimental results do not agree with your hypothesis, reject the experiment." This temptation to see patterns because we want to see them is endemic. All analysts have been trained

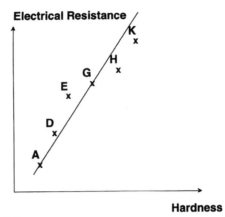

Figure 8.2 Enriched data

on the basis that life is rational and that there are, underlying the surface chaos, relationships between the factors.

Bavelas, at MIT, carried out some fascinating experiments with students. In preparation he took a set of 900 light bulbs, set in a rectangular block 30 × 30, and with each bulb he inserted a randomising device which switched the light on and off at random. A series of photographic plates were then exposed for random periods of time and so Bavelas produced a set of random pictures consisting of white dots.

Students were then told that they would each in turn be shown a series of patterns which they had to classify as either type A or type B. The patterns would be shown on a screen and at the desk in front of the student would be an A button and a B button. They would press one of these appropriately and then an indicator light would show whether they were correct or incorrect in their choice. They were to learn from the responses and when they felt they had grasped the classification criteria involved for A or B, they were to say so.

What they were not told was that the response to their selection of A or B was preordained and purely random. Even so, each student eventually was sure that he or she had spotted the link. Bavelas then produced, for each of these students, a fresh student, new to the whole thing and asked that the new students should be taught by the "experienced" students how to do it.

Eventually Bavelas got them all together again and revealed what he had done and showed them that the whole process was completely random. At this the students rose up in anger – *not* because they had been deceived but because, as they all put it, "You may think it was random, but there *was* a pattern and we spotted it." We are so used to pattern that we can spot it where it does not exist and this is especially dangerous as we can then spot something because it is what we want to see.

A study carried out for a food manufacturer was to estimate the effect on the sales of their product of their sales service staff. These were people who visited the retail outlets. They did not take orders but simply improved the display of the company's own products and put up advertisements and promotional materials in the shops. The company was not sure whether this actually achieved any real effect in the increase of sales. For sales purposes the country was divided into nine areas (corresponding with the TV areas) and data were available from the sales records of the proportion of outlets called on in each of these sales areas. Sales figures were more difficult. Sometimes, for a major chain of retailers, sales were made not to an outlet, but to a central warehouse which may not be in the sales area itself. There were problems of getting the best kind of sample on which to base the share of market figures and there were even difficulties of defining the particular market of which the company had a share. But data of the share of market in each area were provided by the company's market researchers. When plotted there was an encouraging result (Figure 8.3).

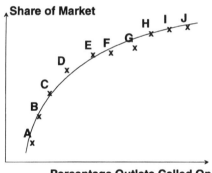

Figure 8.3   Original data. Market share and display

The company management seized on these results. It was clear that H, I and J had too many service men while A, B, C needed more and the gains to be made in share of market by moving A, B, C to the right would much more than compensate the losses incurred by moving H, I, J to the left. Service men and their families were moved from area to area and the research was forgotten.

It remained forgotten until one day the market researchers produced a "better" way of estimating the share of market figures and of redefining what is meant by an "outlet". They stated that they had always been uneasy at the previous method. At this, the analyst was pleased as it should, he thought, smooth out the points in Figure 8.3. However, when the new data were plotted, for the same period analysed previously, they gave (Figure 8.4).

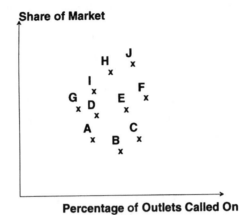

Figure 8.4   Corrected data. Market share and display

Had the first relationship looked like this, the analyst would have questioned it with the market researchers and been told that they themselves were uneasy at the sampling process and were changing it. But because the plot showed a relationship that the researcher liked the market researchers were not asked about the basic data.

A final way in which the analyst can be biased is illustrated by an experiment by de Bono. He gives to a subject a set of shapes, a triangle, a square, a rectangle etc., one by one with the requirement that each shape should be added to those already received so as to make a pattern which can easily be described in words (Figure 8.5).

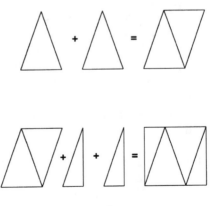

- and so on

Figure 8.5

This process continues in sequence until one piece is produced that cannot possibly be added appropriately to the existing shape. But if the whole shape is broken down into its components and the new piece added, they can be formed into a square.

The moral is that we can be influenced in our view of the whole by the order in which we have received information about parts of it. This is a very very strong influence on the analyst. As we shall see in Chapter 10 we often start with a simple view. This is added to as we gain experience, rather like a Lego set. But the structure of knowledge we finish with can depend on the order of the process.

This can be seen acting on the managers with whom any analyst deals. For example, until recently, in UK banks, all recruits, usually aged 16–18, started life working in a branch, and at that time the height of personal ambition was to be a branch manager. The attitudes they gathered, and their view of the world was entirely dominated by this. So much so that when the nature of banking was revolutionarily changed by the introduction of competition and the coming of the IT revolution, the business and the profits of branches became much less important than that of the corporate and interbank business at headquarters, while the free availability of an immense amount of information meant that control of branches was removed to other centres. These people then found themselves overtaken by others brought in from outside – not because they were deficient in skills but because their view of the world was no longer important. As a result they became embittered and this rubbed off on the customers.

The analyst is not immune from this danger of being overtaken by a changing world. He or she can be taught in a way that is technique dominated and can, by achieving skill, and having an interest in particular techniques, see the world through the spectacles of particular techniques. For twenty years a large UK oil company had an operational research group which was related solely to mathematical programming. Larger and larger models were built for production, distribution, marketing until there was nothing left to explore by this technique. The group was then disbanded and nothing was left. In their day, the group was a centre of excellence, but excellent for only one technique. A similar example in UK industry over the same period was where one group approached every problem through simulation. The time came when there was little else left to simulate and the group closed.

In these cases the results of inbuilt bias are brutal and can be seen. We must, however, realise that we are all biased and prejudiced. How can we discover an unbiased and unprejudiced analyst? Is it not like the case of the standard plate and the standard shot? There seems to be no pure unbiased set to which we can compare. We are biased in problem selection, in problem definition, in measurement (especially in measurement), in objectives and goals, in technique and in presentation. (Can this chapter be re-written in an unbiased way?) There is one way in which the analyst can lighten his conscience. It is easy. It is always avoided. It is to produce the managers involved.

Our subject is burdened by its literature being anecdotal. It is very rare that any case study identifies where it took place, when and who was involved. Kipling refers to the six serving men:

> I keep six honest serving men,
> They taught me all I knew,
> Their names and what and why and when
> And where and how and who.

The analyst is concerned with all six. So often, however, any presentation tells all about the *what*, the *why* and the *how* (especially the techniques of the how). But avoids carefully any discussion of the *when*, the *where* and the *who*.

At presentations of work at conferences it is almost unknown for the analyst to be accompanied by the manager or executive for whom the analysis has been performed. But this is the one way to remove subconscious distortion. And until this happens we have to ask – what has the analyst to hide? Is he hiding his audience from his manager or is he hiding his manager from hearing what the analyst is saying? Perhaps the fault, dear Brutus, is not in our stars.

What is often ignored is the *Weltanshaung* of the analyst in all of this. There is, inevitably, a depressing homogeneity within the analyst community. They are nearly all graduates and are drenched in the academic mores. Reading, argument, analysis, are their staple food. The evidence they consider is so often purely of recorded nature – documents, discussion groups, minutes of meetings, accounts, i.e. the staple food of the middle management and of the middle class. Although to themselves they are conscious of a great diversity, to the outsider they are the grey men and the grey women. Within their own field they have their climactic debates. Some statisticians can hardly speak to each other across the a priori, a posteriori divide. Modellers can be bitter across the hard versus soft science divide. Mathematicians and practical researchers may find it difficult to talk to each other and yet all these divisions are hardly visible to the outsider. Indeed the analyst, him- (or her-) self, finds it difficult to understand or communicate with both the manager and the shop-floor worker. The backgrounds are so different and the university trained analyst can use words with such felicity that communication becomes almost impossible. This inevitably makes cross cultural research very difficult and the well-meaning analyst will find that verbal felicity is not a bridge but a barrier.

It is in the problem of communication that analysts have their great difficulty. For they are engaged in an elitist activity. Even within their middle-class links, their attitude of mind is different from that of professional colleagues – not least with quantitatively orientated accountants. And outside their own class the barriers are also there, for even the working-class woman or man who goes to university finds difficulty when returning home in vacations in conveying what academia is like and what its value systems are.

The analyst must break out of this prison of words and attitudes into what is misleadingly called the real world – for the world of the analyst is every bit as real as the outer world. It is a question of being able to see the world and its problems from the perspective of other people. This is difficult since the analyst will have spent at least 16 years in the knowledge industry with all its rites and ritual dances, with its value system and esoteric modes of communication. But unless this is achieved and the analysts can see and hear the world through the eyes and ears of the others involved, they will be speaking into the wind and writing on sand, even though their words are spoken at professional meetings and their writing is in refereed journals.

Competitive Tendering for Conner Mining

The Eighth Principle: Napoleon's principle applies to objectives. "On s'engage et puis on voit."

INTRODUCTION

There has so far been no example of a competitive study. In every Life assumptions have been made which imply that we do do not provoke a response that negates our analysis. However, even in areas of competition we can often simplify what would be a horribly complicated situation, by assuming that our competitors' reaction to what we do will be sufficiently sluggish for us to treat it as nature. That is, something over which we have no control and which is independent of our own actions.

The case study in this section is based on research carried out in the US oil industry in bidding for undersea oil exploration rights. It also illustrates how management can be wedded to statements of objectives which are clearly capable of improvement, but are not changed for what can be purely emotional reasons.

Anecdote (Probably Untrue)

In World War I, the Royal Flying Corps developed a weapon for attacking enemy troops, particularly on open gun sites, or on troops sheltering in trenches. These were very large darts, weighted with sharpened metal points. A plane could carry many of these and drop them, all together, over the troops. It was important to know the area of the ground which would be covered from different heights of the drop, the pattern over the ground and the density of darts over the target area.

A trial was carried out in a back area. An aircraft dropped a load of these darts on to a target field. A photographer climbed up a tree and took photographs of the darts impaled in the ground to show their distribution over the ground. Unfortunately when the film was developed the darts were not easily visible.

A second trial was then held. This time the photographer was armed with a pad of white sheets of paper and before taking the photograph he walked round the field, pulled each dart out of the ground and stuck it back through a white sheet of paper, so that the papers would be clear in a photograph.

As he completed this, a cavalry officer rode up and, seeing all these pieces of paper each neatly pierced by a dart, asked the photographer what he was doing.

"We are carrying out a trial of using these darts as weapons to hit enemy troops, and you can see how each dart has landed", he replied.

The officer looked again. Each and every piece of paper speared by a dart.

"Good heavens!" he replied. "Had I not seen it with my own eyes, I would never have believed such accuracy was possible."

Moral of the Story

Objectives can cause a lot of bother. It is easy to avoid the bother by having as objectives that which we are already achieving. In this way we can all sleep at night.

Objectives must always be achievable – but they must take us away from the now and into a new future state. The one characteristic of a dead person, or a dead organisation, is that it does not move. Movement requires a direction: Objectives provide this.

So be careful of accepting too easily the first statements of objectives since, as we have seen, the objectives will gradually emerge during a study. It is sensible not to be dogmatic but to move in to a problem, observing and listening. Then, metaphorically, we throw something into the pond and see what happens.

COMPETITIVE TENDERING FOR CONNER MINING

Introduction

Memorandum to OR Manager
From Director of Resource Acquisition, Conner Mining

As you will know, one of my responsibilities is to ensure the acquisition of sufficient areas of land which are potentially oil bearing and we discussed this problem very briefly at the firm's annual dinner. I was interested in your comments, especially as I had always assumed that OR was exclusively concerned with algebra, computers and mathematics. It might be useful to take this a stage further.

We are always planning ahead and indeed our lead times on resource acquisition are longer than most industries. Periodically the government gives notice of an auction for a number of stretches of land (lots) which are potentially oil bearing. All the rival companies are given details and are allowed access to the area involved. There is a deadline by which sealed bids have to be submitted which will give a "favoured company" concession if we then want to negotiate for a future 30 years.

On the deadline date all bids are opened and declared and, naturally, the highest bidder on each lot gets the concession. The whole thing does seem fair and, so far as we know, no one gets any hint of who has bid on what and how much, neither from the government nor from espionage by one company on another. No doubt there have been attempts. But no leaks.

Once we receive notice of auction our geologists survey each lot and estimate its potential. It would be excellent if we knew its potential for a certainty but this is not an exact science. All our geologists will give us is what they call an "X" value, on a scale from 0 to 100. It is very subjective and the only firm thing about it is that an X of zero means that the area consists of solid concrete ten miles deep, while an X of 100 means that if you stick your thumb into the ground a little jet of oil will shoot up! In between, X is very subjective and personal.

This bidding process is a real pain in the elbow. We do not win as often as we need, which means we have to buy crude oil from our competitors. The alternative is to put in very high bids to be sure of winning. There is, I should say, one member of the board who informs me of the excess of our winning bid (when we do win) over the next highest bid and announces this as our MDTD index (Money Down the Drain). The general criterion by which I am judged is the total amount of X values which we acquire in a given auction.

As you will see we do have quite a bit of information available. Incidentally, in three months' time there is a sale of three lots put on the market at the same time and with the same deadline. The board have given me a total of 2100 units to bid for these. The X values are 30, 50 and 60.

What is your advice? Can you help us?

Stage 1

Memorandum to Head of RA from Head of OR

Thank you for your note with its interesting suggestion. Before we go any further, I am concerned at the implied objective of resource acquisition. Is it simply to acquire as many X values as possible?

Surely this should be to minimise the purchase cost per unit of X acquired? And in any event, all this assumes that the Xs are additive, that is, you view as equally attractive one lot with an X of 70 and two lots with X values of 40 and 30.

Could we meet and discuss this?

Letter to Head of OR from Director of RA

Dear Anthony,

It was good to have such a useful lunch the other day and as promised I summarise, as tactfully as I can, the response to your earlier query about objectives.

It is of course absolutely true that our objective criterion should be to obtain the Xs we need at a minimum cost per unit X. But the board's view is that they have to get financial backing from our bankers to cover the bid(s) made and bankers are unwilling to think in terms of statistical expectation. That is why, on the face of it, the bid is made solely within a budget constraint. I say "on the face of it", since because of the MDTD factor I have to protect my vulnerable and tender parts. This is why I do not simply bid the budget limit. Indeed the board like to see me working inside its budget and in my annual assessment they quote "money saved" as the sum of my budget reductions on bidding.

In the case of the big deal auction of three lots, I feel inclined to bid up to the limit. Incidentally it would be excellent if you could give the board a ball park estimate of the odds on winning a sale as this affects the forward position on our holdings of oil land.

On the addition of X values I now see what you meant. But I do not see any alternative to assuming this. Life is too complicated as it is and I have (so to speak) too many balls in the air already so don't let's complicate things.

Yours sincerely,

Jeremy

Letter to Director of RA

Dear Jeremy,
Many thanks. Can you let me have some data on past auctions, for example, who bid how much and on what?

Yours sincerely,

Anthony

Stage 2: The First Data Emerge

Dear Tony,
It was good to have a drink together yesterday and I enclose some data. I only hope it means more to you than it does to me. In view of the great secrecy attached to this I have disguised the units of money.

Yours,

Jerry

There is now an important step which we must take. We are analysing the bidding of the competition and will change our own bidding policy in the light of what we discover. Therefore in what follows we shall omit the data concerning the bids that Conner Mining has made in the past (Table 1).

Letter from Tony to Jerry

So far not much progress has been made. We have looked at the overall pattern of bids and of winning bids and the spread is so wide as to be useless. We have also looked at the behaviour of particular rivals – especially your biggest rivals (MGA), (SAG) and (SSO) but nothing presents itself. (*The reader should verify this.*)

We have also examined the five separate auctions into sets to see the extent to which one set is in fact differentiated from the others. Our view is that we can take all bids on the 23 lots as one coherent population. (*Note:* The reader should verify this from a histogram of all bids and observing the separate auctions.) We really do need a key to this. The main component missing at present are the X values for all these lots. Can we have them?

Table 1 Bids made on 23 lots in one year

Lot	UTL	ABC	MGR	MA	SSO	NBG	BHR	ABR	CBR	DBR	SA	SAG
							Company					
1		526			558	382	660	756	454	724		622
2	467	689		501		533	861	987		1009	579	
3		591	764	571	631	1055		983	727		807	
4	624					550						
5			413									1082
6				393	682		719	837	1008	756	452	
7	535	502			1085		379		827	945	686	
8			403	746				766	904		607	
9		381								495		
10	757			1147	796	367		499		749	803	1123
11	616		1203	1107	549		628	942		759	645	1142
12	403		485				699		521		639	
13			745	549						605		498
14		533		408	658	612	882	471	471	875	586	
15		1077	763									516
16	978	905		711	881			727		832	622	
17			674		477		391	793	934			632
18		492			470		345			404		
19			235				845					
20	771			571	711	689				934	548	860
21	620	459	697			1088	765	1215			952	1003
22		254										330
23		853	828	672	640			787	1009		951	

Note: The table divides, as shown, into five separate auctions.

Stage 3: Problems with the X Values

Letter from Jerry to Tony

Dear Tony,
I was afraid you would ask for the wretched X values. I will have to get them from the geologists and it is going to be like pulling teeth from a tigress with a gum abcess.

Geologists hate publishing their X values. In the past they used to do this. They then found that if they assigned a high X value, and later on little oil was discovered, it was regarded as their fault; but if they assigned a high X value and much oil was then discovered, it merely confirmed how excellent the drillers were at deciding on the best place to sink the well. So since then they do not keep historical X values. But I will do my best.

Letter from Jerry to Tony

It was just as bad, even worse, than I feared. I have now got the X values but under conditions that make a confessional seem like a public broadcast. So can you treat all this (Table 2) as *top secret*?

Table 2 X values as estimated by company geologists (top secret)

Lot	1	2	3	4	5	6	7	8	9	10	11	
X value	56	42	66	66	29	77	50	45	16	88	92	
Lot	12	13	14	15	16	17	18	19	20	21	22	23
X value	43	37	35	59	75	45	25	14	72	84	24	91

Stage 4: First Analysis

If you are Jeremy, carry out the analyses referred to in stage 2. Do you agree with Jeremy's conclusions?

Stage 5: Use the X Values to Answer Anthony's Problems

Refer again to *your* histogram of all bids. The spread is from 254 up to 1215. A range of nearly 5 to 1 is far too large. We have to reduce it. Incidentally you may have classifications in your histogram that are too wide. You should have the bid data divided into about 10 ranges, giving at least two bids in each range.

Stage 6: Reducing the Spread

One way of reducing the spread is to plot only the 18 winning bids (excluding our own three winners). But this gives a very thin histogram. (*Do this.*)

Stage 7: Enter the X Values

Plot on graph paper the X value for each of the 18 plots (as x-axis) and as y-axis the winning bid.

But then reflect, what use is it? What we need to know is the answer to this typical question: "If I bid a given amount on a lot with a given X value, what is the probability that I shall win?"

We have to think in terms of all the bids that are made. Since we only have 21 sets of bidding we shall have to create general laws and relationships. To produce probabilities we must at least have a histogram. This leads us to try and find a key statistic which will allow us to create a (skeletal) probability distribution.

The natural first attempt will be to use the X values – they are the only values that link past history with the future.

Stage 8: Using X as a Key Variable

Take Table 1 again and place at the end of each row the X value for the lot in question. What do you notice?

(1) When X is high the bids seem higher than when X is low and (2) when X is high there seem more bids than when X is low. That is, more people bid on high X values and their bids are higher.

Stage 9: Confirmation

Test this. Plot two graphs. On one take the x-axis as the X value, and plot the points representing the *average* bid (A) on each lot (not counting our own bid) and on another plot, *n*, the number of bids (excluding us) for each lot. At this stage it is best to be realistic and only take two significant figures (Figures 1 and 2).

Stage 10: The Key is X

It should look interesting. Use what ever methods you like to plot two curves, one for A against X and the other for *n* against X. Curves drawn by eye may well suffice.

They should also look encouraging enough to conclude that given X we

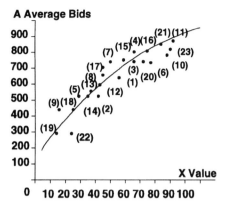

Figure 1 Average bid v X value

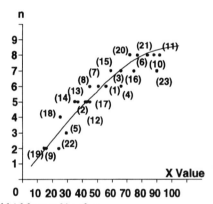

Figure 2 Number of bidders v X value

can now forecast the number of rival bids there will be and the average of those bids (Table 3).

But we still need to answer the question in stage 6 and so we still need all the bids to be brought into play. There are a number of ways of doing this but one of the best is shown in stage 11.

Table 3 X values, average bids and number of bidders

Lot	1	2	3	4	5	6	7	8	9	10	11	12
X	56	42	66	66	29	77	50	45	16	88	92	43
A	640	523	741	800	525	734	740	660	440	782	870	594
n	6	5	7	6	3	8	6	6	2	8	8	5

Lot	13	14	15	16	17	18	19	20	21	22	23
X	37	35	59	75	45	25	14	72	84	24	91
A	555	527	751	807	703	440	290	740	850	290	818
n	5	5	7	7	5	4	2	8	8	2	7

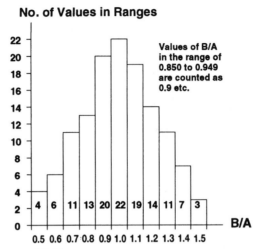

Figure 3 Histogram of B/A

Stage 11: Bring in B

Our problem is that having started with an X and estimated the A, we have to use this to estimate the chance of winning. The two things we shall have are estimates of A and n for any value of X and we want to try out a bid, B. So why not divide each of the bids (B) in Table 1 by the average of the bids in its row. This will give a histogram of B/A, which will of course be centred about B/A = 1.

The reader should now take Table 1 and divide each bid by the A for that row. This forms Table 1 (revised) and provides the raw data for the histogram shown in Figure 3.

We are now in a position to answer the question of stage 6. Reflect. If I have a lot with an X of 50, Figures 1 and 2 estimate the expected number (n) of rival bids as 5.5 and their average (A) as 690. Therefore if I bid *800*(B), the value of B/A = 1.16 and so my bid will beat any bid with a B/A of less than this. The probability of this can be estimated in Table 4 or from Figure 4 as 0.76. (*Note*: This is the author's graph. That of the student may be different.)

Table 4 Cumulative of B/A

Up to	0.55	0.65	0.75	0.85	0.95	1.05	1.15	1.25	1.35	1.45	1.55
Number	4	10	21	34	54	76	95	109	120	127	130
Percentage[a]	3	8	16	26	42	59	73	84	92	98	100

Note: [a]This is the estimated percentage probability that a bid with a given multiple of the average will beat one rival bidder.

The probability of beating one rival bidder is therefore read off the graph (Figure 4).

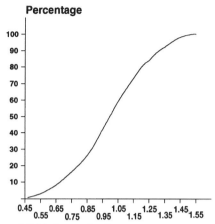

Figure 4 Cumulative of B/A (smoothed)

But the estimate of the number of rival bidders is $n = 5.4$ and so our chances of winning an X value of 50 with a bid of 800 is $p^n = (0.77)^{5.4} = 0.24$. In a similar way we can evaluate the probability of winning an X of 50 with any other bid. We calculate the relative p and raise it to the power of n, where n is the estimated number of bidders.

Stage 12: Do It Yourself

(Note: You must do this yourself with your own Figures 2 and 3 relationships. This will give you a different A and n. Use your own and compare. There is no right answer!)

Stage 13: Now Take Stock

We have established a method for estimating the probability that a given bid on a lot with a given X value will win.

This process has five stages: For a given lot:

1 What is the X value?
2 Use your own Figure 1 to estimate A and n.
3 For any prospective bid B, calculate B/A.
4 Use Figure 4 to estimate p.
5 The probability of winning is p^n.

Stage 14: Calculate the Bids

We can now move on to the next part. There is a sale announced with 3 lots, X values 30, 50 and 60. Take the first of these. For X of 30, read off your own A and n on Figures 1 and 2. For each of the bids 200, 250, 300, 350, 400 and 450 calculate B/A and estimate p for your own table.

Estimate n and in each case calculate the probability of winning, that is, p^n. The following is calculated from the graphs and tables as printed above, but you should use your own and compare. For each of the three lots, there is an estimate of A and an estimate of n:

Plot	1	2	3
X	30	50	60
A	500	690	760
n	3.6	5.5	6.5

For any proposed bid B on each lot we calculate B/A and follow stage 11. These give Table 5 but remember that your calculations may well give different results because your graphs are different.

Looking ahead we can make an additional calculation. Our objective is to maximise the total of the X values which we expect to obtain. Working on the basis that if there is a probability of 0.30 of winning an X of 50 then the average (or expected) amount we can expect is 30% of 50, that is, 15. In Table 5 therefore we have multiplied each probability of winning by the corresponding X value to give the average or expected amount of X which for shorthand is written as E(X).

These values of E(X) can be graphed against the bid, B, so as to show the relationship between the bids which might be made on each lot with the corresponding value of E(X). This should now be done and may be compared with Figure 5.

Stage 15: The Final Steps

How can we use all this to achieve the objective? The problem is to discover the three bids in Table 5, totalling 2100 such that the sum of the corresponding three values of E(X) is as great as possible. In general for a large number of lots this is a mathematical programming problem but, with only three lots, less exotic methods will suffice.

It can be verified that for a total bid of less than 1450 there need only be one bid of 800 on lot 1 and nothing on the others. Also for a total bid of more than 3000 the best bids are 800, 1050, 1150 on the three lots. Our total of 2100 is in between these two extremes and it can be seen, by trial and error, that the best allocation is 0, 1000, 1100 for which the E(X) total is 100.

It is of course trivial to put this on a PC and the computer literate could

Table 5 Probabilities of winning

	Lot	1			2			3	
	X	30			50			60	
	A	500			690			760	
	n	3.6			5.5			6.5	
	p	p^n	E(X)	p	p^n	E(X)	p	p^n	E(X)
450	0.33	0.02	1						
500	0.50	0.08	2						
550	0.66	0.22	7						
600	0.79	0.44	13						
650	0.88	0.60	18						
700	0.95	0.83	25	0.53	0.03	1			
750	0.99	0.97	29	0.65	0.09	4			
800	1.00	1.00	30	0.76	0.22	11	0.59	0.01	1
850				0.82	0.32	16	0.69	0.09	5
900				0.88	0.47	23	0.76	0.17	10
950				0.94	0.69	34	0.83	0.30	18
1000				0.98	0.97	48	0.89	0.41	25
1050				1.00	1.00	50	0.94	0.67	40
1100							0.98	0.87	52
1150							0.99	0.94	56
1200							1.00	1.00	60

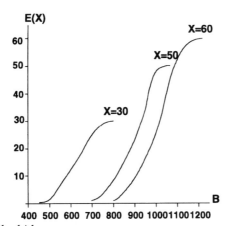

Figure 5 Sharing the bids

derive their own processes for solving problems of this size. We have now completed this task at the cost of making some rather sweeping assumptions.

Assumptions

Controllable variables.
   Our own bids
   Our estimates of X
   The total amount bid

Uncontrollable variables.
   The bids of rivals
   The number of lots
   The dates of the auctions

We Assume

1 That the behaviour of rival companies will not be changed and that they are not themselves learning.
2 All bids are independent and there is no collusion.
3 We have no information regarding our rivals' bids and they have none about ours.
4 The objective is as given.

What are the other assumptions made?

COMPETITIVE TENDERING

Report by Manager of Operational Research. To Director of Resource Acquisition

Introduction

We were asked to study the factors influencing the relative success of our sealed bid tendering for the acquisition of land lots which are potentially resources of minerals in the series of government auctions.

In particular, we were asked to formulate a set of bids on three lots being offered in the next auction such that the total amount bid is fixed at 2100 and so that the potential gain in resources is maximised. The company's geologists have assigned to these X values of lot 1, 30; lot 2, 50; lot 3, 60. This report summarises our analysis and presents the set of three bids.

Reservations

We have, at the outset, to list two reservations:

1   It would, we feel, be more logical to present a solution in terms of the total amount of money likely to be paid on the winning bids themselves rather than the total amount bid. History shows that only about one bid in five is successful and the present objective, while the reasons for it can be understood, is not in our view appropriate. Nevertheless we have, of course, accepted it, but could, if wished, recalculate the solution in terms of other objectives.

2   The objective refers to "resources". We have had to adapt this to a quantitative basis and have used the X values by which the company geologists estimate the resource value of a lot of land. In consequence we have to assume, for example, that the attractiveness of two pairs of lots with X values in the first pair of 25 and 65, and in the second pair of 40 and 50, are both the same at 90.

Data Available

We have used the data given on the bids made by all companies in the auctions of last year. An analysis of these data can be summarised in Table 01 which now follows in terms of:

1   The average of the rival bids on each lot, (A).
2   The number of rival bids (n).
3   The value as estimated by our company geologists.

Table 01

Lot	1	2	3	4	5	6	7	8	9	10	11	12
X	56	42	66	66	29	77	50	45	16	88	92	43
A	641	521	742	799	529	741	737	660	438	780	872	592
n	6	5	7	6	3	8	6	6	2	8	8	5

Lot	13	14	15	16	17	18	19	20	21	22	23
X	37	35	59	75	45	25	14	72	84	24	91
A	560	522	749	808	702	439	290	741	850	292	820
n	5	5	7	7	5	4	2	8	8	2	7

Data Analysis

It is interesting to note above that when X is high, both A and n tend to be high and when X is low, they tend to be low. Graphical analysis confirmed this and these relationships between A and X and between n and X are key points in our analysis.

The other key is the pattern of the bids themselves. We found that when each bid on a lot is compared with the average of the bids made on that lot a very clear pattern emerges. In an actual auction, combining this pattern, using the estimated average of all the bids which might be made on a particular lot with the estimate of the number of rival bidders we can obtain an approximation of the probability of a particular bid winning. Applied to the particular auction with which we are now concerned, gives Table 02.

Although Table 02 gives approximate probabilities of any size of bid winning, there is one further step needed. The objective is to maximise the total X values that we expect to obtain. What is meant by 'expected' and how do we maximise it? We shall use the idea of an average. If every time there is a lot with an X of 30 on offer we then bid 650, the above table suggests that we would win 60% of them and so the average return of bidding 650 on a lot with X = 30 is 60% of 30, i.e. 18. Applying this concept of the average return to Table 02 means that each probability should be multiplied by the corresponding X value. This gives Table 03.

The Solution

It only remains to obtain the best allocation of 2100 in bids over the three lots. This can be done by trial and error and gives:

Lot 1:	Zero	
Lot 2:	1000	Expected (average) X: 48
Lot 3:	1100	Expected (average) X: 52
Total	1100	Expected (average) X: 100

Table 02 Probabilities of bids winning

	Lot 1	Lot 2	Lot 3
X	30	50	60
A	500	690	760
n	3.6	5.5	6.5
Bid			
400	0.00		
450	0.02		
500	0.08		
550	0.22		
600	0.44		
650	0.60	0.00	
700	0.83	0.03	
750	0.97	0.09	0.00
800	1.00	0.22	0.01
850		0.32	0.09
900		0.47	0.17
950		0.69	0.30
1000		0.97	0.41
1050			0.67
1100			0.87
1150			0.94
1200			1.00

Table 03 Expected (average) return from bids (in X value)

Bid	Lot 1	Lot 2	Lot 3
450	1		
500	2		
550	7		
600	13		
650	18		
700	25	1	
750	29	4	
800	30	11	1
850		16	5
900		23	10
950		34	18
1000		48	25
1050		50	40
1100			52
1150			56
1200			6

A Warning

A note of caution. We are dealing with probability and uncertainty. The only thing of which we can be certain is that we shall never gain exactly a total X of 100. On average, however, we feel that this is the best strategy we can offer.

The Future

It is helpful to set out the stages of the method for use in future auctions:

1 Decide what is the total amount to be bid.
2 Obtain the X values.
3 For each lot on offer estimate the number of rival bids (*n*) and their average (A).
4 Take a series of possible bids and for each estimate the probability of it winning.
5 Change each probability into an expected X.
6 If the number of lots is three or less, allocate the total bid by trial and error.
7 If not, there are standard techniques by which this can be done.
8 Having derived an expected return in the light of the total amount to be bid, calculate what might happen if this total is changed. Is this a sensible total?

Caveat

We have had, as is always the case, to make a number of assumptions:

1 The objective is subject to the remarks on p. 207.
2 There is no leakage of information.
3 Rival companies will continue bidding as before.

Acknowledgements

We are grateful to all those who have helped us in this work, especially the members of the resource acquisition department and the company geologists.

Note

This is a difficult report to write as it involves taking a view on the extent to which the executives involved will be able to follow the technical arguments of the earlier pages. Here we have given only the minimum and it may be thought that this is too little. One can only decide this in the knowledge of the potential recipient. We always have to write with a particular person or group of people in mind and should never start without asking the questions:

- What is the state of mind and knowledge of those who will read this?
- What is the state that I would like them to be in when they have finished reading this?

For an interesting case study of competitive bidding see: King, M. and Mercer, A. (1991). Distributions in competitive bidding, *J. Opl Res. Soc.*, **42**, 2, 151–7.

NOTE FOR THE FILE (BY OR MANAGER)

This work came about as a result of informal discussions between ourselves and the Director of Resource Acquisition. The report to him outlines the data and the conclusions.
    Further points to be made are:

1   The objectives are eccentric and curious. We had to accept them this time but on any future occasion we should go higher than the director and have the objectives revised to take account of the fact that only about one bid in five wins and we should think of the total expected cash payment likely rather than total amount bid.
2   The additive nature of the Xs is rather dicey. But what would be better? (Let's avoid getting the utility of a set of Xs. This will not be understood by management, or even, perhaps, by ourselves.)
3   The sensitivity of our solution should have been discussed before. For example, the curves we put through the data were drawn by Guess and God. How robust would the solution be to different curves being drawn?

Reflections

Perhaps the most important assumption is that the rival companies will continue to behave as before. In the real study on which this is based, after the new scheme had been implemented a rival company hired some of the bidding team and the method had to be revised.
    No one would maintain that the solution is accurate. But it is better to have an approximate solution to the real problem than an exact solution to the approximate problem. It is often the case that once a probability is estimated for the first time, the improvement in performance is highly

significant. So always try to get an estimate of probability based on historical data. Beware of estimating probabilities by asking management to make a guess. The odds are they will give you a number just to get you to go away.

Further Work

1 Try (3) in the Note for the File (above).
2 Suppose the objective is changed in two different ways: (a) How should a set of bids be made so as to maximise the expected return in X values for a given expected payment on winning bids. (b) What is the total amount that should be bid so as to maximise the expected X value gained per unit of expenditure on winning bids?

As mentioned in the reflections above, in the actual case study, the company concerned applied the solution successfully but after a couple of years one of their bidding staff was seduced away by a rival company who had noted the company's improvement in performance. What would your advice to our company now be, if we assume this rival company would use our method?

Chapter 9

The Anatomy of Organisations

Hardy's *Tess of the d'Urbervilles* ends with the sentence "The President of the Immortals had finished his sport with Tess." Reflecting on the nature of the organisations with which we are concerned, we have to ask the question which Hardy provokes. What is the nature of our subject matter? We are aware that in every problem we approach, the signals we are seeking are masked by much noise. Quite often, once we get behind the ordered surface mask, we find chaos. Decisions taken are often ignored. Senior managers are given control levers to pull, but often those levers do not seem to be connected to anything. The calm orderly structure so often imagined in textbooks is replaced by a continuing struggle for survival. Departments and individuals fight each other – indeed executives can use tactics on their colleagues which would not be used on rival firms because they would be unethical. Organisations, supposedly, serving the same national interest, seem to (and do) hate each other intensely.

Is such chaos the natural state – are we fighting against the second law of thermodynamics? Is our task as management or management analysts to impose order on chaos by writ of force? Or is the natural state an orderly one and does the chaos arise from our own blundering and our own stupidity? The scientist knows that the common feature of how things work in nature is an ordered statistical simplicity. When a phenomenon is really understood we find order, pattern and common sense, whether this be at the heart of matter, or in a tulip, or in the furthest reaches of the universe. At the heart of management problems there are nearly always embedded simple relationships and our task as researchers is to tease them out. The common sense is not what we put there, it is what we find there. Simplicity comes last.

Some of this chaos is due to sloppy thinking, some is due to a failure to understand human beings. When an exasperated manager proclaims that the staff, the customers, the suppliers, the board or (especially) his or her spouse are thoroughly irrational, what is mostly the case is that these others are behaving rationally within their own value systems and the manager does not appreciate that their value systems do not match his or her own.

What we need therefore is an understanding of the motivations (generally concealed) and objectives of all those concerned in the operations being studied – and the analyst must include himself in all this. Objectives, real objectives, can often have no relationship to the published objectives circulated by public relations development.

The author carried out a survey of organisational objectives, by referring to management research groups in a large number of UK industries: private, public and nationalised. Over half the research groups were unaware of any statement of the objectives of their own organisations. Of those that were aware, with one exception, they fell into two categories – the aggressive and the benign. The exception (which proved to be the only objective in which one could could have any real confidence) was a private printing company in East England which stated "This is a privately owned family business. It is our intention that it remains so."

One company, had a wide and well-deserved reputation for strong excellent management, but also was one where people up to and including director level had been fired, and out of the building within an hour, in a clinical, ruthless way. This company's publicity stated that its objectives included a "mutuality of esteem, respect and service between ourselves and our staff, our customers and suppliers".

A large publishing company has a formal statement of over 20 goals, mostly anodyne and with internal contradictions – "high quality" and "low prices", "high profits" and "high salaries".

Such public statements of objectives and goals are useless – to understand real objectives and goals one has to look at the decisions that are being taken and to deduce what they imply. In a similar manner if one wishes to understand a person's goals it is not helpful to ask the person concerned. What is much more important is to observe how he (or she) spends their money or, even better, how they spend their time.

Conflict within organisations is endemic and bitter. It is not necessarily counter productive since the competitive element can yield greater efficiency. However, the division of a total whole into units which have their own goals can generate wasteful conflict. Within the community care sector there is endemic conflict between the health service and the social services and, within the nursing staff, between district nurses, practice nurses and health visitors. Occupational therapists employed by health trusts and those employed by social services are at each other's throats.

This can be observed everywhere. A research team was invited to study the production problems of an engineering company. This company consisted of a number of vertically integrated units which bought and sold to each other along the process of production, but which could also buy and sell outside. In this situation transfer pricing, which is a zero sum game so far as the main board is concerned, is the life blood of the profits of an individual unit. At the beginning of the research, the managing director of the unit involved impressed on the team the need for treating all information with great secrecy. When the team leader replied that of course nothing would get out to rival companies the response was impolite, but politely summarised it was "I do not worry about my competitors – it is the other units within my organisation I am concerned about."

As has been shown in Chapter 3 the well-being of the whole does not necessarily (in fact only rarely will it) coincide with the well-being of each part. If one was designing an engine, the best total engine would not consist of the linkage of the best design for each bit. The best football team will not be the one with the best possible player in each position.

Organisations can be cybernetically unsound in the way in which they divide their operation into functional parts. Criteria of performance are imposed on each part which have meaning only when applied internally to that part and do not relate to its interaction with other parts.

These internal measures, are not concerned with the whole. This is not an easy problem – perhaps the most difficult task of top management is how to create criteria of performance for the parts which coincide with the performance of the whole and – more importantly – how to motivate the managers so that they keep one eye on their own part and the other eye on the whole.

The list of criteria in Chapter 4 showed the inevitability of conflict within organisations and a quick reputation for wisdom can be obtained by an analyst who, on his first tour of a manufacturing organisation can say to the head of production: "Do you find that your production facility works at less than total capacity because marketing are consistently changing specifications or delivery dates?" Or who can say to marketing: "Do you find that production looks on it as your duty to sell that which they produce rather than for them to produce that which you can sell?"

There are equivalent wisdom producing questions elsewhere. In the field of health for example the interface between the consultants (specialists), the doctors, the nursing staff and the administrators will all, sui generis, have inevitable conflicts. Within political parties the tensions within a party are much greater than those between parties. Such conflicts are endemic and are a state of nature, just as inevitable as the fact that dogs chase cats up trees.

A symptom of the existence of mismatch in objectives is a regression to extremes in a sequence of decisions – that is, a feedback mechanism which is not homoeostatic. There is such an example from the fashion industry in ref 1 which gives an example of the purchasing and sales departments of a fashion store. Purchasing as usual are judged by the total cost of buying goods for the retail departments, less the value of stock left over, while the retailers are judged by what they sold. It is inevitable therefore that retailing will be more optimistic than purchasing in their own assessment of the relationship between forecast sales and planned selling price (Figure 9.1).

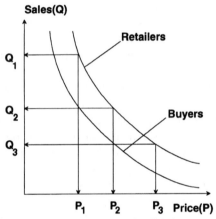

Figure 9.1 Sales and purchasing. A positive feedback

The purchasing manager had previously worked in retailing and knew their relationship of price and sales. In pre-season planning the first step was for the retailing manager to state his price P_1 and to order from purchasing the amount Q_1. But purchasing, knowing from the size of Q_1, what P_1 was involved, decided that they were being optimistic and ordered Q_2. When retailing heard of this they increased their price to P_2 to which purchasing's reaction was to set the order at Q_3 and so on. The consequence of this was a progress to the extreme of high price and low ordering. Such an extreme progression is the first symptom of over communication and confusion of goals and also illustrates a positive feedback.

Sloppy thinking is endemic when setting goals and objectives. The senior executives of a large clearing bank met in a weekend retreat to discuss what sort of bank they wanted to be in 20 years' time. What were the changes in society which might be expected in that period? Since the policy of the bank had been to recruit staff mostly at age 18, with some graduates of 21, and to offer them a career for life, the bank was largely locked into its present staff, and all the senior executives for the next 40 years were work-ing somewhere within it. (This has now changed.) But in the light of all this – what were the objectives? The discussion was largely qualitative and at its conclusion a statement that emerged was "We should try to be the Marks and Spencers of banking." This was very flattering to M & S. What did it mean in real terms?

A feature of M & S is that in style and product it is not necessarily inno-vative and is not a trend setter. It offers staple wear of excellent quality. But M & S do not seem to have many customers under the age of 30 and it is the 18–20 year olds at which the bank wishes to target its marketing. The bank did *not* need to be the M & S of banking.

There are at least three levels at which we need to think; these can be called objectives, goals and criteria. *What* they are called is unimportant. What is important is the content of these concepts. An objective is a state of the organisation to which we would like to move. It is an ideal; it may not be a place to which we think we shall ever get but it gives a sense of purpose and direction. It does not have any date or time within it. It is often not mentioned openly. The objective of a political party is to win the next election. But the party publicly is only concerned in the national inter-est. A goal is a state we want to be at, at a specific moment or period of time. It must be attainable – if it is a carrot, it is a carrot that can be eaten.

A criterion is a state we are in *now*. It is a current index. All of these, objectives, goals, criteria, must be *measurable*. There will be more goals than objectives and more criteria than goals. It is easy and facile to have simple emotional statements of objectives, such as being against sin and in favour of motherhood and apple pie. An organisation's objective can be "high employee morale" or "high level of innovation". A first test is to take the converse and if it is obviously not wanted then the obverse is redundant. One has yet to meet an organisation which wishes for "low employee mor-ale". So what does high employee morale tell us? However, if it is insisted upon then it must be stated how it should be measured. There are many surrogate measures of morale, labour wastage, labour turnover, accident rate, sickness rate, industrial disputes. An executive must not be told how he will be judged without being told the measure. If one is going to be hanged one should be shown the rope.

Measures must not be used unthinkingly. It is well known that often there are two main factors which influence labour wastage: the age of a person and the length of service, whether in the organisation or in the pres-ent job. These relations are similar in shape (Figure 9.2).

If a part of the organisation is doing well and is set to expand, senior managers are often distressed to observe that once it is expanding, the loss rate of staff increases and a symptom of loss of employee morale has arisen. Why should this be so, they ask, particularly since this part is supposed to

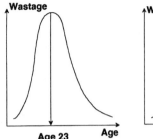

Figure 9.2 Wastage factors

be so successful? But it is inevitable and nothing to worry about. It is therefore important to be very careful in the selection of measures and to understand their arithmetic, logic and structure.

Criteria will always betray what the decision maker thinks is important and this may show the latent objectives and goals in an embarrassing way. Arithmetic is very important. A railway company can use the number of trains arriving at the destination within 5 minutes of schedule as a measure of its performance. However, since the late trains are mostly rush hour or crowded trains, this measure would be quite different if it logged the percentage of *passengers* arriving on schedule.

Enquiry bureaux use the time it takes for telephone calls to be answered as a measure of their performance, omitting to estimate the number of calls which never get through because the lines are busy. Airline safety can be measured in deaths per million passenger miles, even though most accidents occur on take off and landing. A telephone company can boast that 90% of breakdowns are dealt with inside 2 working days. But relating that to how long customers wait gives a different answer because Saturdays and Sundays are not working days. Analyses of traffic accidents on motorways in terms of the vehicles involved is much more favourable to coaches and minibuses than it would be in terms of the number of people involved. Criteria can hide and mislead.

THE PROGRESSION OF MEASURES

There is a progression in this hierarchy of criteria, goals, objectives. Objectives give long term direction, goals give locations for next year and for some years after while criteria tell where we are now and the sense of momentum.

Within each organisation there will be tension – and in well-run organisations this tension will be creative. The old style hierarchies are breaking down, which means that the old style of problem classification is also breaking down. The communication system is the nervous system. Formerly there was one brain, head office, where the nervous system (in the form of accounting data) came together and from where instructions and constraints emerged. The analyst worked within the system – either being located functionally (as in the liver or the pancreas) or geographically (as in the left leg). But now the anatomy can be changed. Access to information via the PC is now widespread and so every part of the body has its own nervous centre.

This manifests itself in two ways. First is the impact of the IT revolution. Information is potential power. It was because he or she was at the centre of a communication system that the accountant emerged in a position of power. It was because he knew more than others that the mediocre managing director could hang on to power. The emergence of the open information system means that power is now open to all who can grab it. No longer will the unfit survive because they are in a small category of those in the know. Perhaps even the accountant will find his long domination threatened, especially if the IT specialist turns to face the organisation rather than the computer. The second way in which the organisation will change is that because IT extends the span of control of a single person then middle levels of management will disappear.

The task of the analyst is to understand the anatomy of the organisational body, the motives, the goals, the communication system, all this before the model is formulated. If not, he will find himself solving the wrong problem.

Reference

1   Ackoff, R.L. (1978). *The Art of Problem Solving*, Wiley, New York.

Buttermere Oil

The Ninth Principle: If you want to kill a problem quickly and painlessly, do not mess about. Go for the jugular.

INTRODUCTION

Every problem is a mixture of the qualitative and the quantitative. It is also a mixture of objectives, constraints, certainties (occasionally) and uncertainties (always). At the beginning, one is faced with a tangled mass of actions, reactions, causes, effects, feedback, etc.

In this situation the first principle is, do not panic. Look for order, pattern and common sense. Look also for one or two particular threads which dominate. We can sometimes discover these by massive data analysis – but this is not the best way out. Even if such an analysis yields a dominant factor, it still has to be explained. Better it is, to think. Examine the variables – read and listen to what people have to say and identify what ought to be happening. There is no substitute for understanding.

Anecdote (True)

A research team in the USA was invited to study the buying of raw cotton. At the beginning of the cropping season the cotton buyers started working their way across country, inspecting the cotton plantations, and buying cotton. The cotton is classified by grade and by staple and in the textile mills blends of grade and staple are spun and woven to meet the mill order books. These two characteristics can be measured accurately in a laboratory but in the cotton fields and gins (warehouses) it has to be hastily classified subjectively by the buyers. The buyers concerned in this study were the best in the business. At the end of each day they telephoned head office, logged in their purchases and got up-to-date mill order information.

When the study began the research team looked for a matrix of order quantities classified by grade and staple and the maximum price at which any quantity should be bought for any grade and staple and the extra amounts which should be bought at different discounts. They soon discovered the hostility of the buyers to any such solution – they would not deal with any solution with more than four numbers in it. The team realised that it was better to buy accurately classified cotton at less than optimal price than to buy wrongly classified cotton at optimal price.

Moral of the Story

The parameters in a problem vary in importance. Initially the estimate of their importance is affected by the history of the analyst. This will not necessarily reflect their real importance.

BUTTERMERE OIL

To Operational Research Manager, Dr Pat R. Dale
From Site Planning Director, Mr E.C. Gullie

As you may have seen from the minutes of the general purposes committee, the company has decided to treat Lake City as a special development area. This city, of 2 m inhabitants is part of the government's strategy for enlarging the national effort in electronics and systems control and will require a great deal of the support services in banking and finance. There is strong academic support from the local university. We anticipate a higher than average growth rate in population, particularly the upwardly mobile group, and in incomes per capita. We will obviously benefit on our service station side, but we must move both quickly and carefully.

At present we have 22 filling stations in the area with a highly varied sales return. We want to know:

1 Are our present stations offering the best mix of facilities? In particular:
   (a) Have they the right number of pumps?
   (b) What effect on the sales of petrol is gained by having a shop selling food, beverage etc.
   (c) Sometimes stations have a rival station close by. What sales do we lose because of this?
   (d) Some stations offer special promotions, e.g. coupons which can be exchanged for gifts. Do these have any effect on petrol sales?
   (e) Is there a yardstick by which we can judge what the sales at our present stations "ought" to be? This is very confusing at present as

there are so many different factors affecting sales. It is only when you work in this industry for at least 20 years that you develop a feel for this, so personally I doubt whether any newcomer can get hold of this problem. But I would like you to confirm that this yardstick is solely a matter for experience.

2 Stemming from (e) above, how should we decide where to locate new filling stations? What are the best sites?

The only information I have about this is some market research carried out by one of my staff who I eventually persuaded to seek fame and fortune elsewhere. He spent a year changing the number of pumps at each of our stations. A lot of trouble was caused with our station managers and some refused to cooperate. As you will see some stations with 4, or 6, or 8 pumps did not change their mode. But some 6 pump stations did close down 2 of their pumps for some weeks and some 8 pump stations closed pumps for varying periods. For what it is worth the data are sent herewith. (This follows as Table 2, page 226.)

Personally I do not think this is worth anything as everyone knows that if you have more pumps then you sell more petrol. In addition, the two grades of petrol we sell are leaded (L) and lead-free (F). Although we always have the same number of pumps selling each, in my wide experience the more pumps you have the greater will be the proportion of leaded sold, compared with lead-free. I don't know why this is so, but you can take it from me that it is true.

I would be grateful if you would now follow this up, by visiting the area manager for Lake City, Mr Glen Cathrer, to whom I am sending a copy of this note.

Do please come and see me when you have been to Glen, but also remember that we must have answers to the above questions within 8 weeks.

(Signed Eric C. Gullie)

PROGRESS NOTE

LAKE CITY STUDY. DR P.R. DALE

Report of Visit to Mr G. Cathrer, Area Manager, Lake City

I spent a whole day with Mr Cathrer and discussed with him Mr Gullie's note. In particular I sought information on the following:

1 The plans and descriptions of all 22 stations in Lake City.

2 What does he think is gained from a shop at a station? Which stations have shops?
3 Which stations have special promotions?
4 What factors does he think are important in affecting sales?

His replies were:

1 The plans and descriptions were available and photo copies of these are in this file.
2 A station shop is very important. Mr Cathrer's personal friends are all enthusiastic about the shops and only use stations which have them.
3 The stations with promotions are as follows: (all stations are classified on a code list as simply numbered 1 through 22). Stations with promotions are 1, 4, 6, 7, 10, 11, 12, 17, 19, 21, 22.
4 These factors are a matter of experience. Mr Cathrer had written to the eleven best marketing managers in the company and asked each to suggest what, in his view, were the two most important factors. They are as follows (Table 1) where the numbers indicate the votes each received.

Table 1

	Factor	No. of managers who think this important
1	Price of petrol	4
2	Personality of the staff	4
3	Location	3
4	Speed of service	3
5	Shop	2
6	Special promotions	2
7	Proximity of nearest station	2
8	Design of station	2

Personal Note by Dr Gullie

The above list is not as helpful as it might be:

1 On discussion it appears that all stations of all companies in Lake City keep their prices very similar. At all stations there are two grades of petrol on offer – leaded (L) and lead-free (F), the prices of these are always nearly the same with a difference between the two grades of 3.0p. per gallon.
2 How do we define "personality"?
3 Location. All stations are on main roads in and out of the city. Appar-

ently they all sell mostly to commuters and so most sales are in the rush hour. This is from 7.00 a.m. to 9.00 a.m. and 4.30 p.m. to 6.30 p.m. Monday to Friday. But there is only one effective rush period for each station as car drivers will not cross the road in a rush hour.

4 Since we know which stations have a shop we can check on this.
5 Promotions were listed by Mr Cathrer.
6 Proximity. This seems a double edged sword. If no rival station is near, it looks hopeful. On the other hand, if others are near maybe it is because there is a greater sales potential?
7 How do we measure "design"?

Proposed strategy:

(a) Examine the factors listed to see on which we should concentrate to begin with.
(b) How do we measure sales? Is it volume of F and L separately, or of (F plus L?) Is it sales receipts, or in contribution to profits?
(c) So far as the second objective of the study is concerned (location of new stations) how do we bring together (a) and (b)?

(Signed P.R. Dale)

We now assume the mantle of Pat Dale. First we shall take (a) above.

Stage 1: Isolate the Factors on Which to Concentrate

It is useful to take what the experienced managers tell us are the main factors and look at their potential. But what are we looking for? By what criteria do we select the short list? By now it should not be a great surprise to suggest that in looking for what ought to be our critical list of variables we require that the variable should have five characteristics:

1 It should be one to which the outcome is sensitive. One way of testing this is by an argument to extremes. When the variable is at an upper or lower limit, should its effect be greater at one limit than at the other?
2 It should take as many values as possible, i.e. a continuous variable is preferred to one which only takes discrete values.
3 It should take values over as great a range as possible.
4 It should be objective rather than subjective.
5 It should be controllable, it must be something we can select in terms of the overall objectives.

For the time being, we can keep the objective to be able to estimate what "should" be the sales (however measured, either in volume, in receipts or in contribution to profits) at a particular station in a particular location, and use this to set controllable variables so as to maximise the achievement of

Table 2 Sales of petrol (from market research) (gallons per day)

Station	4 pumps			6 pumps			8 pumps		
	L	F	Total	L	F	Total	L	F	Total
1	1060	680	1740 (30)	1180	720	1900 (22)	–	–	–
2	1220	720	1940 (20)	1500	900	2400 (10)	1910	1170	3080 (22)
3	–	–	–	1460	1190	2650 (27)	1810	1370	2180 (25)
4	960	720	1680 (52)	–	–	–	1560	960	2520 (32)
5	1270	710	1980 (10)	1430	870	2300 (10)	1830	1430	3260 (12)
6	–	–	–	1510	1150	2660 (40)	–	–	–
7	1220	820	2040 (52)	–	–	–	2020	1300	3320
8	–	–	–	–	–	–	1750	1070	2820 (40)
9	1330	690	2020 (6)	1400	820	2220 (6)	1140	860	2000 (32)
10	–	–	–	1050	730	1780 (20)	–	–	–
11	–	–	–	1560	970	2530	–	–	–
12	1130	820	1950 (15)	1520	1060	2580 (15)	1710	1300	3010 (22)
13	–	–	–	–	–	–	1920	1280	3200
14	930	570	1500 (52)	–	–	–	–	–	–
15	–	–	–	1500	960	2460 (30)	1790	1050	2840 (22)
16	1140	870	2010 (27)	1480	1020	2500 (25)	–	–	–
17	–	–	–	1250	830	2080	–	–	–
18	1150	650	1800 (30)	1330	850	2180 (10)	1430	840	2270 (12)
19	1100	940	2040	–	–	–	–	–	–
20	–	–	–	1420	1080	2500 (25)	1800	1250	3050 (27)
21	–	–	–	1380	920	2300	–	–	–
22	–	–	–	–	–	–	1800	1140	2940

Note: Where the number of pumps in a station was changed during the (52 week) year, the figures in parentheses give the number of weeks with the relevant number of pumps in operation.

this objective. This would be the first stage, and then having done this for one variable the problem can be reviewed again. If having selected a variable we find that it does indeed have a significant effect on the objective we can move on with some confidence. However, if it is found to have but little effect then we shall repeat the process until success is achieved.

The following is the list of factors suggested by the marketing managers together with our comments:

Price

All personal experience tells us that price is important. All economic models include price as a main variable. We know what it is at any time and what the competitors' prices are. However, we are also told that all prices keep in step and there is no difference between stations for a given grade of petrol. So far as sales competition within Lake City is concerned, then, for a given grade, small changes in the price are irrelevant. Since we are told that most sales are to commuter traffic in the rush hour we shall not sell much to out-of-town or through traffic. Price will have an effect so far as contributions to profit of the two grades are concerned and we must remember to deal with this.

Personality of Staff

Comparing with our check list of the five criteria for critical variables, we can see that we have no means of arguing by extremes. There is no information and this variable is highly subjective. It is better to keep this one in reserve lest all else fails.

Location

How is location measured? We are told that these stations are all on roads into town and they are used by commuter rush hour traffic. Proximity to other stations is dealt with separately but traffic must be important. On the argument to extremes, no traffic means no sales and much traffic *should* mean high sales. This variable might also satisfy the other critical criteria. Traffic flow is objective, we can find out what it is and although it is not controllable for the stations we have, it can be treated as controllable when selecting the site for a new station. We can put an *action* tag on this variable.

Speed of Service

Again no information. This might be very important, but for now it is kept in reserve.

Shop

We have information on which stations have shops. As we do not have information on what is in the shop, we have therefore no means of using the argument to extremes, and we should keep this as a secondary variable.

Special Promotions

The same comments apply as for "Shop" above.

Proximity

This could be important but we are unsure about the argument to extremes for reasons mentioned previously. What do we mean by "proximity"? It could simply be the distance to the nearest station (whether or not it is one of ours). But, be careful. We are told that traffic rarely crosses the road and so we must think in terms of distance to the nearest station on the same side of the road, remembering that it is the nearest station, irrespective of brand.

Design of Station

How is this measured? Can it be measured? Is it visibility from a distance? Is it "attractiveness"? It seems impossible to apply any of the five critical criteria.

With all this in mind, Dr Dale, presses on with the collection of further data and information. He writes to Glen Cathrer and receives the following reply.

1 *Price.* There is no price difference between any stations, both we and our rivals move in step with each other.

2 *Personality of staff.* Confirmation that there is no information except that cashiers seem often to be bad tempered and Mr Cathrer is concerned at this.

3 *Location.* Stations are indeed all on main roads. Dr Dale visits and observes there is a common design. Stations have either 4, 6 or 8 pumps. There is evidence in the rush hours of bunching and queuing of cars. The rush hours are 7.00 a.m. to 9.00 a.m. and 4.00 p.m. to 6.00 p.m. Monday to Friday. Saturdays seem "pretty busy all day" (sic) and Sundays fairly light. Most sales are certainly in the rush hours on week days. Dr Dale's team takes traffic flow counts during the rush hours

Table 3   Traffic flow (rush hour; vehicles per hour)

Station	Morning Same side	Other side	Evening Same side	Other side
1	720	77	69	695
2	1100	115	120	1170
3	139	1420	1400	138
4	600	64	61	620
5	89	930	900	87
6	126	1310	1300	135
7	124	1180	1250	115
8	1600	153	168	1640
9	960	99	90	950
10	63	630	650	68
11	1450	141	150	1430
12	121	1160	1180	130
13	1500	148	156	1520
14	550	57	55	570
15	100	1020	1030	108
16	1280	126	120	1290
17	87	830	850	79
18	79	820	800	75
19	1060	109	110	1050
20	1070	109	100	1090
21	101	950	1000	113
22	1150	124	113	1170

and establish that the flow is fairly constant from day to day. These data are in Table 3.

4 *Speed of Service.* Apart from the queuing mentioned in 3, no data were collected. It was noted that it could be collected if necessary. But so far as total time in the station is concerned perhaps the number of pumps in the station could be important?

5 *Shop.* Observation showed that there is a variety of types of shops. Some sell only confectionery and cigarettes. Others sell selections of food, beverages, microwave heated burgers and franks, hosiery, books, children's toys, newspapers. For the time being Dr Dale puts this down as simply "Yes" or "No" in Table 4.

6 *Promotions.* When promotions are held – and they are on in selected stations continuously – they are for fixed periods of time being immediately followed by another one. They also vary in nature considerably.

Table 4 Stations with shops and/or promotions

		Shops	
		Yes	No
Promotions	Yes	1, 4, 6, 7, 10, 11, 12, 17, 19, 21, 22	——
	No	——	2, 3, 5, 8, 9, 13, 14, 15, 16, 18, 20

The stations concerned are listed in Table 4. It is seen that shops and promotions go together. The younger members of the team reflect that it is a pity no one told them. The older members know that this sort of thing happens all the time.

7 *Proximity.* Driving along all the roads and using the trip distance measure in their cars the team estimate the closest stations on the same side of the road in kilometre measure, to be as in Table 5. It is seen that the team used three classifications. Do you agree with them? It is a question of balance, the more classifications, the better – as long as there is a minimum of about 5 in each. The reader can use a different set of criteria of differences if wished. But it will not make any change in the conclusions (confirm this: see Table 6).

8 *Design.* See p. 228 above.

Table 5 Proximity (same side in metres)

	Near (less than 500m)	Medium (500m to 1000m)	Far (more than 1000m)
Station	2, 6, 11, 14, 15, 17	1, 5, 8, 9, 12, 18, 21, 22	3, 4, 7, 10, 13, 16, 19, 20

Note: The team divided these into ranges with as near as possible equal numbers in each range. Why three ranges? Why not? It is a question of balance – the more ranges the better, as long as there is a useful minimum in each. Try it with four ranges if you wish (see Table 6).

Table 6 (revised for enthusiasts)

Proximity	0–350	350–700	700–1050	Above 1050
	2, 6, 15	1, 9, 11, 14, 17, 18, 21	5, 8, 10, 12 16, 19, 22	3, 4, 7, 13, 20

Stage 2: The Basic Question

We now face the question we have been avoiding: What measures of sales should be used? We have been told that the contribution to profits of L is 9p/gal. and F is 12p/gal. The first task is to compare the implications of using L and F separately or to take total sales of (L + F). The latter is preferable, as it reduces the number of variables but also we shall have to take some weighted average of 9p and 12p if we look at profit maximisation.

However, it is permissible to use T = L + F if the proportions of L and F at all filling stations is the same (or approximately so). Reference to Table 2 shows that for all stations and all pump numbers, whether 4, 6 or 8 the proportion of L and F is very close to 0.60. to 0.40. (*Note*: confirm this.) We can therefore simply use total sales as our index of performance.

Stage 3: Variables for Analysis

This being so, which variables of those discussed on pp. 225–229 should be taken? That discussion can be summarised (see Table 7). We now use this table to select our prime variable. This will be an inspired guess to see if there is one factor which might dominate the picture. Reference to the table indicates that the best variable as first choice for the jugular is traffic flow with promotions/shop and proximity as secondary. But speed of service might be implied by the number of pumps in use so this should be taken as an additional variable.

Table 7 Discussion of variables

Variable	Sensitivity (using argument to extremes)	Range of values	Many valued?	Objective or subjective	Controllable or Uncontrollable
Price	Probably high	Nil. Price is fixed	No	Objective	Controllable
Personality	Unknown	Unknown	Unknown	Subjective	Uncontrollable
Location	High?	High?	Yes	Objective	Uncontrollable
Traffic flow	High	High	Yes	Objective	Controllable
Speed of service	Probably high?	Not known	Not known	Objective	Controllable?
Shop and promotions	Not known	Yes or No	2 values	Objective	Controllable
	Not known	Yes or No	2 values	Objective	Controllable
Proximity	Not known	Doubtful	3 values	Objective	Uncontrollable

Traffic Flow

How should this be measured? We are told that few vehicles cross the road and that most sales are in the rush hour. As a first attempt therefore we shall take traffic flow per hour in the rush period on the station side of the road (this means that sometimes it will be the morning rush hour and sometimes in the evening). The relationship to be plotted is therefore

> As x value: Traffic flow as defined above (1)

> As y value: Total sales for both grades, in gallons/day (2)

Where, as is usual, the x is the independent and the y is the dependent variable.

But *what* total sales? At some stations there are separate periods of 4-pump sales, 6-pump sales and 8-pump sales. These could give an overall average per week, by weighting the sales according to the number of weeks at each level. This is very messy. We can easily bring the number of pumps into consideration by plotting three relationships, one for each number of pumps and so by implication bring in the speed of service factor.

Stage 4: Plotting the Variables

Bring together therefore the traffic flow figure to be used from Table 03 (as x) with the total sales, from Table 2 (as y). Distinguish on a plot the 4-, 6- and 8- pump data. (Preferably use your own colour code.)

Stage 5: Plotting the Relationship

Examine the plot that you have prepared. Is there a relationship for all the points? There seem to be three relationships, one for each number of pumps, rather than only one relationship for all the points. Draw your own three relationships, whether by a computer fit, an algebraic least squares fit or by divine inspiration. Figure 1 is a suggested fit – but if this is different from yours there is no real need to be concerned. Follow your own curve and also follow this argument.

What is the Relationship?

Note that it is not linear. There is a curved relation; for all three curves it grows at the same rate initially and then, in order of pump number, it becomes horizontal. Do they do the same in your case?

Remember: There is a missing point through which all three curves go that has not been mentioned. No traffic = No sales. Therefore all three curves pass through (0,0) and if the curves are drawn on a large sheet in this way it is seen that initially they grow together linearly.

What is the significance of this? It is indeed highly significant. Consider the implications. If the whole relationship was linear it would imply that no matter what the traffic flow, a constant proportion of traffic uses the station. This is very reasonable, but it is not true in practice. The proportion using the station decreases as traffic flow increases until the sales achieve a saturation level. This level is reached sooner with 4 pumps than with 6 and sooner with 6 than with 8.

This must be because at high traffic flows fewer people use the station and is probably due to motorists not wanting to go in to a station which is already over full with cars waiting.

Intermission

It is not sufficient to state that the 4-pump, 6-pump and 8-pump curves are all above each other without a corroboration. For example, if all the 4-pump stations have low traffic flow, all of the 6 with medium flow and all the 8-pump stations with high traffic flow, then it could not be concluded that extra pumps cause more sales. But here we are assisted by the fact that for many stations, while all other factors, including traffic flow, remain constant, increasing the number of pumps increases sales. This is true at every station where the number of pumps is changed (see Table 2). It is therefore safe to conclude that increasing the number of pumps increases sales and decreasing the number of pumps decreases sales. At this point we can silently render thanks to the much maligned market researcher whose competence was misjudged by Mr Cathrer.

In the above figure the filling station numbers are in parentheses and apply to the point(s) vertically above.

Stage 6: The Other Variables

We have now established that traffic flow is a key variable and that the number of pumps is important. This is gratifying. But what about:

- Shops/Promotion?
- Proximity?

In Table 4 the stations were classified according to these variables. Using Figure 1 an estimate of the possible effect of these variables can be obtained by taking the residual differences of the sales expected (E) as given by the graphs, from the sales obtained (O) for the 4-, 6- and 8-pump stations.

In Table 8, on page 235, E is the number of gallons expected from the curve and O is the number of gallons obtained (i.e. sold).

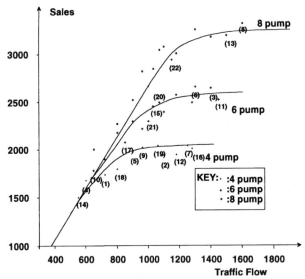

Figure 1 Sales in terms of pumps and traffic flow

Using the value of (E – O) from the relationships (we repeat—the reader should use his/her own data), we can test whether shops/promotions and proximity have any effect. The point is that the three curves give estimates of sales based only on traffic flow and number of pumps. The differences of the actual sales from these estimates is the result of three other causes:

(1) Possible effect of shops/promotions.
(2) Possible effect of proximity.
(3) Residual effects – other possible causes not examined and simple randomness.

Tables 4 and 5 listed the stations according to (1) and (2) above. If we take for each station, the average value of (E–O), (note a simple arithmetic average is good enough) for the 4-, 6- and 8-pump curves taken together we obtain the results shown in Table 9. The averages of these are shown in Table 10. (Once again, a simple arithmetic average is good enough.)

We note first that the average of all these is not zero. This is because either, or both:

1 The curves were not least squares best fits.
2 The draconian manner in which the averages have been obtained.

In any event the numbers are very small. We are left with Figure 1 as the relationship between sales per week, in gallons, number of pumps and traffic flow. Of the latter two, only the number of pumps is controllable. So what should it be?

Table 8 Comparison of graphs with actual sales

Station	Pump 4 E	Pump 4 O	Pump 4 (E – O)	Pump 6 E	Pump 6 O	Pump 6 (E – O)	Pump 8 (E)	Pump 8 (O)	Pump 8 (E – O)
1	1790	1740	50	1940	1900	40	–	–	–
2	2000	1940	60	2450	2400	50	3000	3080	–80
3	–	–	–	2600	2650	–50	3250	3180	70
4	1640	1680	–40	–	–	–	–	–	–
5	1920	1980	–60	2240	2300	–60	2610	2520	90
6	–	–	–	2580	2660	–80	3200	3260	–60
7	2000	2040	–40	–	–	–	–	–	–
8	–	–	–	–	–	–	3280	3320	–40
9	1980	2020	–40	2320	2220	100	2780	2820	–40
10	–	–	–	1820	1780	40	1920	2000	–80
11	–	–	–	2600	2530	70	–	–	–
12	2000	1950	50	2500	2580	–80	3100	3010	90
13	–	–	–	–	–	–	3280	3200	–10
14	1550	1500	50	–	–	–	–	–	–
15	–	–	–	2390	2460	–70	2890	2840	50
16	2000	2010	–10	2580	2500	80	–	–	–
17	–	–	–	2150	2080	70	–	–	–
18	1850	1800	50	2080	2180	–100	2310	2270	–10
19	2000	2040	–40	–	–	–	–	–	–
20	–	–	–	2420	2500	–80	2950	3050	–100
21	–	–	–	2350	2300	50	–	–	–
22	–	–	–	–	–	–	3070	2940	130

Table 9 Values of (E–O)

		Near Station	Near (O–E)	Proximity Medium Station	Proximity Medium (O–E)	Far Station	Far (O–E)
		6	–70	1	35	4	–40
	Yes	11	70	12	20	7	–40
		17	70	21	50	10	–20
Shops/				22	130	19	–40
Promotions							
		2	10	5	–70	3	10
	No	14	50	8	–40	13	80
		15	–10	9	10	16	35
				18	–6	20	–90

Table 10

		Near	Medium	Far
Shops/	Yes	20	60	−30
Promotions	No	−20	−20	10

Taking the marginal contribution to profits as 9p for L and 12p for F and the proportion of L to F of 0.6 to 0.4, then a total of 100 gals yields a contribution to profit of £10.20, or £100 per 1000 gals (approx.). We can use this approximate figure without any sleepless nights as there is a great deal of approximation elsewhere of a more heroic kind.

The optimal number of pumps can duly be estimated if we know the cost of an extra pump. When this question is put to the accountants of Buttermere Oil there is a long period of silence. The eventual response is that there are two answers. For an existing station the marginal cost of replacing 4 pumps to 6 and 8 pumps respectively is £9000 p.a. and £24 000 p.a. A 6-pump filling station would cost £15 000 p.a. to convert to an 8-pump station.

If a station has 4 pumps it is worth converting to a 6-pump station if the extra sales are worth more than £9000 p.a. With the marginal profit of £0.10 per gal. and a 300-day year, extra volume necessary is 300 gals per day. A conversion from 4 to 8 pumps would similarly be sensible if sales increase by 800 gals per day.

Reference to Figure 1 shows that a 4-pump station with traffic flow of more than 900 vehicles per hour should achieve the required increase in sales by installing 2 extra pumps and that if the traffic flow is more than 1000 vehicles per hour the extra sales is over 850 gals per day which would make this change worth while. Similarly a 6-pump station with flow of more than 900 v.p.h. should install an extra 2 pumps.

We have therefore the following conclusions. On the basis of an analysis of sales as a function of traffic flow, number of pumps, promotions, presence of a shop, proximity of the nearest rival station on the same side of the road:

1 Traffic flow is the dominant determinant of sales.
2 The number of pumps has an additional significant effect.
3 The optimal number of pumps is:
   - Rush hour traffic flow less than 900 vehicles per hour: 4 pumps.
   - Traffic flow between 900 and 1200 vehicles an hour: 6 pumps.
   - Traffic flow more than 1200 vehicles an hour: 8 pumps.
4 There is no evidence that shops, promotions or proximity affect sales. However, in all the 22 stations analysed, whenever there was a shop

there were promotions and vice versa. Hence we must include the reservation that this conclusion is not valid if the effects of a shop and of a promotion are in opposite directions.

We can now write our reports.

BUTTERMERE OIL COMPANY

Report to Site Planning Director from Operational Research Manager

Introduction

The Operational Research Department was invited by the Site Planning Director to carry out a study of the location of and facilities offered by our 22 service stations in Lake City in order to answer the following questions:

1 Are our present stations offering the best mix of facilities? In particular:
   (a) Have they the best number of pumps?
   (b) What effect on the sales of petrol is gained by having a shop, selling food, beverages etc.?
   (c) What sales do we lose because of rival stations near by?
   (d) Some stations offer special promotions, e.g. gift coupons. Do these have any effect on petrol sales?
   (e) Is there a yardstick by which we can judge what sales ought to be at our present stations?
2 Stemming from (1) (e), how should we decide where to locate new filling stations? What are the best sites?

The OR department has carried out this survey, using data from the marketing department and market research as well as observational data collected by visiting all the 22 stations. This report summarises the study and answers the questions listed.

Problems of Definition

It will be noted that two of the words in the terms of reference need careful definition. These are "best" and "sales". There are a number of choices but in the event which choice is taken does not matter. There are good reasons for this.

As is known, Buttermere Oil offer two grades of petrol, leaded (L) and lead-free (F). The profit margins on each of these are 9p and 12p per gallon respectively. If "sales" is defined as contributions to profit, this difference in margins could be important. However, at all stations the relative volume sold of the two grades is very close to 6:4 and so maximising total sales, as an indicator of "best" will yield the same result as maximising contribution to profits. It may be protested that margin depends on selling price. This is true, but in Lake City all the rival petrol stations move prices in concert with each other so the relative profits will be unchanged in terms of price levels. Of course, however, absolute profits will vary with margins, but the choices made as to what is "best" will not be affected.

As sales are so concentrated into the rush hour period we have simply used the traffic flow vehicles per hour in the two-hour rush period corresponding to the flow being on the station side of the road.

Data Availability

The previous market research, extending over a year, gave weekly sales for each of the stations, classified according to the number of pumps working (4, 6, or 8). During that experimental year the number of pumps was varied from time to time and this gave useful data.

Stations were classified according to whether or not they had shops and whether or not they had promotions. In the event all the stations with shops had promotions, and vice versa.

Traffic flow was more difficult. Station managers told us, and observations confirmed, that:

1   There is a strong tidal flow in rush hours.
2   Most sales are made in rush hours.
3   During rush hours in particular, drivers are very unlikely to cross the road to get petrol.

The result is that at each station sales tend to be concentrated into two hours, either morning or evening, but not both (see Table 01, p. 240).

Factors Affecting Sales

Table 01 presents the basic data on total sales and the flow of traffic in the rush hour. Although traffic flow is clearly of importance there are a number of other factors which must also be considered and we have taken the following as possibilities:

1   Existence of a store at the station.
2   Promotions.
3   Layout and design of stations.
4   Number of pumps.
5   Personality of the staff.
6   Price.
7   Traffic flow.
8   Proximity of other stations.
9   Speed of service.

Of these, (3) and (5) present problems in being quantified. Price (6) is the same for all stations in Lake City, (9) (for reasons that will become apparent) can be dealt with implicitly and so the analysis has concentrated on (1) and (2) taken together, (4), (7) and (8) in the above list.

Table 01 Traffic flow (rush hour, same side) and sales

Station	4 pump	6 pump	8 pump	Traffic flow (veh. per hour)
1	1740	1900	–	720
2	1940	2400	3080	1100
3	–	2650	3180	1400
4	1680	–	–	600
5	1980	2300	2520	900
6	–	2660	3260	1300
7	2040	–	–	1250
8	–	–	3320	1600
9	2020	2220	2820	960
10	–	1780	2000	650
11	–	2530	–	1450
12	1950	2580	3010	1180
13	–	–	3200	1500
14	1500	–	–	550
15	–	2460	2840	1030
16	2010	2500	–	1280
17	–	2080	–	850
18	1800	2180	2270	800
19	2040	–	–	1060
20	–	2500	3050	1070
21	–	2300	–	1000
22	–	–	2940	1150

Results of the Analysis

Figure 01 shows the sales of all 22 stations, separated into the number of pumps operating, plotted in terms of traffic flow in the relevant peak period.

It can be seen that there are three distinct relationships, for 4, 6 and 8 pumps respectively. There is a real effect of pump numbers since in all cases where different numbers of pumps have been used at different times of the year, sales at a given station are always increased when the number of pumps increases.

The form of the curves is important. They all increase initially along the same straight line. The 4-pump curve diverges first to level out at about 2050 gals per day, then the 6-pump curve diverges and levels at 2600 gals and the 8-pump curve levels at 3250 gals per day.

A straight line relation would have indicated that irrespective of traffic flow, a constant proportion of passing cars used the station. But this is not so. Our conclusion, which was confirmed by observation, is that as traffic flow increases there are more cars entering which then queue for a pump

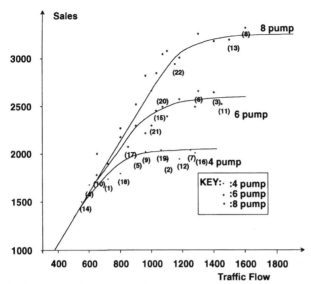

Figure 1 Sales in terms of pumps and traffic flow

and this queue deters others who might have joined. This happens sooner with 4 pumps than with 6, and sooner with 6 than with 8 pumps.

The curves therefore show vividly the effect on sales of traffic flow and the number of pumps. The relation is not exact and the residual differences of sales from the curve estimates are due to a mixture of the other factors listed and random chance.

These residual differences are really too small to matter but, even so, there is no evidence to relate them to promotions, shops or proximity of another station.

The annual cost of increasing the numbers of pumps has been contributed by the Finance Department, to whom we express our thanks. Adding two extra pumps to a 4 or 6 pump station involves both extra capital and running costs. Expressed as an annual charge these can be put as:

4 pumps to 6 pumps £9000 p.a.
4 pumps to 8 pumps £24 000 p.a.
6 pumps to 8 pumps £15 000 p.a.

The deduction which can be drawn from Figure 01, therefore, is that the optimal number of pumps in terms of traffic flow is:

Traffic flow per hour	<900	900 to 1200	>1200
Pumps	4	6	8

We have not considered reducing the existing number of pumps as the advice of the Finance Department is that when the pumps are in operation there is little to be gained in terms of cash flow by closing them.

Conclusions

1 There are two dominant factors which affect the sales of petrol. The more important is traffic flow but the number of pumps is also very significant.

2 An increase in the number of pumps will not decrease sales but if the cost of installing extra pumps is taken into consideration then the numbers that maximise contribution to profits are:

Peak traffic flow (veh. per hour)	No. of pumps
Less than 900	4
900 to 1200	6
More than 1200	8

3 If profit margins or the cost of pumps change then the figures in (2) will change also. But they can be re-calculated for any traffic flow from Figure 01.

4 There is no evidence that any factor other than traffic flow and number of pumps affects sales in a significant manner.

5 So far as new sites are concerned it is important to take account of the potential sales in Figure 01 when negotiating a buying price.

6 The terms of reference included whether the existence of a shop brought in extra sales of petrol. As stated, this is not proven. But it would be worth analysing the relative profit per square metre of ground space of a shop compared with extra pumps and, indeed, the profitability of shops per se.

Acknowledgements

We would like to thank all those in the Site Planning, Finance and Marketing Departments for their help and advice. In particular we express our gratitude to Mr E.C. Gullie and Mr G. Cathrer.

NOTE FOR THE FILE

Buttermere Oil

As an exercise write a note summarising:

1 How and why the project arose.
2 The availability of data, including a criticism of its usefulness.
3 Why the particular measures defining the "best" filling station were used.

4   The central part of the analysis was using Table 02 to isolate one princi-
pal factor (traffic flow) and one major subsidiary factor (number of
pumps) together with two less important factors. Critically summarise
the arguments involved in the lead up to Table 02.
5   A note of vulnerable points in the study – where were guesses made
and in what respects might the study be in error.
6   Any follow-up work which might be useful.

Table 02 Discussion of variables

Variable	Sensitivity (using argument to extremes)	Range of values	Many valued?	Objective or subjective	Controllable or Uncontrollable
Price	Probably high	Nil. Price is fixed	No	Objective	Controllable
Personality	Unknown	Unknown	Unknown	Subjective	Uncontrollable
Location	High?	High?	Yes	Objective	Uncontrollable
Traffic flow	High	High	Yes	Objective	Controllable
Speed of service	Probably high?	Not known	Not known	Objective	Controllable?
Shop and promotions	Not known Not known	Yes or No Yes or No	2 values 2 values	Objective Objective	Controllable Controllable
Proximity	Not known	Doubtful	3 values	Objective	Uncontrollable

Reflections

We always have to make do with what we are given. Clearly price is an
overwhelmingly important variable, but in this case we are told that stations move together on price. Is this really so? If it is so, then the analysis
is made easier because dealing with differential pricing is always messy.
We must avoid the temptation of enquiring too carefully about factors
which can cause extra work and will not yield significant improvement.

The shape of the curves in Figure 01 is interesting. We could have made
the initial assumption that a constant proportion of cars use the stations. If
this was true then Figure 01 would have only linear relationships. The
curves probably are the result of baulking – that is drivers are put off by
the queue. But they could result from drivers not wanting to stop at all for
petrol when traffic was heavy as it might then be difficult to exit from the
station. It is interesting that the curves confirm the conclusion from queue-
ing theory regarding the effect of baulking.

Finally, this is a competitive situation, but as in Conner Mining we have been able to ignore the fact of competition by having a lag period before the competition responds to what we might do. Note also that if proximity has no affect, and if our rivals think that it does, then sites near rival stations may be cheaper because our rivals do not want them, yet the sales potential is there. (Is this true? Are we deducing too much?)

Further Work

1 The Reflections finished with a question. Answer it. After all, if we build a new station adjacent to another, surely sales will suffer at both stations? Where is the fallacy? Is there a fallacy?
2 Extrapolate Table 01 by drawing the hypothetical curve for a 10-pump station. What reservations might you have?
3 Carry out the same analyses as in Figure 01, with the same y axis, but with the x axis being: (a) The number of pumps (4, 6, 8) or (b) Proximity (500 m, 750 m, 1000 m).

This should show the wisdom of taking traffic flow as the first variable to be analysed.

Chapter 10

Bridge Building

This book is deliberately entitled the *craft* of modelling. In the main and major section we have taken a tour round the craft shop, observing what it is that we are trying to construct and critically examining various aspects of the craft.

Interspaced with these narrative chapters have been the Nine Lives. These illustrate some of the experiences through which the aspiring analyst will learn. They are less dogmatic than are commandments, and in any event they are one short of the required number. They are cautionary tales, pieces of advice. A craft lies in the area between an art form and a technique. It is more formalised than an art form, although teaching a visual or performing art involves elements of discipline, and less formalised than a technique. A technique is a vehicle which will take its passengers from the boarding point to a destination. As such, techniques are very powerful vehicles provided one is at the boarding point and the destination is acceptable. There can be a heavy fare to be paid, not least in the form of the assumptions that have to be accepted and the alternatives which must be rejected. So a craft is what we present and as with all crafts there is a fascination in observing craftsmen at work.

This particular craft is that of research and research lies across a spectrum. From the researcher's point of view, at one extreme it will be concerned with understanding, with managing and "solving" problems, which at the time of meeting them are insoluble. There is no certainty of success and often a high probability of failure. In these cases the temptation is to redefine the problem so that it can be solved and it must be confessed that this is often done. In Chapter 13 we shall discuss this more fully. At the other extreme are those situations where the problem can be analysed to produce an acceptable answer and it is known from the beginning that this is so. It is often the case that management knows the answer it requires from the beginning and the researcher is required to produce that answer.

What is certainly the case is that when the probability of success is less than unity, there will be no formal set of logical steps which will ineluctably yield a solution. If the problem is on one side of the river and the solution is on the other then the analyst is not like a civil engineer who knows the materials, the start and finish points and which standard process of construction will get him across in the shortest time or at minimum cost.

SIX IMPERATIVES

There are six absolute imperatives. The most important of these is now listed as it is so very important:

1 Do Produce an Answer in Time

The Other Five Imperatives

2 Do *go* to the source of the data. Find out how they are collected, what are their value, and how accurate are they?
3 Do *listen* to people – what is the structure of the problem area, what is its technology?
4 Do *read* about the background of the organisation, its history and its management.
5 Do *understand* the people involved. Not just the management but all the stakeholders. What is their history, their motivations and their differing perceptions of the problem area?
6 Do *consider* whether there might be a simple lateral thinking answer.

Or: *go, listen, read, understand, consider and produce.*
Here once again are the highly advisory principles from the Lives:

THE NINE PRINCIPLES

1 It is not enough to think you understand what you read. Ask also what other people will understand.
2 Always question the data.
3 Think before you analyse.
4 Do not expect all distributions to be normal.
5 Objectives are not absolutes – they change even during a study.
6 Be ultra cautious in handling estimates of probabilities where there is no possibility of validation.

7 Examine the problem boundaries.
8 On s'engage et puis on voit.
9 Go for the jugular.

Part Two

Chapter 11

Focal Points

This is a convenient point at which to draw together some of the threads of the argument. The preceding sections have shown a number of different problem types and of morals to be drawn, and we shall see some features which are common to many of these.

The First Life

The First Life, was in the nature of a (real life) story and made the point that it is not enough for the researcher to be able to understand and interpret procedures, but also to know how other people do this. Life is rich in examples of differences in verbal or written interpretation and of misunderstandings. It is the staple of comedy. It is the starting point of tragedy. It occurs to each of us every day. Unfortunately the student may not be taught this. Examination questions are clear and unambiguous. Teachers strive to be clear and positive.

Sometimes the misunderstanding is cultural and linguistic. If a lecturer wishes to give a hint to students before an examination he could say: "You might find it useful to check up on this." British students hear the message as an imperative loud and clear but those from other cultures hear the word "might" and regard the remark as an idle throw away. On other occasions differences in educational background can lead to different interpretations. Often these can be legalistic and there will be confusion between the letter of the law and its spirit.

Almost all the exposure of the analyst will be with managers. He or she will be dealing with those who give instructions and not those who interpret them. The misunderstandings which ensue are largely unnoticed.

252 _____ The Craft of Decision Modelling

The Second Life

The Second Life turned upon the interpretation of data and how the scale of origin can affect its interpretation. Published health data give an infant mortality rate of 10.7 per 1000 for those below the poverty line and 9.8 for others. This looks much less serious when expressed as live births — 989.3 and 990.2 per 1000, respectively. We can, out of pressure of time or sheer laziness, take data as given, in terms of original units of measure, in an unthinking way and so miss out on a vital relationship. In this case the unexpected variable was time, or rather a time delay. In the terms of the original question it was indeed unexpected and only arose because the data were looked at in a new way.

The Third Life

The Third Life dealt with robustness. Not all the variables in every problem are important and sometimes care and attention can be lavished on variables which have no effect. For example, the object of university brochures is to encourage more students (1) to apply and (2) to accept offers made. To this end the universities themselves are mainly motivated by what other universities are doing and proceed to expend effort with no understanding of the effect on (1) and (2) of different styles of brochure. Every parent will know the sinking feeling of depression when faced with yet another university brochure. These brochures are frequently produced to impress a peer group within the university and fail to impress the customer. They are often not tested, in any market research sense, on potential students who receive them with sighs of resignation, as most parents will know and as most students will remember. All the effort expended has but little effect.

The Fourth Life

The Fourth Life took the problem of incomplete information. We should always be thankful that our information is incomplete, for we are certainly unable to deal with the complete story. It is here for the first time that we induce from our experience. The fact that certain statistical distributions are common in particular situations means that we can bring into our analysis fresh information which lies outside the data. In addition, of course, there is a range of alternatives that are themselves robust. In statistical practice it matters little whether we use a normal or a Cauchy distribution, indeed even a triangular statistical distribution, can be good enough. We are not therefore bounded by the data we have. Although each problem may be unique per se, it is generally part of a pattern and part of the mainstream of life.

The Fifth Life

The Fifth Life was (probably refreshingly) brief and shows how objectives can change as we exchange ends and means. Objectives can also change as perceptions change. A common reason for failure in OR is that the culture of the client has not been understood and the client has therefore not been understood and the client's objectives have been misinterpreted.

The Sixth Life

The Sixth Life introduced the widespread occurrence of the logistic curve and brought it in as a possible general statement for a group of similar examples. It also for the first time uses this approach not just to estimate the expected value of a variable (in this case end of season sales) but, much more importantly, the variance of the estimate. Expected values, which are the basis of the first case studies are of limited use, since they yield little information about probability. The combination of expectation and variance is much more powerful. We can obtain an estimate of the probability of a given level of total sales being achieved and this in its turn yields another expectation: of profit. At this stage we were content not to obtain the variance of this expected profit.

The Seventh Life

The Seventh Life, like the fifth was, for purposes of variety of presentation, in a different form. It is based on an actual study in the social services sector and shows how government departments each trying to do the best for themselves, end up by doing less than the best for those in need and for the taxpayer. It is an example that the traditional breakdown of management into manageable bits, each with its perfectly reasonable yardstick of performance, is counter productive. There are many cases where the performance of one part of the whole has to be degraded, as measured, in order for the whole to improve. This is a hard lesson for many managers.

The Eighth Life

The Eighth Life makes an important point about constraints. All problems in real life, as discussed and analysed, have some form of objectives involved. It is rare that we can, with clear conscience, "optimise". As previously mentioned, optimising can only take place with confidence where only one variable is involved and single variable problems arise mainly at the tactical level. In addition to the objectives there are also constraints. These can be technical (the characteristics of a machine), managerial (customers must be supplied within three days), social (all staff will eat together), personal (we take pride in the quality of our product), professional (once patients leave hospital it is up to the local GP what their continuing treatment should be), philosophical (we have to trust our suppliers).

Some constraints are explicit, some implicit. The former are known before the analyst starts his work, the latter are often known only when a proposed solution is rejected for unexpected reasons. The worst constraints of all are those in the mind of the analyst, of which he or she may be unaware and it is sad that so often the analyst does not apply to his own thinking that rigorous process applied to others.

Until this point in the Nine Lives, the consequences of our actions have always been in terms of what we do and of the natural variability of life. There is no malign opponent. Now in this case, Eight, there is. We have the introduction of competition but have managed, as is often the case, to ignore it and treat it simply as natural variability. Where the reaction or learning time of our competitors is longer than the interval between successive decisions then it is useful, subject to periodic checks, to treat them simply as nature.

The Ninth Life

The Ninth Life leads to an important principle of analysis where many variables are involved. It is easy, fatally easy, when such diversity of possible causes are available simply to take one of the many computer packages for multi-variate analysis and to run the data through. It is the 'simply' that causes the problem, for it has a seductive attraction to the lazy mind. Undoubtedly if we try for long enough some relationships will emerge, but it would be both foolish and dangerous to rely on any relationship which cannot be explained in some rational way. Life does have meaning and there is a dividend from rational analysis. Even if, and when, multi-variate analysis shows an association between two variables that association still has to be explained. There is no substitute for thought, and thinking about a problem beforehand has the added advantage of economising in the time and effort spent in data collection and analysis. Indeed sometimes, as will be seen in Chapter 12, p. 257, thinking time can dissolve a problem, not just solve it.

This Life also illustrates the important tactic of going for the jugular. The variable traffic flow, is shown to be the critical variable and the reader should note the logical process by which its potential was identified. Having identified this variable its effect is taken out. This residual variability is what remains when traffic flow is accounted for. In this study the other possible causes of the residual are not continuous. The distance to the nearest station on the same side of the road, which is continuous, is only available in one of three ranges and shops/promotions are available in the form "Yes" or "No".

In practice, the effect of traffic flow in this example is so great that what remains is rather trivial and would be ignored. But if the residual was still significant it could be tested against plausible causes one by one.

It is important to place this book within its own constraints. It is a first primer setting out the basic stages of analysis where we agree what the problem is and there is confidence in this agreement. But the reader should put all this in a contextual relationship and the following sections will do this. These sections will also develop the growing influence on our craft of the immense changes in information technology (not withstanding the important caveat above).

Chapter 12

The Analytical Process

What should we do? As often described the scientific process on which OR is supposed to be based is:

1 Define the problem.
2 Collect information and data.
3 Analyse the data.
4 Produce a hypothesis relating causes to effect.
5 Test the hypothesis with trial implementation.
6 Implementation.

In practice, none of this now applies. It was of universal application at one time but those days have gone. It is a useful construct, especially since all these stages do exist. The progression from 1 to 6 does not now occur in the linear manner implied and the work involved in each of these is complex and interacting. We take the implications of these, spurred on by the first realisation that, apart from examination questions, no real problem ever turns out to be the one which is first proposed.

We can now identify a number of concerns:

1 How are problems defined and described?
2 Is there any such thing as a value free neutral fact?
3 Can the analyst stand in some sterilised zone?
4 On whose behalf is analysis carried out?
5 What are the pitfalls?

In this chapter we shall discuss these topics and, having done so, we shall in the final chapters suggest some of the causes of success and failure in practice and the principles which underlie the stages in a research project.

How Are Problems Defined and Described?

This is not the real first question, for what is the purpose of defining or describing a problem? We immediately move into semantics. For "problems" imply a desire to find how to deal with them. What does "dealing" mean? Dealing can imply disposing of a problem by:

1 Absolution
2 Resolution
3 Solution
4 Dissolution

Ref 1 outlines these four stages and the first stage is often the most common way of dealing with a problem, not only by an organisation but also by each of us individually in our personal lives. For absolution involves ignoring a problem and hoping that it will fade away. Often it does but, if it does not, then it can well get worse.

Problem resolution means that there is not any "correct" answer, since all the parties involved have different value systems. Resolution stems from a willingness of the parties to trade off their values. Bargains will have been struck, recognising the essence of a bargain between parties is that all parties feel that they are better off with the bargain than without it.

Solution means that a universally acceptable answer is found, an answer that in some way is "correct". Academic courses are rich in such problems, which generally turn out to be exercises.

Dissolution, or the dissolving of the problem, is a change of mind of the participants that means the problem is seen in a different way, often leading to the view that although the separate value systems are unchanged, the values themselves are trivial compared with other considerations.

It must be confessed that problem definition and description have received little consideration in the development of classical OR. To begin with, problem definition was the perogative of management. It was the task of OR to receive questions and answer them (an attitude of mind which can influence teaching programmes in the subject). The boundaries of the problem were also set by management. Those classic and exciting first military problems were all tactical in nature and were all, of necessity, taken as given. In the early years of OR in industry and government, the OR scientist appeared on the scene, like a regimental bandmaster invited into the officers' mess and was told what tunes to play. All he could do was to select the instruments.

Right from the beginning of industrial OR there was a discussion of how it might be possible to "solve" problems without any data and by sheer logic. Once the process of OR became well established analysts were increasingly concerned with working with management on problem description as a joint activity. However, in the early years analysts had not the self-confidence to set the problem agenda and the setting of terms of reference for an investigation was the task of management.

Soft OR springs from the academic study of the process of problem setting adds a joint activity between the manager and the analyst (refs 2 and 3). Soft systems methodology takes as its building blocks six constructs:

1   Who gains or loses from the activities?
2   Who performs the activities?
3   Since every activity of any living process involves:
    Input → Transformation → Output
    What is the transformation?
4   What is the viewpoint that makes this definition meaningful?
5   Who can stop the activity?
6   What are the constraints?

This approach (see refs 4, 5 and 6) is a powerful catalyst in refining the view of the problem. Often these approaches make a distinction between the analyst's view and "the real world". It may be commented that this "real world" is itself as subjective as the analyst's view. Indeed some philosophers maintain that the real world does not exist. Alternatively the world of the analyst is every bit as real as the "outside world" and to talk of the "real world" can be a warning signal that the analyst does not feel part of it.

Those who have experienced OR carried out in industry or commerce or government will have sympathy with this. It is so difficult, so often, to obtain a valid universal consensus of what is "really" happening that one can doubt that "reality" exists. (The reader is left as an exercise to define the reality of the situation in Northern Ireland.)

But real or not, the world has to be dealt with and, SSM is established as a successful way of leading to a coherence of view between all those associated with or affected by a purposeful activity. It is useful to ask what is the robustness of this coherent view; if another analyst had acted as catalyst or if another process of discussions and resolution had been followed would the conclusions have been the same? Most would agree that the answer to this question is "No". And what happens if the discussants refuse to agree?

There is one question which is akin to Sherlock Holmes's dog which did not bark in the night. This is the question of the effect of language on the process of problem description. We have referred to the point that all data are value laden and therefore include a hidden bias. Language itself contains a hidden bias and this is illustrated and discussed vividly by de Bono (ref 7). All OR, including soft systems OR, is discussed in language which may then be translated into mathematics and back out again into language. de Bono points out that the English language is excellent for description but poor for perception and the process of model construction is one in which perception is more important than description:

> In a sense language is a museum of ignorance. Every word and concept has entered language at a state of relative ignorance compared to our present greater experience. But the words and concepts are frozen into permanence by language and we must use these words and concepts to deal with present-day reality. This means that we may be forced to look at things in a very inadequate way.
>
> The word "design" should be a very important word because it covers all aspects of putting things together to achieve an effect. In fact language usage has made it into a word with very restricted meaning. We think of design only in terms of graphics, engineering and architecture. To many people it simply means visual appearance as in fashion.
>
> Language means that we can only see things as they were, not as they might be.

There is, however, another serious criticism of the process of problem definition and description. This is the tendency of the researcher to define problems in such a way that he will be able to "solve" them. Since problems do not exist in any concrete form but rather as ideas in our heads, there is a latent subjectivity. No one wants to be useless. There is an internal pressure on each of us to define any perceived problem in such a way that we then become useful to its solution. This pressure is present in SSM but it is not often explicitly acknowledged. Since problems are ideas, the use of the words "problem owner" in soft systems analysis is unfortunate, for who can own an idea?

All processes of reasoning have one characteristic that is inevitable but curiously unremarked. This is that the process is oral (mostly) and written (occasionally) but is always verbal. Verbal reasoning is a highly elitist activity and such processes erect a large keep-out sign to those of lesser educational achievements. Quantitative methods are more open to more people to understand and to participate in than the processes of logical qualitative arguments.

We have seen how a group of experts reacting to the death of an elderly woman each diagnosed it in terms of their own expertise. Who can say that the OR analyst would refrain from saying that the problem was an OR problem of the allocation of resources from limited budgets? Would the soft systems methodologist refrain from stating that it was really a problem in which root definitions were needed from an SSM approach?

Can they all be right?

Probably they can all be right, but many of them would be loath to concede the problem to the others or even to concede that other approaches were equally good. The point, that is so often overlooked, is that the analyst is not some neutral castrated body sitting in the theatre seats commenting on the action. He is not even the part author of the drama, he is up there on stage acting his head off. Moreover he is doing it in his own interests, even though he may feel completely benign.

It is a sad fact that most analysis is carried out in self-contained boxes in which the approach to a problem can be mathematical, or "soft", or "hard" or via information technology (IT). The sadness is induced because often there is no concern with other boxes. It is still rare in practice for a soft systems approach to incorporate the leverage of sophisticated IT and even more rare to read of an IT solution which starts from a "soft" basis. And in all these there is no mention of the time by which an answer must be provided. Similar criticisms can be made of the mathematical modeller, who may start from an objective which must be expressible algebraically and a "hard" modeller who may accept too easily the problem as handed down by management and then fail to consider a full range of options.

We can conclude that if we want to be effective, all those concerned with the drama, all the actors, must agree on the reasons for the work. They will all have different objectives and desires for what they will get out of it, but they must at least agree to allow it to proceed.

Are There Any Value Free Data?

If so trivial a case as calculating the cost of driving a car from London to Bristol is so difficult, (see p. 20) what can one say about the really complex problems involved in deciding whether to close down a factory? The point is that, unlike physical sciences where mass, volume, velocity, density are definable, measurable and exist independent of purpose, costs can only be related to purpose and it is meaningless to ask an accountant the cost of anything without specifying the purpose to which the information will be put.

All information of a quantitative nature is in a unit of measure. The purchase cost of a newspaper is 35p per copy no matter how often one reads it nor how many people read it. The cost of going to the theatre is £20 per person per visit. The implicit assumption is that one's time spent in reading the newspaper or in going to the theatre is not part of the cost. In the health care field, it is by a particular value system, namely that the consultants' time is of infinite value compared with the time of the patient, that hospital appointments systems have been structured, and this is even more extreme (if it is possible to be more extreme than infinity and zero), in the way in which court cases are scheduled by a criminal justice system.

The analyst should always look at data and information to discover what the value system is. The decisions taken by management tell one a great deal about the latent value system, and the data which management uses tell one much about the management itself.

Where data are kept and how it is classified are clues to a value system. To look at the way files are classified is also instructive. For example, until recently, the UK National Health Service filed data on patients according to who provided the service to them. A patient who went from GP to hospital outpatients, and then to a stay in hospital and then subsequently was transferred to another hospital, and from there to a consultant and back to another GP would have had a set of separate records kept by each service provider. There would not have been a single file just for the patient alone. This suggests that the value of the NHS is as a provider of service and employment and is not primarily related to the patient.

To summarise so far, there may be neutral facts, but there are no neutral data. The value system is implicit in:

1 What is available.
2 What is used.
3 What is ignored.
4 The units of measurement.

In general, information and data are personally retained by an individual within a system for one of two reasons:

1 There is a compulsion, legal or managerial, that it must be retained and available.
2 The information will enhance the status and power of the person who holds it.

Can the Analyst Stand in Some Sterilised Zone?

It seems to be the case that many analysts assume that they are invisible and most of the accounts of how to carry out research assume that the analyst acts as an enabler in a purely benign way. There is, unfortunately, no way of confirming or refuting the effect of the analyst.

In the original classic mode of OR, the analyst took a problem as defined, collected the data and analysed them. There seems to be no interaction between the analyst and the analysis. A linear programme is a linear programme is a linear programme. But there is in fact a very rich interaction. Within the LP mode there will be assumptions and choices to be made by the analyst – even the assumptions of linearity itself. Using LP assumes that there is a unique single objective function and universally acceptable constraints.

Why use LP anyway? The discussions which lead to the problem being defined, in which the analyst himself will take part, will influence the technical approach. Most analysts will lean to particular techniques and these techniques will even significantly affect the objective function and, in doing so, they will also affect the type of objective which can be dealt with.

Of course, the interaction does not end at this minimal level. The process of research will involve the analyst in constant discussions to tease out objectives, priorities, forms and units of measurement and all those underlying motivations which are never explicitly stated. In all of these the analyst will be interacting at many different levels with all those actors and participants in the problem arena. This relationship is certainly not that of master (management) and servant (analyst). Nor is it one of patient (management) and psychiatrist (analyst). At its best it is a symbiosis between equals, but the analyst must always remember that he has no skill in management to offer per se.

This does not make the task of management easier. Indeed OR demands a higher level management to face the real problems of choice. It also takes the analyst beyond the arithmetic and the algebra. Arithmetic and algebra are easy because there is always a right answer and only one right answer to boot. But this process also takes the analyst into problems of morality and ethical behaviour.

On Whose Behalf is the Analysis Being Carried Out?

In all human activity there are moral and ethical dimensions and this applies particularly in modelling. We are surrounded, in this activity, by various stakeholders – those who pay, or employ, us to model, our employers (not necessarily the same), the fellow workers, the owners (for a local authority, the council; for a commercial enterprise, the shareholders), the public at large. The list is almost endless because society itself is a system.

The greatest difficulties are caused when modelling in the public domain. A local authority invites us to consider the planning problems of building a new factory, or helping decide the line a motorway will take. We may personally find it immoral that people may be turned out of their homes, with poor compensation, if certain alternatives are taken. The local authority – elected representatives – may wish some alternatives to be kept secret as long as possible, while still being within the law, in order to maximise the chance of their "pet scheme" going through. One can fabricate scenarios at will.

Many, perhaps most, analysts, may feel that as long as what they do is legal and is professionally competent, then that is sufficient. It is in the "Render unto Caesar" case, where the principle is simple and its interpretation is complex, that difficulty lies. It is certainly the case that one's environment dominates. Academics have much more freedom of choice as to what they do, and their ethical problems are minor compared with those who are in commercial, competitive and (especially) governmental environments.

By their own nature and because of their desire to contribute to the public good, analysts face the problems more starkly than others. There is no slap on, user friendly answer. Those entering the profession should be aware that if they really think about what they are doing, then they will be faced with choices. The only principle is that when one does have a dilemma one should be open and honest about it and declare how one has reacted.

What Are the Pitfalls?

The first pitfall to be avoided is that of being drawn into a discussion of whether or not this process of modelling in general, or of operational research in particular, is a science. Those who declare OR to be a science or not to be a science do so without defining what they mean by a science and what they mean by OR. In these terms anything can be defined as a science or defined as not a science. Different bodies classify it in different ways. The establishment view is that it is a science, in the sense that it is recognised as such by the British Royal Society and is covered for financial support by the Science and Engineering Research Council. In universities in the UK it can be classified either in the hard science area or in some area related to business studies. Many American universities group it with economics and finance, i.e. in the social sciences. The reality is that philosophically, apart from pay and rations, it does not matter one bit. It does, however, give some people a wonderful excuse for getting cross with each other.

Chapter 13 will deal with the practical organisation of research. The assumptions which underlie the practice are first that we are dealing with "problems". Problems are not those exercises so beloved of some academics in which there is a unique correct answer, which can be achieved by the techniques of the preceding chapter in a textbook. As we have seen, a problem is ephemeral and highly subjective. Our assumption is that the "problem" which exists only in the mind can be revealed, described and discussed in words of language.

Words are clumsy instruments and their very meaning can be different in subtle ways to different people. Just as we have no means of ever knowing whether the word "red" describes the same colour as seen by different people, so we have no means of knowing the personal reaction to words. The first big assumption is that language can cope with the process of description and reasoning and that all can join in the discussions on an equal footing.

The second assumption in modelling is that what we can describe can be measured. The measure may be a direct attribute (the size of a pay packet) or it may be a surrogate (such as labour turnover to measure morale).

The third assumption is that these measures are descriptions of a system of causes and effects, that there is an underlying logic in the problem area and if some things occur then these occurrences will affect the probability of other things occurring.

The fourth assumption is that there are decision points and that the continuum of life is, or can be, fractured by separate moments when, so to speak, the points on the railway line can be changed. To confuse the analogy even more, the assumption is also (fifthly) that at these points we can stop the world, get off, build a model and then get back on again and find everything the same.

The sixth assumption is that the process of collecting data does not change the data themselves. For example if one asks a sales manager the probability that next year's quarter's sales will exceed 5000 units, the very fact that he has assigned a probability may affect the probability itself. For if he estimates the probability as 80% he may then concentrate his efforts on making it happen.

In the face of all this it is small wonder that much interesting research is in the area of problem description. There is a danger, however, that the interest is restricted to the description per se. In many accounts of problem structure and management there is no consideration of time – that is – "When is the answer required?" There are many cases where the problem is clear and the time scale pressing. The moment the *Titanic* hits the iceberg is no time to discuss whether icebergs really exist.

Equally, because we are dealing with living systems which are changing during our research there must be a sense of urgency. Tristram Shandy remarked that when he started writing his autobiography it took him two years to write the story of the first six months of his life. When OR fails, it does so, not because of technical incompetence, but by the time a solution is proposed the problem has gone away, or it has been solved by someone else or most commonly, it has been wrongly defined.

It is easy in the early stages of an OR study to get involved in detailed reflective discussions. There is, however, no substitute for trying something out, or in the vernacular, to get stuck in. The principle of Napoleon in fighting a battle – "On s'engage et puis on voit", was repeated by Lenin. "On s'engage et puis on voit", is a good principle for research.

References

1 Ackoff, R.L. (1978). *The Art of Problem Solving*, Wiley, New York.
2 Rosenhead, J. (1989). Rational Analysis for a Problematic World, Wiley, Chichester.
3 Bryant, J.W. (1989). *Problem Management*, Wiley, Chichester.
4 Checkland, P.B. in Ref 2.

5   Checkland, P.B. (1988). Soft systems methodology: overview, *J. Appl. Sys. Anal.*, **15**, 27–30.
6   Checkland, P.B. (1981). *Systems Thinking, Systems Practice*, Wiley, Chichester.
7   de Bono, E. (1990). *I Am Right, You Are Wrong*, Viking, London.

For a considered professional view of the Practice of OR see: Report of the Commission on the Future Practice of Operational Research. *J. Opl. Res. Soc.* (1986), **37**, 9, 829–86.

Chapter 13

Practical Matters

The paradigm of the scientific approach with which the last chapter began is worth inspecting again. It appears logical in a textbook but life is never like that. In a laboratory this process might well apply but a laboratory is a machine for isolating research from environment effects and OR is essentially a study of the environment itself. From the first day possible "solutions" lie embedded in the muddle and the mess of the reality with which we are grappling. If we can understand the problem the answer will come out of it, because the answer is not separate from the problem (ref 1). The first theories we formulate which carry within themselves possible solutions arise simultaneously with the problems (ref 2). There is a parallel with the work of the sculptor who approaches the block of marble or granite not with the concept of imposing his or her own structure on it by writ of force but rather by liberating from within it the figure which will emerge.

If no study could start until the objectives are known then very few studies would start at all. In almost all studies an initial statement of the objective tends to be very fuzzy: "We are worried about our stock out rate." "We think we ought to increase our acquisition rate of new accounts." "How can we reduce the queues of vessels waiting to enter the port?" "What provision need we make for extra domiciliary care for old people?" All of these relate to real case studies and all of them are changed several times during the studies themselves.

Research groups no longer, or should no longer, wait patiently like taxis on a cab rank, for customers to arrive and give a destination. This is an interactive science not a reactive one and analysts must know their parent organisation well enough to suggest where help can most usefully be given. Note should be made of the assumption in the preceding paragraph that the proper place for this research is within the organisation being helped. Outside help from consultants or from academics is specially needed:

1   To provide skills and experiences that do not exist within the organisation.
2   To externalise the stress which may occur from a study in a highly sensitive area – this can include the need for secrecy.
3   To meet a peak load.

There is a difficulty for those who have never been employed inside an industrial, commercial or governmental organisation in that they may not appreciate how the problem looks from the manager's side of the desk and it is dangerous to assume one acquires this knowledge by spending a sabbatical in industry or government.

To return now to the main argument, what are the criteria to be used to assess those areas where research can help? First we should remember the parrot cry of management at the end of so many studies. "Your answer is only plain common sense" hides a great truth. We are indeed dealers in common sense, as it is called. The difficulty is that it is not all that common and can sometimes be badly wrong. It is a pity that some OR training assumes that common sense is possessed by everyone and that it is always correct. The consequence is to concentrate solely on techniques rather than skill. Hence OR scientists, when asked by management what they can do, may list a set of technical tricks, or problems defined in terms of techniques. Other specialists – economists, accountants, social scientists – do not fall into this trap and exhibit themselves as bright, intelligent, perceptive and sensitive people. Management, particularly senior management, are interested in the diagnosis of the patient and not in the surgeon's instruments. Analysts should have more self-confidence.

This difference between technique and skill is very important. The *Oxford English Dictionary* defines technique as the mechanical or formal part of an art and quotes Grove: "A player may be perfect in technique and yet have neither soul nor intelligence." Skill is defined as "Practical knowledge in combination with ability". Skill in fact is the delivery of technique under pressure.

This is not the digression it might have appeared. Its importance is that the analyst must never look on project opportunities in terms of techniques. Of course a very strong subconscious pressure will be for an analyst to define, describe or approach a problem in such a way as to maximise the probability of "solving" it. As has been remarked, most failures in OR occur because the solution proposed "solves" the wrong problem. To approach all problems by the same technique means that eventually there will be no problems left which can be solved in that particular way and the OR group will be disbanded.

PROJECT SELECTION

There are two ways in which a research group can list potential problem areas. The first is by logic, and the second is by emotion. In the logical approach, the organisation is mapped, rather like an old-fashioned management tree, in terms of the decision points. What decisions are taken, where and how are they taken and by whom? This (long) list is then sorted and culled by four criteria:

1 For which of these are quantitative data available or can be obtained?
2 In which is there a real range of choice?
3 Which of these are sensitive in terms of the goals of the organisation?
4 Is there a willingness to change?

We take these in turn:

1 Remember that in this section, as indeed in the rest of this book, we concentrate on analysis via a modified scientific method. The basis therefore is number and quantity. The fallacy is to accept quantitative data because they are there, irrespective of the measurements and assumptions involved. We are also concerned with those illuminating problems where a combination of fresh thinking, lateral thinking and "common sense" yield a solution (ref 3). We do not have any management skills to offer, we have a skill in data collection, analysis and synthesis. The quantitave must always be present.
2 Often the range of choice is much more restricted than we might think. Incoming governments who have gained office by promising wide and radical change, find themselves making small changes, because the room for manoeuvre is much less than they thought. Often the range of choice of big decisions is pre-empted by many small decisions which have already been taken. A parent's decision to change to another job can be restricted by the need not to move house to another district, for reasons of children's schools, or even because new carpets have just been fitted at home.
3 One reason why so many organisations survive is that for many decisions the sensitivity is low. In other words over a wide range of choice the consequence is approximately the same. There will be other decision variables which are highly sensitive, for example, when interest rates increase many decisions yield very different payoffs and, indeed, bankruptcy rates spiral upwards. But as has been seen in the Third Life,

the reorder process in inventory control, which is affected by interest rates, has but little effect on costs over quite a wide range. It is always useful to have a crude and simple check by taking alternative decisions to extremes. Sometimes in a transportation study the effect of the constraints is such that the difference between the least cost and greatest cost solutions is very small.

Not only sensitivity itself is important. There is also the question of whether the project is significant. Sometimes OR seems to consist of large brains being applied to small problems and this should be anathema. The small problem can demand sophisticated mathematics or computing power but the result has negligible effect, even though the sensitivity range between the extreme solutions is relatively great. From time to time, for reasons of goodwill, such problems may have to be analysed, but care should be taken to avoid the inevitable result of being looked on as a small problem group staffed by big brains.

4 The researcher is not necessarily invited to study a problem because the manager wants to have it resolved. Sometimes the invitation is extended so as to allow time for a lengthy piece of work, which will last long enough for the manager to get out and move to another job. (Politicians are adept at this.) In other cases a team, even an in house team, can be invited to provide an alternative target for frustration and anger and thereby to take the heat off the management concerned. Alternatively the research can buy time for the problem to dissolve or simply to disappear. Research teams have to be wise as serpents in not taking on nonprojects offered for self-saving by management. Another aspect of this is that the project should not be in a sacred cow zone, that is, aspects of an organisation that will not admit of particular forms of change.

These logical steps to determine a problem area may not always be appropriate, especially so as they are time consuming. The alternative is the emotional method of taking a thermometer around the organisation to see where the temperature rises. This is the same as to follow the sound of gunfire.

The Emotional Approach

No organisation is a happy band of brothers and sisters marching into battle under a banner carried by its chief executive. Organisations divide into parts. These parts are given different criteria of performance and objectives and, almost always, these criteria build in conflict. Reference has already been made to the effect of criteria of performance applied to parts of an organisation creating conflict. Where different parts of a company buy and sell to each other by internal transfer prices then great anger exists between the most lovable people.

In many years of analysis of management problems, from the manufacturing and production problems in the early days of OR right up to the social problems of today the writer has always found without exception that conflict within the organisation looms very large on the agenda of management. Following the sound of gunfire takes one to the centre of real problems, but be careful. Gunfire means that the bullets are flying and the researcher himself may get hit. As mentioned in the last chapter it is always prudent to assess whether the problem can be resolved or dissolved.

The First Questions in a Project

Having now obtained a project which satisfies these criteria, what are the most important questions to be faced? There are three:

1 When is the answer needed?
2 How accurate must it be?
3 What form must it take to be usable?

When is the Answer Needed?

This is the most unasked question of all. Timing is very important and it is better to have half an answer on time rather than perfection too late. This can affect the process of the research itself. A method such as a large-scale mathematical programme in which darkness reigns until the last second when the light shines should be avoided if a "quick and dirty" answer is likely to be needed. Actually in most research there is a gradual revelation of the answer. On the other hand, there is the danger of the answer to the above question being given as "Today". Sometimes it is needed today and then quick methods can be used. Beware, however, of the managers who want everything today. This betrays that lack of forward thinking and planning which is inimical to research itself.

There is a natural process to research, since it must always be based on understanding and understanding cannot be hastened. Quick answers of necessity demand a prior understanding of how the organisation works, (what might be termed the "management technology"). Equally, rapid data handling can provide answers too quickly to allow the researcher time for gestation. Some managers seem to believe that if it takes a woman nine months to have a baby, then nine women cooperating together should be able to do it in one month.

How Accurate?

At one extreme the answer may only need to get the sign right. Arguments from economists about taxation and its effects are not only about the measurement of the ensuing change in inflation but even whether the effect is inflationary or deflationary. If only the sign can be forecast then a major victory will have been won. The effect of advertising on sales may well have to be approximate and, given the very complex nature of the interaction of computing sales policies, advertising and promotions in a market place, an approximate answer may be good enough.

But for product blending in oil distillation, a precise answer will be needed, not only because experience shows that the maximum improvement one might expect is of the order of 4% but because an improvement of only 0.5% of a very large sum of money is still a large sum.

The Form of the Solution

Everyone has methods of working and we all view the world through different spectacles. There have been many cases where impressive solutions have been produced which cannot be implemented because the organisation does not work that way.

There is a (true) story about this. A company could run itself excellently without any day-to-day involvement by the owners (who were the President, and two Vice Presidents). One of the Vice Presidents noted that although the company's share of market was increasing steadily, the market itself was declining and unless there was a change of course the company would disappear.

Their thinking was to introduce a new product line and an academic consultant was asked to help. He studied the production technology and the modes of sales and distribution, following this with a search for products with a similar technology, sales and distribution. The first one was obvious – plumbing. But when the owners were presented with this they were disappointed. They said they want something "better" without defining "better", but that they would certainly recognise "better" when they saw it. So the search continued and came up with exotic tools used in aircraft maintenance. This was an improvement on plumbing but still not acceptable. Successive ideas were rejected until one day, while driving to the company, the consultant heard on his car radio a discussion on the recently developed transistor and at his subsequent discussion threw in desperation, the idea, "what about transistors?" "Great, wonderful, marvellous, this is it!" Came the response, followed by the supplementary question: "What is a transistor?"

This gave a strong hint of what was meant by "better": it meant that they wanted more fun out of the business and to be more involved in it. As Townsend of Avis later put it: "If you're not in business for profit or for fun, what the hell are you doing there?"

Subsequently the three owners went into the hydraulic coupling and valve business and lived happily ever after.

How to Conduct Research

Having decided on a project and on how to progress it, what should be borne in mind by the research team? There is a very important *don't*.

Don't take the project away from management, and then work on it in the back room of the research team even if you report back on time. If the research is taken away from the people who are going to apply it, then no matter what else is done, it will not be implemented.

Don't get pushed down into lower and lower levels of management. In the author's personal experience this renders the research useless before you start. There must be regular contact either with a single senior manager or, preferably, with an ad hoc group of those who will affect, or be affected by, the research. This group should meet regularly, according to the progress of the work. There will be three important dividends:

1 Access to data.
2 Criticism of data and constraints.
3 Implementation.

Access to Data

Research is an inconvenience to line staff who are not judged by their helpfulness to researchers. Help will be avoided, denied or be positively misleading. But the knowledge that the data or graphs produced by a junior or middle manager will leap-frog intervening levels and land on the desk of the big chief causes the most angry lion to coo like a dove, especially if his/her name is on the data. Access therefore is easy.

Criticism

From the outside of a problem, the pattern of causes and effects can be misleadingly simple. There is the net curtain syndrome. What goes on in a household of an apparently loving family, behind the net curtains in the window, is sometimes unknown and often distorted. Similarly in a management setting, the reality behind the management tree, mission statements, job descriptions, responsibilities and duties can be murky indeed and will distort not only the perception of the observer but also the possibilities of implementation. For an in-house research group this can be difficult but it can be even more difficult for those imported to carry out a study unless the managers find it easier to unburden themselves to strangers. *Always* be suspicious of mission statements.

A steering group can help the research through the minefield of personal relationships. But it does much more than this. It can, and will, comment on the validity of the data by, for example, cutting back on marketing departments' inevitably optimistic sales projections and increasing the capacity figures of production, which are over-pessimistic because slack has been added. Subjective estimates can be confirmed or refuted in this way.

There will, finally, be the formulation of constraints. Some of these will belong to the culture of the organisation. For example a major US brewery specialising in beers at the top end of the market, rejected considered analytic advice that they could make even more profits by expanding into the lower end of the market, with the response that they took pride in their product and did not want to be associated with the production of rubbish. Other constraints will be in terms of behaviour. A research team has to adapt to the colour and texture of surroundings – the parallel with the camouflage of animals in the bush is exact. Place yourself in the culture of the organisation. This does not mean changing yourself. It means understanding other people.

Research teams can unwittingly cause cultural offence. A team visiting coal mines in Kent found that the underground temperatures were so high and the atmosphere so humid that the mineworkers were naked apart from boots, belt (to hold the cap-lamp battery) and hard hat. The following week in a Yorkshire coal mine, the same team caused offence by walking to the showers without a strategic towel.

Other constraints can be technical or managerial and frozen out of history. The XYZ company may have priority for a particular product for no known reason except that it has always been so. In a university, particular departments which once were important can continue to get good treatment, even when they have become a backwater. These constraints can only be teased out – the fact that something has always been so means that it can be accepted without question. (Analysts should not be complacent about this – it is endemic in their own research also.) The best way to discover the unspoken and the unquestionable is to go first of all for a constraint-free solution and then to observe the responses "We cannot do that because . . . "

Remember the working rule that often it is better to remove a constraint and take any feasible solution than to optimise within the restricted set of constraints.

Implementation

Undoubtedly some senior managers will come to the first meeting of the steering group with feelings of resignation – like martyrs going to the stake.

But this work is fascinating and exciting and any researcher who cannot transmit this excitement to others is in the wrong job.

The managers will be so fascinated, that there is the danger that they will want to do all the research themselves. They should be resisted, but they should always be a part of the team. It is often the case that during the research the outline of the solution gradually emerges and so the implementation does not consist of the planting in the earth of management a new tree, but rather the gradual grafting of a shoot which will imperceptibly grow. The one thing no one in charge wants is to be surprised.

An enthusiastic head of an internal OR group (not the writer) was invited to meet a senior director to present the results of a study. On entering the office, he sat down opposite the director, opened the file, fixed his director with a steely gaze and said, "Sir, I have a great surprise for you. Do you know how much money you wasted last year?" The meeting was short. After leaving it at high speed, the head remarked, "These really are very difficult people to deal with. I thought he would have been pleased."

Small wonder that the senior director was displeased. He was being put in the spotlight for failure. The researcher should have said, "Sir, I may be mistaken but I think there is a way in which you might be able to reduce your costs quite significantly next year." The object is the same, but the message gives the glory to the director.

Such disasters should never happen in a steering group, for its members will feel that they are responsible for all the achievements of the research. It is not only glory which is the prize. There is also an awkward moral dilemma which can be resolved. Often at the end of a study, which does not have a steering group, the researchers will know what the organisation should do. It might be that on balance of costs and probabilities the decision ought, for example, in the opinion of a team planning for a hospital building programme, to be to build a new 800-bed hospital in Derby. There will be some medical administrators and consultants in favour, others (pace Machiavelli) will be against. Those against may be people who want the hospital in a specific other town, or consultants who are angry because their speciality is neglected or reduced in the new hospital. All of these have the common aim of rejecting the report, even though some may favour Leicester and others Nottingham, and others favour orthopaedics. The team leader faces a dilemma. To what extent does he push what he regards as correct? He probably knows more about the alternatives than anyone else, for the others know only their own case. He will inevitably be asked by those against such questions as:

- "Are you certain of your cost data?"
- "Are you satisfied that you have measured patient need properly?"
- "Are you certain of your clinical and diagnostic forecasts?"

- "Are the loadings you have assumed for surgical wards, pathology laboratory, X-ray laboratory, domiciliary visits, outpatient follow up, all correct?"

To these his truthful answers will be uniformly "No, No, No and No". He will then be torn to shreds by those who are anti, he will be publicly humiliated and the wrong decision may be taken. On the other hand if he answers uniformly "Yes, Yes, Yes and Yes", he will not be speaking the truth but the right decision may then be taken.

The problem is that no one knows what is the correct decision because no one knows the "correct" answers to the four questions. In this case it is no use dissolving the problem and looking at something else, because the money is in the budget, it has been allocated, it cannot be spent on anything else and a hospital is going to be built somewhere.

The steering group solves the dilemma. To them the researcher can be totally honest. The data, estimates, forecasts can all be laid out and their provenance examined. Redundant, or dominated, solutions can be excluded. Robustness can be calculated and gradually a solution will emerge. Sometimes it does not matter which of two or three alternatives is undertaken and where there is dispute over some of the input data solutions can be presented in the form

$$\text{If } A \rightarrow X \tag{13.1}$$

$$\text{If } B \rightarrow Y \tag{13.2}$$

$$\text{If } C \rightarrow Z \tag{13.3}$$

The argument following the publication of the report will be on the higher level of A, B or C (the data input) which does leave the *amour propre* of the protagonists and antagonists relatively undented. In those cases where the steering group themselves are universally agreed on what should be done, then they themselves will fight for the solution with a dedication, energy and animal cunning, such as to leave the research leader breathless.

The composition of the steering group should be small enough to enable everyone to attend all meetings and large enough to encompass relevant interests. There will probably be a lead department for the research, two or three other affected departments should be there, plus those connected with the data, e.g. the accountant, together with the team leader who acts as secretary. (This has the advantage that he is seen as the servant, while in effect he is the most influential of them all.) The lead department should supply a (very) senior man as chairman and no one should be invited to join the working party simply because they have time to spare. People who have time to spare, have it to spare because they are not very useful.

Location of Research

No study has any chance of success unless management, and relevant specialists, are involved. The other necessary conditions for success are that the team should have:

1 Access to the decision takers.
2 Access to data, information and mores.
3 Access to the corridors of power.
4 Responsibility for the success or failure of its recommendations.
5 Security of tenure from political attack from within.

Everyone would like to report directly to the chairman of the board or, at the lowest, to the managing director. But there are dangers in operating at that level. These stratospheric and exotic creatures can be transient phenomena and a sympathetic MD can easily be replaced by a hostile one. Additionally if one wants to play ball in the major league one must have a major league research team. At the top level perspectives are different and it is of little use if the research team can answer any questions put. Their task at that level is to set the agenda of questions, to be proactive not reactive.

An alternative is to put the team in a major operating department, for example; marketing, production, purchasing. The difficulty is that very soon one then becomes regarded as *de facto*, if not *de jure*, the spokesperson of the parent department. Another choice could be the management services group. The problem here is that some groups are, frankly, backwaters staffed by line management failures. To put OR in such a group gives it the kiss, if not of death, then certainly of debility.

To locate OR within an IT department has greater attractions. We live on information and to be able to take part in the flow of an organisational life blood is exciting. It is of interest to note that there is no accepted doctrine. Some larger organisations put OR into IT, others, where OR and IT are together, then force them apart. It all depends on what sort of IT department one has. We have reflected that one reason for the rise and rise of accountants is that not only did they create the information and distribute it, they also knew its value, interpreted it and presented it in a manner which was compatible with the needs of management. At present it is not universally evident that IT specialists are following that example. So often they seem to be facing their wonderful systems and have turned their back on the management – only turning round to talk to them when they need money to buy even more wonderful systems.

If the IT is outward looking, interpretive and aware of management's needs (as distinct from what they want) then this is a good home. The broad hint of the last paragraphs lead us to suggest that putting OR in with the accountants has much to recommend it. This is provided that it is a

278 _____ The Craft of Decision Modelling

modern, forward looking department. It is of interest that the major commercial consultancies available in OR are provided by the large accounting firms.

In the end, everything comes down to people. The research team and its characteristics, the managers and support staff, the attitudes of mind of those within, the responses of its environment, all come together in a glorious melange. There is no correct answer to the question of how to succeed. We can only point to necessary conditions for success and sufficient conditions for failure.

Reference

1 Krishnamurti, J. (1987). *The Penguin Krishnamurti Reader*, Penguin, London.
2 Popper, K. (1976). *Unended Quest*, Fontana, Glasgow.
3 Ackoff, R.L. (1991). *Ackoff's Fables*, Wiley, Chichester.

Chapter 14

The Future

We start this survey of possibilities and probabilities by reminding ourselves of the vast changes that are taking place in our subject. Even a short
time ago the material in the first section of this book would have been a
sufficient grounding for the embryo analyst. The subjects variously referred
to as management science or operational research were omnibus collections
of techniques, algorithms, modelling processes all linked by an attitude of
mind regarding decision making. For decades past, OR groups had set out
to be interdisciplinary in nature – all human life was there. But this was
no longer the case by the end of the 1970s. Whether by pressure from outside, or lack of will from within, there grew up other relevant areas, ergo-
nomics, cybernetics, probabilistic management accounting, system analysis,
"soft" OR and, most important of all, information technology (IT), so that
classical OR found itself no longer a total orchestra of specialities but an
instrument in an even larger orchestra. No longer is OR called "interdisciplinary", it is often referred to as a discipline in its own right.

This has been seen particularly in universities and in this penultimate
chapter we reflect on the future of OR education. At this first stage, however, we can note the changes in universities' treatment of OR. When the
first university departments of OR were created, they proudly flew the
interdiscipline flag. In doing so they provided a welcome recognition that
the map of knowledge as drawn by older universities needed re-drawing.
The boundaries of subjects, frozen out of history, were outdated. In a matrix
format for example, the history, language, philosophy, culture, art of
France, could for the first time be treated in the context not of five different
subjects, but as one related subject. Even such diverse topics as religious
studies and marketing were brought together. This re-drawing of the map
welcomed a topic such as OR and as long as universities expanded all was

sweetness and light. But it is a law of life that eventually all expansion ends and in universities expansion was followed by contraction, if not in absolute terms, but certainly in terms of resources per unit of output. No longer was there either sweetness or light and there was a retreat into the academic laager. The criterion of judgement was publications and not practice, and publication journals, whose editors were almost totally academic, suffered from the same squeeze and became more pure.

Hence OR retreated into a single discipline and OR scientists had to compete for resources, and for the glittering prizes, as mathematicians. In general, mathematicians looked on those in OR as fallen mathematicians who were doing inferior hack things for money, in the same way, that some kinds of women may regard other women as "fallen women" – for the same reason.

The consequence is that OR at present is uncertain of its professional development. This is strange since the central distinguishing feature of OR, an attitude of mind to problem solving, is both endemic and imperishable. We therefore contemplate the future of the subject within the context of a range of threats, reassured by the fact that these threats, to use a hackneyed observation, are actually opportunities.

The danger for the subject is that there are some parts of it which seem unwilling to coexist. We have referred to the *soft* systems approach which has grown in the past decade and also to the explosive growth of IT. The unfortunate reality of the present situation is that often neither of these seems to recognise the other. With few exceptions, pace Eden (ref 1), the standard texts on soft OR make but little reference to the impact of the availability of information on problem description and on the generation of strategic options. Similarly, texts on IT discuss management problems as though they exist in some uniquely recognisable concrete form. The nature of IT and its explosive growth, a growth that is so rapid that any publication about it is out of date by the time it appears, seem to ignore the strategic possibilities of soft OR.

This is said in no pejorative sense but as a clinical observation. However, one can but reflect on the difficulty OR has in preserving its unity, if two component parts seem not to realise that the other exists. The danger in any subject is that component parts fight each other, in the same way that management departments such as production and marketing, fight each other.

Hayakawa (ref 2) refers to the struggle between species and distinguishes between two kinds of struggle for survival – the interspecific, as between wolves and deer or between men and bacteria, and the intraspecific as between members of the same species as when rats fight other rats or men fight other men. A great deal of evidence from biology, according to Hayakawa, indicates that those species which have developed elaborate means of intraspecific competition often render themselves unfit for inter-specific competition and become threatened with extinction. Cooperation within the species is essential to survival. One can only deplore the zeal with which so many researchers attack the work of others in the same field, who have a different approach, and the extent to which so many university research groups fail to be catholic, or broad church in their approach.

Even at meetings of scientific societies those attending will largely be those who agree with the philosophies of the speaker: soft systems researchers do not often go to IT meetings and vice versa. All this withdrawal into camps, all this view that he who is not with me is against me, will lead, as it has always done, to self-destruction.

So much of what we follow is fashionable for a time and then gets absorbed into the mainstream or else becomes discarded. We have been through periods when the hot topics were work study, standard costing, mathematical models, business games, planning programming and budgeting systems, management by objectives, cybernetics, multi-criteria decision making. Some of these have disappeared from conference agendas and have become part of the fabric of the subject. Others have simply been cast aside like last year's fashions. But OR remains while so many others have melted away.

At the time of writing we do have these two important topics which jostle for our attention, namely soft systems methodology and information technology. The curious difference between these is in their provenance. SSM has largely been developed in academia, nearly every publication is by an academic, while the provenance of IT is almost completely from commerce, industry and consultancy.

Clearly, soft OR has recognised a gap in the traditional mode of OR and reinforces the message of this book that for OR to serve to its full potential it must not only answer other people's questions but must ask the questions themselves. It is in problem description that we now have a much more specific process of evolving those things that management should be worried about, rather than those things it does worry about. In this context we suggest some of the areas in which soft OR should develop. It all stems from the recognition that words are just as value laden, just as misleading, as the quantitative data which we have previously excoriated.

Hayakawa (op. cit.) refers to the delusional nature of words, the dangers of abstractions and that everyone has different subconscious reactions to certain words. Within the process of soft OR maps are produced which link various conceptual abstractions of the problem area. The danger is that these maps can be regarded as the "reality" itself. The world of happenings in which we each live is a very small world.

So far as this world is actually seen or felt or heard, to most of us Sydney, Australia, the British Museum, a violent crowd at a football game, do not exist as if we had been there. If we ask how much we each know at first hand, it is very little indeed. Most of our knowledge is acquired from books, conversation, TV, newspapers and all our knowledge of history comes from other people in words spoken or written. And often these other people did not see the event. Nearly all knowledge comes from this verbal world and not our personal extensional world.

Out of all this we produce, as in soft OR, a map of a world which we have not visited. But a map is not the thing itself. Sometimes the map is obviously false, but is held securely. (People will not sleep on the 13th floor of a hotel, but will do so if 13 is skipped and the 13th is called the 14th.) No matter how attractive the map is, it is useless if it does not show the structure of the territory.

A danger in soft OR, recognised by some of its practitioners, is that the map is accepted as corresponding to "reality" and people use the map to take a journey. These maps are drawn as a result of a process of verbal reasoning by those who, largely, have not gained their knowledge at first hand. It is, of course, language that has made possible the progress of the human race by enabling experiences to be passed on to others. Written language has been a more safe way of preserving the integrity of the communication than the oral. In the oral, not only is there the variability of what is said from one occasion to another but more importantly, the tone of voice, the inflexion and the interplay with facial and body expression play a significant part. The way a word is said can convey a totally different meaning, not only in Mandarin, but also in English. In particular, words and inflexions have cultural connotations that will not exist outside a culture. This can cause not only offence, but actual strife. The use of four-letter words by the inarticulate is excusable as expressing a feeling that does not lie in the vocabulary of the speaker. When a striker from a car factory in the UK was interviewed on TV he remarked to the interviewer, "Its easy for you people who can talk well, but we can't tell you how we feel because we don't know the long words. So p*** off."

This is a cultural problem for all of us. Words within a culture are value laden and misleading – how often do those who come to a verbal contract genuinely have different understandings about what was agreed – but between cultures words can break down completely. The attitudes of mind also differ between cultures. The fact that soft OR is almost completely academic in its origins gives it a rigorous strength but there can sometimes be an unworldly feeling about its practice, what can be an apparently abstract contemplation of the meaning of life. Indeed one standard text lists the important matters to be covered in such an approach but does not include the time factor. One can recall Lyndon Johnson's remark when asked his reaction to attending President Kennedy's first cabinet meeting,

"They were a smart set of guys, but I wish that just one of them had run for office as a municipal dog catcher."

Those of us in research belong to a very different culture from those we are trying to help and for OR carried on in the cosy world of the researcher, it can be so difficult to convey and receive impressions, that the research can break down. The analyst who comes from the manual working class can establish a non-patronising relationship with the less well educated which his own educated children, or his own well-educated colleagues, can never achieve.

The immediate future of soft OR is, we suggest, twofold. Notwithstanding the (constructively) critical remarks above it does indeed have an important part to play, but there do seem two aspects which could be helpfully developed. The first is to work with linguistic philosophers and those who understand the relationship between language, thought and action. If this is not done the trap will be sprung in exactly the same way as the trap was sprung on those who assume that all data are valid and true. If numbers have a profound emotional content, how much more so do words, pictures and maps? The meaning of words is not in the words – it is in us. The second aspect is to encourage much more development and application by practitioners working in the fields of commerce, industry, government and in the social and service sectors. At present there does seem such an academic concentration in the research as to give it the misleading impression of being a game played by academics. This should also deflect the unnecessary hostility felt towards it by some practitioners.

INFORMATION TECHNOLOGY

When information was collected, classified and summarised by marks on pieces of paper, the flow of it could be controlled and could be made to follow the structure of authority. A central function, the brain of the firm, received information from all the organisation and, amongst other things, returned to its parts instructions, advice and also only that filtered part of what it had received which it felt was necessary. The process was much like the system of information and control by which the human body works. When large mainframe computers arrived on the scene, central management was able to use them to increase it own authority. The high cost involved gave a ready excuse for the centre to be in charge and the increase of information availability increased the power of direction of the centre.

There is a remarkable parallel to this in research by Bavelas of MIT. Bavelas was concerned with the effect of communication patterns on the effectiveness of a task oriented group. He took groups of subjects and gave them a group task – for example, to solve a jigsaw puzzle – and imposed on them a structure of communication in which they were only allowed to talk to designated people. Typical patterns are shown in Figure 14.1.

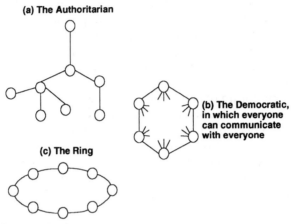

(a) The Authoritarian

(b) The Democratic, in which everyone can communicate with everyone

(c) The Ring

Figure 14.1 Communication structures

There were significant differences in enjoyment and performance by those taking part. The most popular, but least efficient, was the democratic (b). The most efficient but the least popular was the authoritarian (a). There was, however, a very interesting by-product. This was the emergence of a group leader. The authority and leadership exercised by a member of the group was not so much their inbuilt personality but was determined by the number of communication channels they possessed. For example, in the authoritarian group (a), although the diagram by its analogy with a management tree brainwashes us in to assuming that A will be the leader, in fact B emerges as the group leader because of the communication factor.

This has important parallels for management. We observe that although accountants, per se, are neither more nor less intelligent than lawyers, engineers, marketing executives, production managers and researchers, they still have emerged in authority at the centre of affairs because the financial network within an organisation is the most strong and the most centralised. Moreover, the accountant has taken the trouble to learn what the accounting information means for management.

The organisation picture has been until recently, and still is in most cases, one of central control, with an accountant on stand-by, into which data enters and instruction leaves. Every increase in the computing power at the centre sucks in more information and churns out more instructions. The consequences can be seen everywhere. It takes a wise centre to abstain from using the power it has acquired but the picture is changing with the advent of very cheap personal computing. (It is interesting to note that a small computer costing only a few hundred pounds and used by a university student has a power greater than the mainframe computer bought when he or she was born and which in today's terms would have cost over a million pounds.)

There will be an increasing move to work stations, and not only because it makes technical sense. The social ethos is a move to decentralising and away from the large monolithic, unfeeling and uncaring organisations which fill basic requirements in telecommunications, energy and utilities. We can now probably look to profound implications on the pattern of OR practice.

The cost benefit of decentralisation can be enormous. Local work stations cannot only deal with small local problems but with large complex ones as well. They create an enormous demand for their services because of this ability. The cost savings have been very large – a quoted saving in health care costs by a Yale University study, of $50 billion, and in American Airlines a reduction in network computing costs of 80%, by PCs installed at a cost of only $5 million.

The impact of IT on management is just as spectacular. Kaye (ref 3) records different areas of advance:

1 *Corporate frontiers*: the removal of middlemass control of customer/ supplier connections, integration of activities.
2 *Market strategy*: overcoming the complexity of variety. Economies of scale.
3 *Product and service strategy*: managing a larger variety of product. Increasing obsolescence of products which contain information handling devices. Reduction in new product lead time, faster response to market change, increasing market segmentation.
4 *Production and distribution*: exploiting product tracking capacity – "just in time" production.
5 *Human resources*: changing the job – moving to a small number of exceptional problem thinkers, (OR analysts should specially note that), removing barriers to communication.

Kaye also affirms the effect of this on middle management whose relay job will require fewer people but whose problem solving role will be more important, with the integration of data processing across frontiers. It is at the centre that the most important changes are taking place, however, and in many places there will be the introduction of an information manager to the chief executive team.

One of the most important features will be the effect of IT on management structure. The formal structure is a reflection both of a certain mores and of the technology of communication. Take as an example the constitution of the United States. It reflects an attitude of mind to the place of man in society and the distribution of power within a federal society. It also reflects the problem of communicating over a vast geographical area where the fastest method of transport for a person was a galloping horse, and for goods was the speed of an ox. It would be bizarre if the constitution of a United States created today was the same, given the information transmitting power. Nor would the UK national health service have created today the same structure as it did fifty years ago for the same reason.

What IT has done, which is highly significant, is to change the map of organisations by enlarging the span of control of a single person. It used to be one of the physical constants of management that seven was the maximum number of people that any one person should have reporting to them. IT, however, greatly widens the grasp of a manager and the consequence of this is that the number of levels of management is savagely reduced. Great has been the fall-out rate of middle management for this reason and the free availability of information has profound implications for the OR analyst, not least by the disappearance of the boundary between the strategic and the tactical, the short term and the long term, the departmental and the corporate, the regional and the national, the national and the international. Along with all this is the possibility of dealing with fine market segmentation combined with market integration.

Where does this lead the analyst? The experience of American Airlines, to which reference has already been made is, Thomas Cook the President of its Decision Technologies Group, one in which a small backwater group of eight people was transformed into a group of 399 researchers of whom 75 work directly for AA and the remainder work on outside consulting. This group has developed their own turnkey systems and also works closely with the data processing group. It is able, via the sophisticated IT structure to attack the central profit generating task of all airlines, namely where to fly, when to fly and what equipment to use. Old style OR would have taken separate decision models, IT on its own would have developed man/machine models for scheduling but the combination of OR and IT was able to solve high level problems of integration.

Where does this put OR? The first duty is to point to the necessity of not yielding to the temptation of concluding that all this makes the explanatory model redundant. It is easy to utilise the vast speed, power and breadth of an IT system to observe what is happening, to describe it and to "solve" a problem by means of a descriptive model. Such models can indeed be produced almost at will and there is much that can be done with massive and rapid data analysis. It also means that, assuming the future is going to be like the past, simulation models can be created and future scenarios can be generated. But we still have to explain what is happening. We can, for example, have total information about the human body, blood flows and pressures in every part, alkalinity and acidity, chemical, physical and biological data. This can be provided continuously and in profusion, via continuous brain scans and so on. All this will tell us what is happening but it will not tell the why or the how. Unless we have the why and the how answered we cannot develop prevention nor can we cure.

The point of explanatory models is that because they display their own assumptions, they can then be used for extrapolation. Descriptive models used for extrapolation are dangerous because the conditions under which they can be used are hidden. The Babylonian and the Greek models, to which reference has been made, could not have led astronomers to deduce the existence of an invisible star. Using Newton's laws, however, led to a deduction based on the orbits of the known planets and, in particular perturbations in the orbit of Uranus, concluding that there could be the existence of a previously unknown planet, named Neptune. One of the great occasions in the history of astronomy was when on a given day, at a given moment, the great telescope in Berlin was pointed in a given direction, and there was Neptune, seen for the first time. This discovery was only possible because of an explanatory law.

The second consequence of importance for the future of OR is that there will now be a plethora of decision-making points and there will therefore be a vast increase in the client base. Before this IT explosion the most important problems were centralised. This was where power was. This was where the data were. But in the new regime, information (which is power) is spread evenly over the whole structure and wherever there is a PC or a work station, there will be a problem solution capability and these problems will be on a broader base encompassing a wider range. Moreover, whereas previously OR built on a relatively small customer base with much repeat business, there will be many many potential customers and OR will have to move out of its reactive mode, of responding to top managers, and into a proactive mode of anticipating problems at work stations and PCs. The reduction in the number of levels of management means also that the work of the analyst will be more visible to the top management with all the opportunities (and dangers) that implies (see ref 4).

An extremely useful consequence of IT will be that the units of measurement will be standardised. Present practice in accounting, for example, not only makes it impossible to compare costs and revenues in different organisations, because of different accounting conventions, but also allows of different cost bases within the same organisation. Historically this has always happened until a firm central management imposes a discipline on unit measurement. It was recorded in the *Chicago Daily News*, 29 September 1948:

> before 1883 there were nearly 100 different time zones in the United States. It wasn't until November 18 of that year that . . . a system of standard time was adopted here and in Canada. Before then there was nothing but local or

"solar" time . . . The Pennsylvania Railroad in the East used Philadelphia time, which was five minutes slower than New York time and five minutes faster than Baltimore time. The Baltimore and Ohio used Baltimore time for trains running out of Baltimore, Columbus time for Ohio, Vincennes (Indiana) time for those going out of Cincinnati . . . When it was noon in Chicago, it was 12.31 in Pittsburgh, 12.24 in Cleveland, 12.17 in Toledo, 12.13 in Cincinnati, 12.09 in Louisville, 12.07 in Indianapolis, 11.50 in St Louis, 11.48 in Dubuque, 11.39 in St Paul and 11.27 in Omaha. There were 27 time zones in Michigan alone . . . A person travelling from Eastport, Maine to San Francisco, if he wanted always to have the right railroad time and get off at the right place, had to twist the hands of his watch 20 times en route.

Such routines were accepted by the passengers, just as today we accept similar variations in practice, (some financial journalists seem not to realise they even exist). However, at a stroke, IT can standardise measurement units and translate them to any common base for any particular user. It is difficult to see how OR can survive, let alone expand, without working in close relationship. Perhaps one will not be accused of arrogance if we take the historical analogy that OR has to be to IT what the Greeks were to the Romans.

EXPERT SYSTEMS AND ARTIFICIAL INTELLIGENCE

Expert systems are an attempt to reproduce on a computer the decision-making behaviour of an expert manager by using his input information and discovering the factors within it which lead to the decisions which he takes. This then provides a means by which others can take their own decisions, by having the computer replicate for them what the expert would have done. This task is proving much more difficult than expected and the day of ready access to an ES seems almost about as far away as ever.

One can reflect, possibly with naïveté, on the relevance of this to the decision analyst. For the analyst's task is to enable the expert to do even better than before by measuring more, by broadening the scope of the decision, by absorbing relevant history and by specific forecasting. In fact, by expanding the mind of the expert.

As in all model building the problem of verifying and validating the models in an expert system is important. An interesting account of such work is given in ref 5. There are clear links between expert system and the cognitive mapping pioneered by Eden (ref 1), and ref 6 discusses this linkage.

AI operates at a level above this by creating, or attempting to create, a computer "brain" that can imitate the thinking process of a human. A simple test would be to formulate a process by which AI would produce humour or a joke. Humour springs from producing an unexpected pattern, hence seeing an elegant man or woman slip on a banana skin is funny but seeing a cripple do so is not funny. However, not withstanding millions of pounds of expenditure, AI is still grounded and although Turing proved that computers can improve themselves by themselves, AI, like ES, does not yet prove an aid. But the cost of ES is continuously reducing and the analyst must be prepared for the moment when it is ready for use. Some maintain that it is ready for use now.

In the light of the foregoing, the reader is invited to look at the Nine Lives and check where and how those particular problems, which it should be remembered were presented as illustrations of principles, and not as examples of best current practice, would be approached. For example, the Third Life (Berwyn Bank) could now probably be approached by a just-in-time solution. Always remember that the availability of soft systems, of IT, of ES and AI, does not diminish the importance of the nine principles enunciated.

MANAGEMENT

This availability of soft systems, IT, and of good analysis, does, however, change the nature of management and of the quality of managers very significantly indeed. The demands made on managers, if they are to take advantage of all this will be much greater – they will have to be more highly skilled in the understanding of methods and techniques to be able properly to utilise modern analysis and to understand analysts. This in its turn will demand better analysts. The analyst will have to drop her devotion to optimality (if such devotion still exists) and both manager and analyst will have to work for solutions that are capable of implementation to problems that have been adequately described, and moreover work for solutions that are produced in time. The analyst must look on him-, or herself as not only a problem solver, but as problem understander. The analyst must always retain control of the solution until it is fully confirmed and implemented.

The consequence of the increased power from IT is that both analyst and manager must have the ability, and the will, to profit from it. The danger is that standard "slap it on" answers may be used. It will be fatally easy for analysers to have at their disposal quick easy answers to what appears to be standard problems. There are indeed similar problems but the availability of facile software will allow the analyst to take the answers and force the problems to fit them. Experience shows that within most problems there are variations which mean that the standard answers are not appropriate. The future therefore contains great opportunities both for the competent analyst and for the charlatan.

THE STAGES IN RESEARCH

We have rejected the simplistic view of the research model on the good grounds that practice is not like that at all. Practice is much more chaotic and it is only projects written up and recollected in tranquillity which have such orderly progress from stage 1, statement of problem, to stage 6, implementation of results.

Conversely, however, there is no certain set of stages that will solve a problem that has a research content. For no problem that is known from its inception to be solvable within a given timeframe can be termed research. There is therefore no sufficient set of steps which lead to success, but there are necessary steps. The first, before all else, is to understand the anatomy of an organisation as well as its ethos, sociology and history. It may be protested that this adds five years to a project before you begin. That is not so for anyone with experience (and people without experience should be in a research team and not leading it). Comparative anatomy, meaning the structure of management control (the skeleton) and the flow of information relative to the control systems (the nervous system), the forecasting procedures (the sensory system) are all common features of all organisations. Where is authority located? Who has it? What are the environmental influences? What are the relative balances in objectives between survival, growth and well-being? What are the attitudes to risk?

It is hopeful, but not helpful, to abstain from doing anything at all until the objectives are known. This does not apply in the real life style of any analyst, so why should he or she expect to do to a complex system like an organisation that which he is unable to do for himself? Again Napoleon: on s'engage et puis on voit.

Just get in there, observe and listen and read. Do not raise a profile, do not write, and talk as little as possible. Together with management sit down and work through the logical map of the problem area but always remember that the energy which drives the whole thing is emotional and this emotion is the sum total of the ambitions of those involved. This will *not* be put on public display and remember that the map is not the thing itself.

At this stage the first questions which should have been asked will come to the surface. When is the answer needed? How accurate must we be? What form should the answer take? These we have listed in Chapter 13, but now in the future we must always ask about the availability of information and the processes by which we can deal with it. There is a dynamic involved in information flow which can be harnessed to a project but in order that the IT is our servant, and not the other way round, we look at the person(s) for whom and with whom we are working, and ask what is under their control, what is under their influence and what factors work together in a causative claim to influence, together with the constraints, technical, social, personal, the consequences of the whole system of causes and effects.

It is at this stage that technology and techniques enter. We have to remember that the sort of objectives with which we can deal are dependent on the techniques used. For example a deterministic network of causes and effects with linear constraints and a linear objective function will lead us to a linear programming formation which can only optimise. We cannot generate a shortlist of alternative solutions in order to make a personal choice. All techniques are objective constrained, the only exception being simulation for which IT gives a great leverage.

It is also at this stage that we learn two things.

1   The objectives or goals we have assumed are wrong.
2   The solution is unacceptable – often for behavioural reasons.

And the whole process starts again. It may well be that in the rational discussion approach to describing the problem the participants have not been totally frank – the picture is as they would like it to be or even that the picture they believe in, is not correct. We all have great powers of self-delusion, particularly in those things in which we are personally involved, (how many marriages would survive the benign process of soft OR?).

Eventually time takes over. It may be cynical but there will be a moment when we have to grasp the nettle and state:

- This is the problem as we see it.
- These are the data.
- These are the constraints we have assumed.
- These are the assumptions.
- This is what we should do and we shall be here to implement and control the solution.

Finally: we accept responsibility for this solution.

EDUCATION

All this has profound implications for the future of education and training. These are two different but related concepts. Education is a process of maturing and of producing certain attitudes of mind. Training is a drilling process (at least according to the OED). Hence one is trained in linear programming but not educated by it. We are fortunate indeed that OR is both educational and training, for OR is an attitude of mind applied to understanding and solving management problems. Whether or not it is part of the scientific method is profoundly irrelevant. There are three separate, but intimately related parts to this problem of education for MS/OR.

1   The academic institution.
2   The teacher/researcher.
3   The reward system.

The Academic Institution

The problem of the institution is that in general it can be antipathetic to the OR ethos. The important thing about OR is its approach to problems. In general, in the departments of a university, in which OR is most likely to be located, it is the tools, techniques and publications about them which can dominate the reward system. This reward system may take no cognisance of a piece of research which, for example by simulation, increases the throughput of a hospital by 50% without any deterioration in patient care but will be much more impressed by a publication about an interesting facet of the computer simulation algorithm, which reduces processing time by 5%.

A solution to a problem which gets 80% of the answer in 20% of the time yields less glory than a long slog in which 80% more of the time gets a perfect answer. The task of a university should be in research, teaching and service to the community. In many universities world wide the latter is missing and in addition, to call an academic "an excellent teacher" can be the kiss of death for promotion prospects, especially to a chair.

The Teacher/Researcher

The teacher/researcher has to be an integrated being, a person competent to acquire, as well as competent to pass on to the student, knowledge, with a sense of enjoyment and excitement. The problem is that few academics know how good their colleagues are at teaching (it is immensely bad form to sit in on the lectures of one's friends) and, *a fortiori*, have no clue at all regarding how good they are themselves. (Many universities in the USA and some in the UK do have a formal system of assessment of teachers by students.)

The academics themselves must spend time outside in practical work. It is easy to spend time just visiting, rather like an interested outsider walking round a zoo. The essential is to soak oneself in the ethos of the outside world and to take oneself to the problems. Academics must get to know the business. Universities must take the initiative and staff must be willing to prove themselves. They have more to learn than does the organisation they are visiting. The best people for this are those who have spent significant parts of their professional lives working in a non-academic institution, becoming not just in it, but of it. Spending a sabbatical year is useful, better than nothing, but it is easy to delude oneself about its virtue. The most boring person of all is the academic who endlessly recounts the story of his, or her, year in industry!

A study of current university syllabuses in OR (especially in the US) is desperately depressing. Collections of techniques, hewn out of other disciplines, are then stitched together to make a corpus of knowledge like bleeding chunks of butchers meat. The stitching should be in the attitude of mind. The techniques are servant. In general any one can learn the techniques and anyone can teach them. Most competent academics could themselves teach the whole of the technique content of an OR masters course. The essential component is the project. It is a pity that for reasons of academic logistics, the project often only starts when all the theory has been taught. Why not take it the other way round – why not start on the project and introduce techniques (by the students teaching themselves or each other) after the project has started? What can be taught *ab initio* is the anatomy of organisations, basic accounting and computer science (not programming). In these days of user-friendly computer systems, computer programming must, of all subjects, have had the shortest shelf life.

The Student

The most important person in any educational institution is the student. If academics do not give a good course this year then they will have a chance to get it right next year. But the student gives a year of his or her time which is irreplaceable. The student will come to this subject at undergraduate or graduate level, or perhaps as an add on to a course in business, management or accounting. The techniques will probably be presented at undergraduate level as ritual algebraic dances – most closely akin to Morris dancing where no one knows why they are doing it, but only that if they have just jumped, they must now whack sticks.

To these one can only hope that they will also be exposed to case studies. Not, one hopes to finished studies which are, and have all the life and excitement of, post mortems. In general, case studies are for necrophiliacs. Living interactive cooperative studies, of which the Nine Lives are examples, are better at conveying the essential attitudes of mind. At graduate level there must be cooperative work with faculties on outside projects. These are essential. Although the list of projects in an OR department may change every year, there is no reason in fact, why the projects should not be repeated. They are certainly better done by the faculty if they are repeated. For example, in the mechanical engineering department, week 3 of the second term may well always have a project in tribology and this is taken as acceptable. The project is the centrepiece of the learning experience and by far the most important part of it. It needs more care in its approach, even than teaching a course, but rarely receives it.

The Reward System

Not only can the teacher/researcher suffer under a reward system that may be anathema to *real* OR, the student can also suffer in this way. For how is the student examined in some places?

1 By written examination.
2 With no books or notes.
3 Without being able to confer with others.
4 By answering questions to which there is often only one "correct" answer in which:
5 All the information given is faultless, necessary and sufficient for an answer and for which:
6 The student is not allowed to suggest that the question is ill judged and capable of improvement.

Not one of these will apply in the job to which the student moves on graduation. The consequence is that the seal of approval can be given to those who succeed in performing in exactly the opposite mode from that in which they will earn their living. Can anything be more bizarre?

The examination paper should preferably not exist and the project report, examined orally, should suffice. If there has to be an examination, questions could be distributed beforehand and a random selection of them made by the invigilator at the examination, (ensuring that the student covers the whole range in revision). For some topics the student should be able to set his own question and then to comment on an answer given by the examiner. For others, since the best way to learn a subject is to teach it to other people, then in these other subjects each student could be given a topic to teach to others and assessed on his or her performance. It would be salutary for potential employers themselves to set such examination questions for it is certainly the case that the present processes can be almost entirely contrary to the OR ethos.

In summation, at present the examination process is often set so as to reassure the parent institution and hence persuades the candidate that the characteristics necessary to pass are those relevant to his or her future. It seems strange that what is so often packed in to a 12-month experience of being force fed in the class room, should be allowed to be an introduction to 40 years of employment. The important point which some universities have not grasped is that education and training are not mutually exclusive.

References

1 Eden, C. and Radford, J. (1990). *Tackling Strategic Problems*, Sage, London.
2 Hayakawa, S.I. (1974). *Language in Thought and Action*, Allen & Unwin, London.

3   Kaye, D. (1989). *Game Change*, Heinemann, London.
4   Geoffrion, A.M. (1992). Forces, trends and opportunities in MS/OR. Working Paper 395, Western Management Science Institute, University of California, Los Angeles.
5   O'Keefe, R.M. and Lee, S. (1990). An integrative model of expert system verification and validation. *Expert Systems with Applications, An International Journal,* **1**, 3, 231–6.
6   Lee, S., Courtney, J. and O'Keefe, R.M. (1992). A system for organizational learning using cognitive maps, OMEGA, **20**, 1, 23–36.

Chapter 15

Closing Thoughts

Model building is an intensely personal activity and it has been a great strain to write so much in the third person. This is what one is expected to do and one has done it to the best of one's ability.

I hope, above all, that I have conveyed the sense of fun and excitement that there is in model building. I have tried to steer a clear course between contending factions. Some people in this field, as in almost all academic activities, enjoy most of all scoring points off their own colleagues. It seems so trivial and childish and is one of the less pleasant features of the subject. Even so, to me there is nothing half as much worth doing as OR.

1 *It is intellectually challenging.* Do not be deceived by the apparent simplicity of many OR studies. Blackett, later to be a Nobel laureate, stated that military OR was, for him, as intellectually stretching as physics. Do not wash it aside as only common sense. Common sense can be badly wrong. Remember that any common-sense view of the earth is that it is flat.

2 *It is useful and it improves the human condition.* It is this that took me into OR from armaments testing. I think that every project with which I have been associated, in civil service, nationalised industry, competitive industry and university has, in some small degree at least, (and sometimes in large measure) left the world a better place than it found it.

3 *It is enjoyable.* The one thing that, to me, distinguishes OR meetings from those of other disciplines is the sense of excitement. OR is such fun and it is marvellous to be paid for doing something that is so enjoyable.

Bibliography

A Journey into Serendipity

The references within the text have purposely been kept to a minimum. There is of course a vast literature devoted to modelling, in its broadest sense. The following list has been compiled with the assistance of friends and colleagues in operational research and its kindred activities. They range in date over a period of 480 years. It is the equivalent of a browsing section in a bookshop where one can make happy discoveries by accident. There are a variety of approaches covered here. Those specialists who feel passionately about this subject may well reject some of these, but one hopes that none will be universally rejected as being valueless. Given one's personal aversion to extensive bibliographies, which often seem to be presented not to help the reader but to demonstrate the erudition of the author, this list has been kept short.

APPROACHES TO DECISION MODELLING

Computer Based Methodology

Adelman, L. (1991). Experiments, quasi experiments and case studies: a review of empirical methods for evaluating decision support systems, *IEEE Transactions on Systems, Man, and Cybernetics*, SMC-21(2).

Avison, D.E. and Wood-Harper, A.T. (1991). Information systems development research: an exploration of ideas in practice, *Computer Journal*, **34**, 2, 98–112.

Evans, J.R. (1989). A review and synthesis of OR/MS and creative problem solving, *OMEGA*, **17**, 6, 499–524.

Geoffrion, A. (1992). Forces, trends and opportunities in MS/OR, *Operations Research*, **40**, 3, 423–445.

Little, J.D.C. (1970). Models and managers: the concept of a decision calculus, *Management Science*, **16**, 8, B-466–B-485.

O'Keefe, R.M. (1988). Expert systems and OR/MS methodology (good news and bad), *Interfaces*, **18**, 6, 105–113.

Schwenk, C. and Thomas, H. (1983). Formulating the mess; the role of decision aids in problem formulation, *OMEGA*, **11**, 3, 239–252.

Simon, H. (1987). Two heads are better than one: the collaboration between OR and AI, *Interfaces*, **17**, 4, 8–15.

Soft OR

Checkland, P.B. (1972). Towards a systems based methodology for real world problem solving, *J. Syst. Eng.*, **3**, 87–116.
Checkland, P.B. and Scholes, J. (1990). *Soft systems methodology in action*, Wiley, Chichester.
Eden, C. and Radford, J. (1990). *Tackling strategic problems*, Sage, London.
Rosenhead, J.V. (1989). *Rational Analysis for a Problematic World*, Wiley, Chichester.

Systems Analysis

Checkland, P. (1981). *Systems Thinking. Systems Practice*, Wiley, Chichester.
Flood, R.L. and Jackson, M.C. (eds) (1991). *Criticial Systems Thinking: Directed Readings*, Wiley, Chichester.
Miser, H.J. and Quade, E.S. (1985). *Handbook of Systems Analysis: Craft Issues and Procedural Choices*, Wiley, Chichester.
Morgan, R.K. (1981). Systems analysis: a problem of methodology?, *Area*, **43**, 219–23.
Tomlinson, R. and Kiss, I. (eds) (1984). *Rethinking the Process of OR and Systems Analysis*. Pergamon, Oxford.

RISK

Bofinger, E., Dudewicz, E. J., Lewis, G. J. and Mengesson, K. (eds) (1992). *The Frontiers of Modern Statistical Inference Procedures* II, American Sciences Press, Ohio.
Cooper, D.F. and Chapman C.B. (1987). *Risk Analysis for Large Projects*, Wiley, Chichester.
Hertz, D.B. and Thomas, H. (1984). *Practical Risk Analysis*, Wiley, Chichester.

THE SCIENCE CONTEXT

Barnes, B. (ed.) (1972). *The Sociology of Science*, Penguin, Harmondsworth.
Beveridge, W.I.B. (1957). *The Art of Scientific Investigation*, Random House, London.
Bridgman, P.W. (1958). *The Logic of Modern Physics*, Macmillan, London.
Butterfield, H. (1960). *The Origins of Modern Science*, Macmillan, London.
Popper, K. (1974). *The Logic of Scientific Discovery*, Hutchinson, London.
Stebbing, L.S. (1958). *Philosophy and the Physicists*, Dover, New York.

GENERAL READING

Ackoff, R.L. (1974). *Resdesigning the Future*, Wiley, Chichester.
Ackoff, R.L. (1979). Does quality of life have to be quantified? *JORS*, **30**, 1–16.
Ackoff, R.L. (1986). *Management in Small Doses*, Wiley, Chichester.

Beer, S. (1972). *Brain of the Firm*, Allen Lane, London.
Beer, S. (1979). *The Heart of Enterprise*, Wiley, Chichester.
Beer, S. (1986). *Decision and Control*, Wiley, Chichester.
Bennett, P.G. (1985). On linking approaches to decision making aiding: issues and prospects, *JORS*, **36**, 8, 659–669.
Bryant, J. (1988). Frameworks of inquiry: OR practice across the hard soft divide, *JORS*, **39**, 5, 423–435.
Bryant, J. (1989). *Problem Management*, Wiley, Chichester.
Descartes, R. (1637). *Discours de la Methode*. English version by D. Curtis (1984). Grant and Cutler, London.
Eden, C. (1982). Problem construction and the influence of OR, *Interfaces*, **12**, 2, 50–60.
Friend, J.K. and Hickling, A. (1987). *Planning Under Pressure*, Pergamon, Oxford.
Jackson, M.C., Keys, P. and Cropper, S.A. (1989). *Operational Research and the Social Sciences*, Plenum, London.
Gregory, G. (1983). *Mathematical Methods in Management*, Wiley, Chichester.
Gregory, G. (1988). *Decision Analysis*, Pitman, London.
Machiavelli, N. (1513). *The Prince*, translated by B. Penman in 1992, Pub. Dent.
Majone, G. and Quade, E.S. (eds) (1985). *Pitfalls of Analysis*, IIASA, Wiley, New York.
Mangham, I. and Pye, A. (1991). *The Doing of Managing*, Blackwell, Oxford.
Martin, M.J.C. (1971). *Case Exercises in OR*, Wiley, Chichester.
Moore, P.G. and Thomas, H. (1976). *Anatomy of Decisions*, Penguin, Harmondsworth.
Phillips, L. (1984). A theory of requisite decision modelling, *Acta Psychol.*, **56**, 29–48.
Popper, K. (1966). *The Open Society and Its Enemies*, Routledge, London.
Teilhard de Chardin, P. (1955). *Le Phenomene Humain*. English version by B. Wall (1965). Collins, London.
Watson, S.R. and Buede, D.M. (1987). *Decision Synthesis: The Principles and Practice of Decision Analysis*, Cambridge University Press, Cambridge.
White, D.J. (1975). *Decision Methodology*, Wiley, Chichester.
Whyte, W.F. (ed.) (1991). *Participatory Action Research*, Sage, Newbury Park, CA.

RELATED TECHNICAL AREAS

Statistics

Ehrenberg, A.S.C. (1975). *Data Reduction*, Wiley, Chichester.
French, S. (1989). *Readings in Decision Analysis*, Chapman and Hall, London.
Lindley, D.V. (1985). *Making Decisions*, Wiley, Chichester.
Makridakis, S. and Wheelwright, S.C. (1989). *Forecasting Methods for Management*, Wiley, Chichester.
Mason, R.D. and Lind, D.A. (1989). *Statistical Techniques in Business and Economics*, Richard Irwin, Illinois.
Smith, J.Q. (1988). *Decision Analysis. A Bayesian Approach*, Chapman and Hall, London.
Thomas, H. (1972). *Decision Theory and the Manager*, Pitman, London.

Marketing and Distribution

Bonoma, T.V. and Clark, B.H. (1988). *Marketing Performance Assessment*, Harvard Business School, Boston.

Golden, B.L. and Assad, A.A. (eds) (1988). *Vehicle Routing: Methods and Studies*, Elsevier, Amsterdam.

Mercer, A. (1991). *Implementable Marketing Research*, Prentice Hall, London.

Mercer, A., Cantley, M.F. and Rand, G.K. (1978). *Operational Distribution Research*, Taylor & Francis, London.

Accounting and Finance

Layard, R. (1972). *Cost Benefit Analysis*, Penguin, Harmondsworth.

McKenzie, R.B. and Lee, D.R. (1991). *Quick Silver Capital*, The Free Press, New York.

Sizer, J. (1989). *An Insight into Management Accounting*, Penguin Business, London.

Index

Ackoff, R. L.   9, 37, 64, 85, 171, 219
Advertising Models   59
Allocation   96
Ansell, J.   139
Architects   92
Artificial Intelligence   288
Astronomy
    Babylonian   27
    Greek   27
Averages, moving and
    exponential   166

Bavelas, A.   186
Blackett, P. M. S.   40
Bowen, K.   120
Browning, R.   97
Bryant, J. W.   98, 265
Buffa, E. S.   171

Chaos   213
Checkland, P.   95, 98, 265
Cockburn, C.   142
Cockburn, P.   163
Competition   96
Constraint   21
Courtney, J.   295
Critical Path Analysis   135
Cycles   166

de Bono, E.   97, 189, 259
Descriptive models   28 et seq,   287
Discount factor   138
Dyer, J. S.   171

Eden, C.   280, 288, 294
Education   290 et seq
Elasticity   216

Emshoff, J.   171
Expert Systems   288
Explanatory models   28 et seq, 287

Feasibility   21
Finance   90
Fishburn, P.   120

Geoffrion, A. M.   295
Goodchild, J.   37
Gregory, G.   85, 120, 139, 163

Hastings, M.   64
Hayakawa, S.   197, 280
Health service   260
Herodotus   26

Implementation   274
Industrial revolution   6
Information Technology   283 et seq
Internal Rate of Return   138
Intuition   52
Inventory   96

Kant, I.   4
Kaye, D.   295
Kendall, M. G.   4
Keynes, M.   27
King, M.   211
Krishnamurti, J.   278

Language   264
Lee, S.   295

Lindley, D. V.   37, 120
Linear Programming   34, 92, 130 et
  seq

Makridakis, S. K.   171
Marketing   90
Marx, K.   4
McGervey, J. D.   37
Measurement   20
Mercer, A.   211
Mitchell, G. H.   63, 85
Monte Carlo method   134
Morris, C.   139

Newsboy problem   163
Newton, I.   27
Norman, J.   171

O'Keefe, R. M.   295
Objectives   21, 24, 214

Patching, D.   98
Personnel   90
Popper, K.   120, 278
Probability   113 et seq
problems described   258
Production   90
Project management   271
Project selection   269 et seq
Purchasing   90

Queuing problems   56, 92, 96

Radar   7

Radford, J.   294
Reasoning   260
Regression   166
Replacement   96
Risk Analysis   133
Robustness   80
Rosenhead, J.   98, 265
Routing   96

Scientific method   19, 257
Search   96
Sequencing   96
Soft systems   95, 259, 280, 290
Strategic options   280
Submarine warfare   40
Systems   87

Techniques and skill   268
Textiles   211
Toulmin, S.   37
Trend   166
Tversky, A.   120

Uncertainty   22, 113 et seq
Universities   4, 291 et seq

Variability   56

Waddington, C. H.   139
Waters, C. D. J.   139
Wharton, F.   139
Wheelwright, S. C.   171
White, D. J.   63, 120, 139
Williams, H. P.   139